MADOFF
WITH THE
MONEY

MADOFF
WITH THE MONEY

JERRY
OPPENHEIMER

WILEY

John Wiley & Sons, Inc.

For all the legitimate victims of Bernie Madoff's Ponzi scheme,
this story is for you

Contents

If you read things in the newspaper and you see somebody violate a rule, you say well, they're always doing this. But it's impossible for a violation to go undetected, certainly not for a considerable period of time.

—*Bernie Madoff, speaking at a panel session about Wall Street, October 2007*

Prologue

Around nine o'clock on the morning of Thursday, December 11, 2008, the employees of Bernard L. Madoff Investment Securities LLC began drifting into the midtown Manhattan firm's high-tech offices, where everything was in tones of black and gray, the boss's chosen colors. More than a few were a bit hung over. The night before they had all joined in toasting the holidays at the festive annual Christmas party that their respected and beloved financial icon threw every year at an upscale restaurant.

Despite the after effects of all the drinking and food consumption, everyone was feeling fine emotionally, if not physically. Some strong black coffee or a couple of Tums would take care of their ills. The holidays at Madoff were always a joyous time, a time for celebration, and this holiday season was to be no exception. That morning the employees came to work with visions of their promised year-end bonuses dancing in their heads, and with expectations of the usual splendid Christmas presents dispensed by their munificent boss, Bernie, and his lovely wife, Ruth.

Despite 2008 being in the depths of a recession seemingly on a par with the Great Depression, and with the stock market tanking, generous, wonderful Bernie still promised all of them bountiful bonus money. Two traders alone had brought in some $7 million in profits and were pledged 25 percent of the take.

There also was no reason to doubt that Madoff's gifts would be under the tree. Ruth always knew how to spend money, especially around the holidays.

"We used to call it Ruth's 'Twelve Days of Christmas,'" says a Madoff veteran. "Beginning in the early '90s she'd spend at least $150,000 a day, give or take, during the holidays, buying gifts, and who knows what else."

Her expenditures during the holiday time frame were well documented because certain Madoff employees had the responsibility of keeping tabs on Bernie's and Ruth's cash flow.

"They had so much money coming in and out of their accounts they needed five people to keep track of it," the employee asserts. "There was a Disneyland atmosphere. Money meant nothing to the Madoffs."

Accordingly, Madoff employees were thrilled. They considered Bernie one terrific, generous, magnanimous boss. The more money that flowed, the better. Many of them got well-paying positions with him right out of high school, and learned what they had to know on the job. In return for their loyalty, they earned good salaries, better than most were paid in the financial sector, and nice perks, too. And a few very special ones even became extremely well-off, with big homes and expensive cars and boats.

A job at Madoff, if you watched your p's and q's, meant virtual lifetime security. "Bernie seldom fired anyone," says a lifer. "You just got recycled into a different department."

Some invested wisely with Bernie, trusting his financial acumen— after all, the boss was considered an investor's dream, a genius, and one of the most powerful money men on Wall Street. How lucky they were to work for him. They thought of Bernie almost like a father figure, a messiah, and most felt secure that they'd have a very pleasant retirement. Unlike the bleak situation at other financial firms in the terrible economy of the latter part of the first decade of the new millennium, no one from Madoff was joining the growing ranks of the unemployed.

"We were always like one big, happy family," offers one of those Madoff veterans who had invested their life savings. "Bernie was our god, a wonderful boss, eccentric, sometimes scary eccentric, but still wonderful. He was a stand-up guy."

But all of those warm feelings quickly evaporated around 10 o'clock on that wintry December morning. Christmas 2008 for the 180 or so Madoff workers (and for thousands of other Madoff victims across the country and around the world) was going to be far different from Madoff Christmases past.

The weather service had forecast "a wintry mess" for the tristate New York metropolitan area for that Thursday.

For the employees of Madoff it would be more like a horrific terrorist attack.

As one longtime employee sadly observes, "12/11 was our own 9/11." Bernie and Ruth Madoff were about to become as controversial a couple as Julius and Ethel Rosenberg, and as infamous as Bonnie and Clyde.

Around 10 o'clock that morning, the boss's younger brother, Peter, the number two in charge of the family-run firm—Bernie's sidekick for some four decades—entered the trading room on the 18th floor and called for everyone's attention.

His hands were trembling, and he needed to lean against a desk to steady himself. His voice was tremulous.

"I have some bad news," he told the gathered workers. "Bernie's been arrested."

"He looked scared, teary-eyed, and everyone was suddenly in a state of shock," vividly recalls one of those standing there, listening in utter disbelief. "Someone asked Peter what happened, and he said he did not know why Bernie was arrested, or for what reason—or whether it was personal, or whether it was business. He said he didn't know whether it was for good, and he didn't know whether it was for evil. (This was a claim that would later turn out to be untrue.) And he said, 'Don't discuss this with anyone.'

"When we found out later that day what Bernie had done, I remembered how sincere Peter had sounded that morning, and I thought, 'In his next career he could win an Oscar.'"

A close and longtime elderly crony of Bernie's who was permitted by the boss to use a desk and a phone and conduct private business

in the office whenever he wanted to—and was a major investor—
happened to come in that horrific morning.

"Peter made the announcement that Bernie had been arrested, and
all havoc broke loose," he recalls, the memory of the moment indelibly
imprinted. "I immediately thought, 'It's a mistake.' Maybe his passport had
expired. Maybe there was an SEC regulation that the company didn't
adhere to, and they were just going overboard on setting an example."

Though no smoking was permitted in the office, he lit one up and
held his head in his hands for half an hour, contemplating what kind of
crazy jam his chum Bernie had gotten himself into.

Then he left the office in a daze.

"I was in a state of shock, and I actually walked home from 53rd
Street to 83rd Street, and never went back. People started to call me, and
I told my friends, 'It's all a big mistake. I'm going to go to sleep tonight
knowing that tomorrow morning you'll find out it's a mistake.'"

In another section of the three floors on which Madoff had offices
in the striking Lipstick Building, the announcement of Bernie's arrest
was made by gregarious, likable, jeans-wearing Frank DiPascali, who
everyone knew was the boss's right-hand man on the 17th floor. No
one ever really knew what he did for Bernie, or for that matter what
Bernie did in one of those offices on seventeen.

"We didn't have a care in the world that morning," recalls a longtime employee. "Suddenly Frankie comes crashing in telling us the
boss has been arrested by the FBI. 'We're not certain exactly what happened,' he says. 'He's engaged a lawyer. Do not talk to the news media,
period.' That's the first time Frankie ever gave orders like that. We were
all sitting at desks and were kind of thunderstruck. 'What the hell did
the boss do to get arrested by the FBI?' Little did we know.

"A little while later Charlie Wiener, the boss's nephew who was
head of administration at Madoff, came in with two or three other fel-
lows and introduced them as SEC guys and told us, 'They are going to
be camping out here for a while.' There was just a little trading that day,
and then it stopped and we just sat at our desks like the waking dead."

Before the end of the day Bernard L. Madoff Investment
Securities—the firm that engendered trust because the boss's name was

on the door—was taken over by FBI agents, Securities and Exchange Commission investigators, forensic accountants, and federal prosecutors.

There would be no more Madoff bonuses. There would be no more Madoff presents. There would be no more Madoff investment returns. There would be no more life savings. There would be no more Madoff.

All was now gone.

■ ■ ■

My objective in writing this book was to inform the reader about Bernie Madoff, the man—the self-proclaimed *macher* behind the biggest fraud ever perpetrated. Up until now, he has been an enigma. My goal as an investigative biographer was to dig deep and discover where he got his values and ethics—or lack thereof.

This is not another static business book, a primer on white-collar crime, but rather an in-depth profile, weaving together both the forces that shaped this swindler and the world in which he lived—showing the man Bernie really was.

As you read on, you will learn about his twisted family roots; his dreams of power and riches; the questionable characters along the way who aided and abetted him in his meteoric rise from poor boy in a middle-class Queens, New York, neighborhood, to one of the most powerful men on Wall Street; how that power made him feel above the law; and how it resulted in his fall, his public shame and disgrace.

In pursuit of that story I tracked down dozens of people who knew Bernie best—or thought they did. As a result, a true and often frightening portrait emerges from their candid characterizations and often shocking anecdotes—not only about the man behind the scam, but about his family, the reasons he chose Ruth to be his wife, and his sons' and brother's rise in what has now become the infamous Madoff dynasty. The mostly on-the-record accounts shared by those sources for the first time will, I hope, give readers a fuller, more coherent understanding of the most reviled thief who ever lived.

Chapter 1

Beginning of the End

As the economy worsened in 2008, Bernie Madoff was in desperate straits.

Calls from panicked clients had started coming in to his virtually impenetrable 17th-floor private office in the Lipstick Building on Manhattan's Third Avenue—the office later identified by authorities as Ponzi Central, the epicenter of history's most massive fraud—where his billions of dollars in personal investment accounts were handled in strictest secrecy.

With the stock market crashing, with credit tighter than anyone could remember, with unemployment hitting record highs, with the housing market in free fall, with big banks and investment houses failing or pleading for government bailouts (and getting them), and with automaker giants like General Motors and Chrysler teetering on the verge of bankruptcy, Bernie was facing his own private hell, his own private demons.

Big and small investors in his very exclusive club—a privileged circle of financial institutions, charities, billionaires, celebrities, and some

1

few favored Joe Six-Packs and Wal-Mart Moms—who were receiv-
ing steady and huge returns on their investments in good times and in
bad, had begun requesting, and then demanding, that their money be
returned.

In the past, when they needed money from their accounts, they'd
get a check within days. Suddenly, they were getting the stall. Now
Bernie was facing redemption demands to the tune of a whopping
$7 billion. Bernie realized that if he couldn't cover those requests, his
decades-long charade as a self-styled financial wizard and investment
messiah was nearing a horrific end.

Still, the man who was "considered a statesman in our industry" by
a head of a firm that guaranteed the sanctity of stock trades thought he
could elude getting caught, that in a last-ditch blitz of raking in more
new big-money investors—unknowing lambs being led to slaughter—he
could make good on the funds his earlier investors now wanted returned.

His desperation heightened in early summer when he went on a
marathon cash-hunting expedition.

"It was around the end of June when he went to France *really* trying
to get more money from wealthy Europeans, or anyone else he could
find," says a longtime close associate of Bernard L. Madoff Investment
Securities LLC (BLMIS). In the south of France, he had a gated villa in
exclusive Cap d'Antibes, and one of several yachts, all named *Bull.* There
were those who later observed that the *Bull* designation did not represent a high-flying bull market as most thought, but rather was an ironic
insider joke for the bullshit he was throwing at those he was bilking.

Bernie usually had a very calm demeanor, but now he was clearly
in panic mode.

He came back from France in order to attend the very fancy annual
company summer party bash on the expensive sand at Montauk in the chic
Hamptons, where his posh beachfront home was located. Says the close
associate, "Bernie was putting on a happy face for everyone. Then, he left
right away again to try to recoup, to try to get more investors to hand him
more money as more requests came in from those wanting to cash out."

They were people and entities that suddenly were becoming cash
poor, many of them good friends of Bernie's who knew how bad things
were as Wall Street seemed to be laying another egg just like in 1929.

Before the Great Madoff Panic of 2008 was ignited by the worst economic debacle that the United States and the world had faced since the Great Depression, people had begged Bernie to take their money because of the steady and relatively high promised returns. They virtually threw cash at him. They sent envelopes filled with moolah. They made wire transfers in the tens and hundreds of millions of dollars.

If Bernie personally turned them down because they asked too many questions, or because they seemed to be doing their due diligence (which too few did), or because he just felt paranoid about them, they begged their friends who were Madoff insiders to get them in.

Bernie was the Studio 54 of money managers. He and only he could raise the velvet rope and let those hungry for big returns into his private, exclusive club. For a long time the minimum cost of admission was at least $5 million, unless he offered a special dispensation. And he often did. After all, to Bernie money was money.

Just a glance at the web site of Bernard L. Madoff Investment Securities LLC elicited gold-standard trust. The company was described as:

> ... a leading international market maker. The firm has been providing quality executions for broker-dealers, banks, and financial institutions since its inception in 1960. ... With more than $700 million in firm capital, Madoff currently ranks among the top 1% of U.S. securities firms. ... Clients know that Bernard Madoff has a personal interest in maintaining an unblemished record of value, fair dealing, and high ethical standards that has always been the firm's hallmark.

His slogan, "The owner's name is on the door," engendered trust. After all, this was a guy who once was chairman of the National Association of Securities Dealers Automated Quotations (Nasdaq) system. Gimme a break!

Those who couldn't deal directly with Bernie dealt with trusted middlemen, later called feeder funds, who were sending the cash to Bernie in return for hefty commissions, hundreds of millions of dollars in several cases. As it turned out, those investors who placed their money and trust in feeder funds had never even heard of Bernard Madoff—until the end came, and then it was too late.

But now as the frightful economic year 2008 was coming to a close there was little if any big money like that floating around to throw at Bernie. Now a number of Madoff investors wanted their money back. They needed cash flow, even if it meant losing the promised return.

■ ■ ■

As P. T. Barnum once famously declared, "There's a sucker born every minute." It was an anthem Bernie frequently used with certain people close to him when old and new investors showered him with money, says a pal.

The old in late 2008 was one Carl Shapiro, who had begun putting his money with Bernie when he was just a little *pisher* in his early 20s. With a promise from Bernie to reportedly repay with interest or a gain, the elderly Boston entrepreneur and philanthropist who had made a fortune in the garment industry now sent him $250 million.

Still, it was not enough to cover all of the redemptions Bernie was facing.

With the proverbial noose beginning to tighten around his neck, Bernie was overjoyed in early December 2008 when some new millions suddenly came his way—a mere bag of shells compared with the billions he needed to snag, but still nothing to sneeze at.

That infusion of money was the beginning of the end for Madoff, the first in a chain of fast-moving events leading up to his arrest, guilty plea, and imprisonment for running the biggest and slickest Ponzi scheme ever, and getting away with it for decades.

The last person known to be taken to the cleaners was a hugely wealthy businessman by the name of Martin Rosenman, who was president of the heating oil distributor Stuyvesant Fuel Service Corporation, located next to the Cathedral of Deliverance, a graffiti-covered storefront church, in a bleak section of the Bronx, one of New York City's five boroughs.

As one of America's grimmest Christmases in decades approached with hundreds of thousands without jobs, with thousands facing foreclosure on their homes, with the luckier ones desperately holding on to whatever money they didn't lose in their 401(k)s, and with retailers starving for customers, Rosenman appeared to be Bernie's Santa Claus when he called the Madoff offices on December 3.

Rosenman was making a surprise year-end investment—a $10 million offering on which he wanted to start earning a nice Madoff return—now 7 or 8 percent in a time when a measly 2 to 4 percent was available elsewhere.

A friend who had invested with Madoff and done well with him over the years had advised Rosenman to do the same. You can't miss putting your money in Madoff, new investors were being told, Madoff's a sure thing. So, Rosenman decided to give him a try.

Rosenman was from Great Neck, one of the many affluent, predominately Jewish Long Island communities whose wealthy residents, fabled country clubs, and prestigious institutions would soon see their fortunes in Madoff evaporate. From Long Island to Palm Beach, from Europe to South America, there would be many, many other Rosenmans when all became known, thousands of them.

Playing his exclusivity con game to the hilt, Bernie told Rosenman that "the fund was closed"—closed, that is, until New Year's Day 2009. But if Rosenman, managing member of Rosenman Family LLC, wanted to move his money quickly, he could wire the funds to an account that BLMIS had with a popular and trusted bank, JPMorgan Chase & Company. Bernie promised that Chase would hold the money until the New Year, when it would be transferred into the very elite Madoff fund.

Rosenman wired the money on December 5. Four days later the Madoff firm that Rosenman had entrusted with his millions did what any supposedly ethical company would do—Madoff, or a representative, notified Rosenman that his money was in safe hands, and had been invested in the short sale of $10 million in U.S. Treasury bills, or so it was claimed.

With Rosenman's money in the bank, one could envision 70-year-old Bernie Madoff, once a poor boy from Queens who now owned a couple of yachts, fancy cars, elegant homes, and a 50 percent interest in a $24 million 12-passenger sleek Embraer Legacy jet—a tanned and coiffed dandy of sorts who wore $7,000 suits and sported $700 sweaters and $80,000 watches—gleefully and greedily rubbing his hands together. With his sphinxlike smirk, his chipmunk cheeks, and his beady eyes, he was the anti-*mensch*.

As it later would be revealed in various news accounts, JPMorgan Chase and BLMIS had a business relationship. As part of his massive fraud, Bernie was placing hundreds of millions of dollars through his account at the bank—investors' funds that hadn't been invested by him for years. Moreover, the bank reportedly withdrew its own $250 million from one of Bernie's major feeder funds.

And as it would turn out, Marty Rosenman became the very last investor to give money to Madoff in the days before his enormous criminal scheme would come crashing down.

Not surprisingly, there was no record of the Rosenman-Madoff transaction. Moreover, the Treasury bill sale was "never authorized" by Rosenman, bogus or not.

As Rosenman's attorney, Howard Kleinhendler, later stated, "We don't think any securities were bought or sold. To the contrary, we think he [Madoff] was deliberately collecting money. He was trying to get more money in the door for this final distribution he wanted to make."

On December 9, the same day that Madoff let Rosenman know that his $10 million had been invested, Bernie made a surprise revelation regarding the distribution referenced by Kleinhendler. Bernie declared that he planned to dispense fat bonuses to his employees, friends, and family members amounting to as much as a startling $300 million, according to investigators. About a hundred signed checks totaling $173 million were never sent and were later discovered in his desk drawer after his arrest.

Like others among some 14,000 present and former Madoff investors, many of whom were bilked with catastrophic losses, Rosenman sued to get back his money—and seemingly caught a break. Irving Picard, who was subsequently named trustee after the scandal broke to oversee the dismantling of Bernie's evil Ponzi empire, agreed to set aside the $10 million and not put it in the pot that would eventually—it was hoped—be generally distributed to Madoff victims. But a bankruptcy judge later ruled there would be no special treatment for Rosenman, a decision that was then appealed.

Whichever way it turned out, Bernie's fraud didn't leave Rosenman and his family destitute. Far from it. The Rosenman company had been acquired by the Hess Corporation in 2008; the Rosenmans were extremely wealthy. As Kleinhendler noted, the $10 million was not the Rosenman family "nest egg . . . not something that will dramatically affect their life." Many of Bernie's investors fit that profile, a demographic in which $10 million didn't mean the end of the world to them, but that still didn't excuse Bernie's crime.

■ ■ ■

If the Rosenman family wanted its $10 million back, Bernie's wife—the well-coiffed, well-preserved, shop-until-she-dropped Bergdorf blonde who would soon become known to the world and in tabloid headlines as Ruthie—also wanted some millions for herself.

Two days before Thanksgiving 2008, and a few days before she and Bernie celebrated their 49th wedding anniversary, the petite 68-year-old self-styled socialite gave herself a $5.5 million cash present in the form of a whopping withdrawal from her account at a company called Cohmad Securities Corporation, a Madoff tentacle and feeder fund that would come under intense scrutiny by authorities.

Cohmad was the merger of the names Madoff and Cohn—the latter for Maurice "Sonny" Cohn, an old friend of Bernie's. Cohmad, along with Cohn and his daughter, Cohmad president Marcia Cohn, would later be sued by the Securities and Exchange Commission (SEC) for bringing investors to Bernie and ignoring and even participating "in many suspicious practices that clearly indicated Madoff was engaged in fraud."

An SEC official stated that Bernie "cultivated an air of exclusivity by pretending that he was too successful to trouble himself with marketing to new investors. In fact he needed a constant in-flow of funds to sustain his fraud, and used his secret control of Cohmad to obtain them."

Then, on December 10, with the clock ticking like a time bomb on Bernie's fraudulent operation, Ruth withdrew another $10 million. When

her greed was disclosed some weeks later in a court action, the tabloid
New York Post's headline blared: "Shocking Withdrawals on Eve of Bust."

By making those withdrawals, many wondered, did Ruth Madoff
know the roof was about to cave in?

Up to the end, she had maintained an office at Madoff headquarters
where Cohmad also had its office. And in her 50th high school reunion book—an event that Ruth and Bernie attended on November 7,
2008, just a month before his house of cards collapsed—she proudly
boasted: "Bernie and I worked together in the investment business that
he founded."

Was Ruth Madoff helping her desperate husband in his last-ditch
efforts to bring in more money? Or was she just socking away cash
to cover herself in the future? In the coming months there would be
much speculation about that money, and what Ruth knew and when
she knew it.

According to a veteran Madoff executive with close ties to the
family, it appears that Ruth may have been one of her hubby's longtime family partners and participants bringing in investors.

The executive tells the following story:

In late April 2008, a well-to-do elderly couple decided to move
from New York City to Palm Beach. As they were beginning to set-
tle in, the husband suddenly died of a heart attack. In September 2008
the widow, a member of the Palm Beach Country Club, many of whose
wealthy members would lose fortunes to Bernie, "got into a foursome
on the golf course with Ruth and some other ladies," states the Madoff
insider. "The widow had never met Bernie Madoff. But by the end of
September she had all her money with Bernie. So, it seems Ruth was
working for him. I was shocked."

So much was happening, and only a close-knit circle was aware.

On December 8, for instance, an anxious and stressed Bernie blew
his top in a telephone conversation with Jeffrey H. Tucker, co-founder,
with high roller Walter Noel, of the Fairfield Greenwich Group, soon
to be identified as the Madoff firm's largest feeder fund. Beginning
in 1989 Fairfield Greenwich began spoon-feeding Madoff billions of
dollars in investor money and received hundreds of millions of dollars in fees simply for being the intermediary. Bernie was furious with

Tucker because many of Fairfield's investors, frightened by the worsening economy, were pulling out enormous amounts of money, known as redemptions. Bernie wanted the growing outflow of funds halted ASAP, and he strong-armed Tucker.

"Just got off the phone with a very angry Bernie who said if we can't replace the redemptions for 12/31 he is going to close the account," Tucker, a former Securities and Exchange Commission official, wrote in a letter to Fairfield's executive committee. "His traders are 'tired of dealing with all these hedge funds' and there are plenty of institutions who can replace the money. They have been offered this all along 'but remained loyal to us.' . . . Not sure of our next step but we best talk. I believe he is sincere."

The epitome of the con artist, Bernie the bully had successfully intimidated Tucker. Tucker was clearly worried about losing Fairfield's long connection with Madoff. As soon would be disclosed, however, there was no one waiting in the wings, as Bernie threatened, willing to pump much-needed money into Madoff's now relatively empty coffers. Tucker quickly followed up with an apologetic letter to Bernie. "Our firm is very dependent on its relationship with your firm. . . . You are our most important business partner and an immensely respected friend. . . . Our mission is to remain in business with you and keep your trust."

The Fairfield Greenwich Group, like a number of other such Madoff-connected entities, would soon be the subject of a lawsuit for its "complete disregard of its fiduciary duties . . . its flagrant misrepresentations to investors [that] rise to the level of fraud," all of which the firm adamantly denied.

■ ■ ■

On the evening of December 9, 2008, a day before Ruth's $10 million money grab, a highly revelatory meeting took place between Bernie and his top lieutenant and younger brother, Peter Madoff, the senior managing director and chief compliance officer of BLMIS. Bernie is said to have confessed to Peter, who had worked virtually side by side with him for some 40 years, that he had been operating a monster Ponzi scheme on the side. If such a confession was actually made, Peter, as head of compliance, had an obligation to immediately report his brother's criminal activities to the proper authorities, such as the SEC. He did not.

The next day, December 10, Bernie supposedly made a similar confession to his sons, Mark and Andrew, who also had worked closely with their father, and were the recipients in recent years of a whopping $31.5 million in what were claimed as loans from their parents, money that later would become part of the case. Mark was in charge of the legitimate stock-trading arm of his father's firm, while Andy was now heading up a relatively new entity called Madoff Energy, which involved the buying, restoring, and selling of abandoned oil rigs to small oil companies and wildcatters. The Madoff scions were said to have been as shocked as their Uncle Peter when the patriarch of the dynasty told them what he had been up to. After he made his so-called confession to his sons, the brothers contacted a lawyer friend, Martin Flumenbaum, and then filed a report with the authorities.

Like so much in the Madoff saga, though, one has to question the veracity of the confession scenarios that were spun. Many inside and outside the company—investors, investigators, longtime family friends and associates, and the public at large—found it hard to swallow that none of the family members knew about Bernie's nefarious activities, and that Bernie had acted alone. The family seemed too close-knit and too involved with the company that was founded a half-century earlier to be unaware of the patriarch's activities. And there was speculation that the alleged admissions made by Bernie to his sons and brother were a way to protect them from possible prosecution. In other words, they didn't know anything about any of the bad stuff until Bernie told them—just hours before he was busted.

■ ■ ■

On the night of December 10, the employees of BLMIS gathered for the company's annual Christmas party thrown for the second year in a row at festive Rosa Mexicano, an upscale Upper East Side Manhattan restaurant, a short walk from the Madoff offices. Little did the merry partygoers know that this would be their last joyous time together.

Earlier in the day Andy Madoff, the chief executive of Madoff Energy, had told his assistant, Toniann Astuto, an eight-year Madoff veteran, that he would see her later at the party. But neither Andy nor his brother Mark made an appearance, which surprised Astuto and others. The boys were usually at the Madoff employee bashes, having a grand old time.

But the revelers had no idea of the Madoff drama that was unfolding behind closed doors, or of the dynamite about to be ignited.

Neither presumably did J. Ezra Merkin, a close associate of Bernie's who was holding a benefit for the Israel Museum that same night in his Park Avenue apartment, surrounded by his priceless collection of Rothkos and some of New York's wealthiest Jews and patrons of the arts, many of them Madoff investors (most unknowingly). As president of Manhattan's exclusive Fifth Avenue Synagogue and a world-class investor, Merkin headed several huge private investment funds that were feeding billions into Madoff. Merkin would soon become enmeshed in the Madoff scandal, accused of fraud and deception in a civil suit. The clock was ticking on Merkin, too, that night.

Although the Madoff scions failed to make an appearance at the Christmas bash, Bernie, Ruth, and Peter were in attendance. Bernie needed to keep up appearances, even as the end neared.

One longtime employee, William Nasi, who had been Bernie's personal errand boy and messenger beginning in the late 1960s, perceived a change in "the boss's mood" compared to Christmas parties past.

> Bernie always acted like a politician—squeezing the flesh, kissing babies, playing the crowd, going from table to table, playing the role of the boss.
>
> This time when he showed up, Ruth was acting out that role. Bernie just stood there silently. There was total dead silence from Bernie. He never said a word that night. He had that thousand-yard stare, that combat stress stare. He walked like an ambulatory zombie.

Another veteran Madoff employee, Amy Joel, whose late father, Martin J. Joel, had been a trusted friend and colleague of Bernie's and whose surviving family would be one of those financially wiped out, notes that Bernie always rented fabulous places for the Christmas party. "He always did it great, and it cost him a pretty penny," she says. Like Nasi, Joel agrees that Bernie's mood was far more somber at the 2008 party.

> I thought it was odd because Bernie and Ruth sat at a corner table by themselves in the front of the restaurant looking out. I guess they thought the feds were going to come and get him that night. I went over to say something to Bernie. He seemed very tense. Peter circulated and said hello to everyone and wished us a happy holiday.

Meanwhile, the Madoff employees—the traders, the secretaries, the computer guys, everyone—were all having a festive time, though a bit less joyful than in past years.

"The mood was a little bit more somber because obviously the economy was going down the toilet," observes Astuto, who had joined the Madoff organization as the secretary and personal assistant to Peter's glamorous fashionista daughter, Shana Madoff, a lawyer, the company's compliance officer, and a divorcee who had recently married a former SEC official. Shana, who was pregnant, had arrived at the party late and looking unnerved.

"We all knew that things were not going well in the world. And the Madoffs, Bernie and Ruth, weren't around as much at the party as they usually were," continues Astuto. "Bernie, Ruth, and Peter didn't seem quite in a party mood. Normally, especially Peter, you'd see him circulating. He'd come around to everybody, laughing and joking, but not this time. He usually had his wife, Marion, with him. But she didn't come because he said she had a headache.

"I saw Bernie and Ruth in the food line and I wished them a happy holiday and I asked them where Mark and Andy were. Ruth said Mark's wife, who was pregnant at the time, wasn't feeling good, so she wasn't sure they were going to make it, and Andy was running late because of his girlfriend. I said, 'Oh, okay,' but they never showed up, which was a little odd."

Bernie's personal secretary of a some 20 years, Eleanor Squillari, a good-looking, tough-talking, 50-something Staten Islander with a snarky manner, was enjoying the party, but she had been seeing changes in Bernie's physical and emotional makeup as the end drew near. In the office he seemed in a trance. Once strong and dominating, his voice had become "almost inaudible. . . . If he wasn't staring into space, he was looking down, working on figures." She told some of her confidantes in the office that he appeared at times to be "in a coma." Under intense stress and anxiety, Bernie was taking medication for high blood pressure, and sometimes had such intense back pain that he was forced to lie on his back on the floor of his office.

When others in the office asked if the boss was okay, Squillari would tell them no, quickly adding, "But he's not dead," at least that's what she told *Vanity Fair*.

Squillari was to Bernie what Rose Mary Woods was to President Richard "Tricky Dick" Nixon: She was the secretary and gatekeeper who also was the keeper of the flame and the keeper of the boss's personal, intimate secrets. Once a Madoff investor, she had taken her money out some years before, or she would have lost it all.

Still, everyone except for the grim-appearing Madoffs were having a fun time at the party, and better yet the annual bonuses were due soon.

Rosa Mexicano was jumping that night.

"It was a great blast," Bill Nasi thought at the time. But looking back several months later, he compares those hours of fun to the hours before another immense and historic tragedy.

"It was like dancing on the foredeck of the *Titanic* before it hit the iceberg. For us, it hit the iceberg the next day."

■ ■ ■

Around 8:30 A.M. on Thursday, December 11, Theodore Cacioppi, an FBI agent, along with a partner, arrived at the chic and exclusive prewar cooperative apartment building at 133 East 64th Street, a short stroll from Central Park, showed his identification to the doorman, walked through the conservative lobby with its leather chairs and an orchid in a vase—the orchid was Ruth's idea (the Madoff offices always had fresh orchids on display)—and took the elevator up to the two-level penthouse, the Madoffs' 4,000-square-foot, $7 million aerie filled with great art and priceless antiques.

With just two apartments on each floor—it was that elegant a building—the feds easily found the Madoffs' door. More visible tenants inhabited the co-op, such as *Today* show co-host Matt Lauer, who would later complain about his loss of privacy in having to weave his way through the small army of reporters staking out the Madoffs in order to get to his apartment.

Cacioppi, who had been with the Bureau for six and a half years and had been "personally involved" in looking into allegations against Bernie, knocked on the door, but the doorman had already telephoned up, alerting the Madoffs to their early-morning visitors. Bernie, wearing a pale blue bathrobe and slippers, had told him they were expected.

At the moment the FBI agents walked into the foyer of the Madoff apartment they already knew that Bernie had admitted his crimes to several close associates, according to Agent Capiocci's sworn complaint and deposition that was filed with the U.S. Magistrate Judge for the Southern District of New York, Thomas F. Eaton, on the day Bernie was booked for fraud. The close associates, listed as three "senior employees," were known to be his sons and his brother. Peter was told first, and then Mark and Andy—purportedly on the day of the Christmas party at which they were no-shows. Their attorney, Flumenbaum, of the prestigious Paul, Weiss, Rifkind, Wharton & Garrison firm, asserted that the brothers had no knowledge of their father's criminal activity before he informed them the day of the party.

Beginning in early December, according to Capiocci, Bernie had revealed that he had been running a "separate" investment advisory business for clients that was not part of the Madoff firm's trading and market-making activities, and that he had kept the financial statements for that operation "under lock and key." Bernie, who appeared "to have been under great stress," disclosed "he was struggling to obtain the liquidity necessary to meet requests for approximately $7 billion in redemptions." Bernie said he "wasn't sure he would be able to hold it together."

At a subsequent meeting at his apartment he informed his associates—his sons—that his investment advisory business was "a fraud," that he was "finished," that he had "absolutely nothing," that "it's all just one big lie," and that he was running "basically, a giant Ponzi scheme," and "had for years been paying returns to certain investors out of the principal received from other, different investors," according to the FBI agent's report.

Bernie stated that "the business was insolvent, and that it had been for years," and he estimated that "the losses from this fraud to be at least approximately $50 billion." Bernie claimed he had $200 million to $300 million left and he "planned to use that money to make payments to certain selected employees, family, and friends."

He also stated he was going to give himself up to the authorities.

Earlier in the year he had claimed in a government filing that he managed $17.1 billion in assets for just 23 clients, which would turn out to be a lie as enormous as his crimes. In fact, as investigators would determine, there were thousands of investors over the years and as much as $65 billion of their money.

Facing Bernie in his richly appointed apartment, Agent Capiocci said, "We're here to find out if there's an innocent explanation" for what had been alleged. Bernie's response was short and not very sweet. He said, "There is no innocent explanation." According to Capiocci, "Madoff stated, in substance, that he had personally traded and lost money for institutional clients, and that it was all his fault. Madoff further stated, in substance, that he 'paid investors with money that wasn't there'. . . that he was 'broke' and 'insolvent' and that he had decided 'it could not go on' and that he expected to go to jail."

Bernie, the one-time power-broker trader, one of the pioneers of modern Wall Street, a "pillar of finance and charity," as the *New York Times* described him, was then placed under arrest—just hours after he celebrated Christmas with his employees. At the FBI's office, he called his lawyer, Ira Sorkin. "Hi, it's Bernie, I've just been arrested and I'm handcuffed to a chair."

At his arraignment that day, wearing a white striped shirt, no tie, and dark gray slacks, he was initially charged with a single count of securities fraud, a charge that would later escalate. For a time he would remain free on $10 million bail and confined to his fancy apartment—home detention with electronic monitoring—a judge's decision that infuriated Bernie's victims and raised questions in the public's mind about the justice system, a system where common criminals without money or reputation are immediately incarcerated for far lesser crimes because they can't afford to post bail.

A spokesman for the SEC, which would come under extreme congressional and media criticism for ignoring red flags in the past about Bernie's criminal activities, called his fraud "stunning" and "of epic proportions," and the regulatory agency swiftly filed separate civil charges.

Like a tsunami, the news of the arrest of a Wall Street legend, a former chairman of Nasdaq, a noted Jewish philanthropist, spread quickly. On CNBC, the business channel with the stock crawl that was a daily habit for millions from Wall Street to Main Street, the shocking, mind-boggling news was flashed:

"If you are working on a trading desk, stop what you are doing for one second before you walk out the door and clean your desk out for the day," announced anchor Michelle Caruso-Cabrera.

"Bernie Madoff has been arrested."

■ ■ ■

By day's end, the Madoff offices had become a crime scene—invaded by FBI agents, federal prosecutors, probers from the SEC, and forensic accountants who got access to everything—the computers, the laptops, the cell phones, the e-mail.

Over the next few months into 2009, accounts of the crimes of Bernie Madoff would quickly unfold, and the tragic stories of his victims would become public.

Desperately seeking to end his controversial house arrest, revoke his $10 million bail, and put him behind bars, prosecutors went to court with startling evidence that Bernie and Ruth had sent some of the fruits of his crimes in secret packages to relatives and friends over the Christmas 2008 holidays. The booty, which was reportedly worth more than $1 million, included gifts to his brother Peter, sons Mark and Andrew, and other relatives. These "swag bags," according to investigators, ranged from inexpensive $25 cuff links and mittens that cost $200 to eye-popping bling that included diamond-encrusted Cartier and Tiffany watches, diamond brooches, diamond and jade necklaces, and jewelry fit for royalty or a rapper. Later confiscated by the prosecutors, the gifts had been sent by Bernie after he had pledged to the SEC that he wouldn't dispose of any assets. His lawyers claimed it was all one big mistake, and the judge declined to revoke bail and send him to jail.

Then came an overwhelming shocker. With as much as an estimated $65 billion missing, shell-shocked Madoff investors who now had no idea what had been done with their money learned that the stocks and Treasury bills listed in such detail on their account statements had never actually been traded—and Bernie's incredible deception had been going on for at least 13 years. The bombshell was dropped in late February 2009 by Irving Picard. The *New York Times* observed that the revelation "demolishes the theory that Mr. Madoff was an honest man driven into fraud by the relentless market strain of recent years."

Speculation that there would be a federal grand jury investigation, more admissions of guilt, the naming of co-conspirators, and especially a plea bargain deal in exchange for naming names ended on March 12, 2009, just three months after Bernie's arrest, when he pleaded guilty in open court to a cornucopia of felony charges— securities fraud, investment adviser fraud, mail fraud, wire fraud, money laundering, international money laundering to promote specified unlawful activity, international money laundering to conceal and disguise the proceeds of specified unlawful activity, making false statements, perjury, making a false filing with the SEC, and theft from an employee benefit plan.

Wearing a $7,000 custom-tailored Savile Row suit—under which was a bulletproof vest to protect him from furious investors—Bernie pleaded guilty to the biggest swindle in history. As he stood before Manhattan Federal Judge Denny Chin, he stated in a low voice:

> I am so deeply sorry and ashamed. As I engaged in my fraud, I knew what I was doing was wrong, indeed criminal. . . . I am painfully aware that I have deeply hurt many people.
>
> To the best of my recollection, my fraud began in the early 1990s.

He further admitted that he "never invested" the money entrusted to him by thousands of investors. "Instead, those funds were deposited in a bank account at Chase Manhattan Bank. When clients wished to receive the profits they believed they had earned with me or to redeem their principal, I used the money in the Chase Manhattan bank account that belonged to them or other clients."

He said he believed his classic, but monstrous, Ponzi operation "would end shortly, and I would be able to extricate myself and my clients from the scheme. However, this proved impossible, and as the years went by I realized that my arrest and this day would inevitably come."

But perhaps the most shocking statement of all was his claim that he had acted alone, that he had pulled one of the biggest frauds of all time just by himself.

The judge immediately ordered that Bernie be locked in the Metropolitan Correctional Center near the courthouse to await formal sentencing. Rather than his spectacular penthouse, he would now live in an eight-by-eight-foot maximum security cell, as Prisoner No. 61727-054.

All told, he faced a maximum sentence of a century and a half in prison—at the age of 70.

Bernie Madoff, who used to boast that he was "the most powerful man on Wall Street," was destined to die behind bars.

Outside the courthouse, victims of his scheme cheered as he was driven off to his new home under tight security.

"Bernie Madoff in Slammer at Last," screamed a headline in the *New York Daily News*.

His first full day in jail was Friday the 13th of March.

In a lead editorial that day, the *Wall Street Journal* observed: "In a world that seems able to argue about any subject, the Madoff saga isn't open to argument. . . . The condemnation raining upon his head is universal."

Still, with Bernie's guilty plea on record and the swindler behind bars, there were more questions than there were answers.

Nobel Peace Prize laureate Elie Wiesel, who had escaped Hitler's death camps only to be victimized again, and by a fellow Jew no less, to the tune of $15.2 million from his Elie Wiesel Foundation for Humanity, plus the entire life savings of Weisel and his wife Marion, thought he had an answer. He publicly termed Bernie a "psychopath," adding, "It's too nice a term for him. . . . 'Sociopath,' 'psychopath,' it means there is a sickness, a pathology," observed Wiesel. "This man knew what he was doing. I would simply call him thief, scoundrel, criminal."

But the scorn leveled upon Bernie by a man of peace like Wiesel and thousands of others publicly and privately didn't answer the bigger questions:

How did Bernie Madoff become one of history's biggest, most brazen thieves, a financial titan who led a twisted, bizarre double life like some financial Dr. Jekyll and Mr. Hyde?

Where did he learn his values and ethics, or lack thereof, that fueled his twisted psyche?

Who aided and abetted him along the way?

Why did people trust him?

What made Bernie Madoff tick?

Here, now, is the true story of the Ponzi King, his rise and fall, from those who knew him best, or thought they did.

Chapter 2

Growing Up a Madoff

B ernie Madoff was a born operator who always seemed to know his way around the system—even when he was a young punk growing up in Queens.

In English class during his sophomore year at Far Rockaway High School, Bernie and his classmates were assigned to read a book and deliver an oral report. Bernie wasn't much of a student, and cared little about academics. Reading wasn't especially high on his list of things to do.

"Prior to the presentations," recalls classmate Jay Portnoy, "Bernie looked at my book. He just opened it up and said, 'Oh, yours looks boring.' I asked him why and he said, 'It doesn't have any pictures.'"

Bernie essentially ignored the reading assignment, and even let a couple of his pals, like Portnoy and Bernie's best friend, popular and good-looking Elliott Olin, in on the fact that he wasn't going to spend his spare time reading. He felt it was easier to just fake his way through class. Beyond that, he wasn't considered by his pals to be the brightest light in the academic firmament.

"Bernie didn't take the assignment, or school, that seriously," asserts Portnoy.

Even then Bernie was too busy thinking of ways to make money—an endeavor impressed upon him at home by his parents, Ralph and Sylvia.

"Money," maintains a longtime family friend, "was the Madoffs' aphrodisiac."

So Bernie figured he'd just deal spontaneously with the book report when the time came.

And it did, quite suddenly.

Bernie was one of the first in the class to be called upon by the teacher. Unshaken—and thoroughly unprepared—he strode confidently to the front of the room and successfully winged it.

"He gets up there and, looking quite serious, says, 'The book I'm reporting on is called *Hunting and Fishing* by Peter Gunn,'" remembers Portnoy. "And Elliott was in the second or third row and blurted out, 'Peter Gunn!?' followed by some stifled giggles."

Peter Gunn was the name of a suave, sophisticated TV detective.

"Our first inclination was to laugh, and then we realized we didn't want to throw the guy in," continues Portnoy. "If Bernie could carry it off, all the more power to him. We all kept quiet because we didn't want to blow his cover. No one wanted to see Bernie fry. For about 10 or 15 minutes Bernie just went through this whole story about *Hunting and Fishing* and pretty much was making the stuff up as he went along.

"He stretched it out smoothly and talked about a subject very few of us knew anything about, being from Queens. He acted as if he knew about hunting and fishing, which I'm sure the teacher knew nothing about. When Bernie was finished, she asked to see the book. Bernie said he didn't have it. He told her, 'I had to return it to the library.' We all had to stifle a laugh."

In hindsight, Portnoy thought it was possible that the teacher "saw through" Bernie's deception because she was only a decade older than her students "and pretty sharp. But, nobody could really get mad at Bernie. His put-on persona carried him through."

Describing the incident more than a half-century later—and after Bernie was in the headlines—Portnoy believed the book report affair, and other similar incidents that he witnessed during their school days, said much about his one-time chum who became the despised and infamous fraudster.

■ ■ ■

Bernard Lawrence Madoff was born in Brooklyn, New York, on April 29, 1938, just as the Great Depression that had ravaged the country was ending and as the flames of war were being fanned by Hitler in Europe. Bernie, as he would always be called, was the middle child of Ralph Z. and Sylvia "Susie" Muntner Madoff. Sondra, nicknamed "Sonnie," was the first of Ralph and Sylvia's brood, born in 1934, and Peter, considered the brightest of the three, was the last to arrive in 1945.

Bernie's family roots go back to Eastern Europe—Poland, Romania, and Austria. They came to the United States in the early twentieth century, part of the great wave of immigration of Jews from the ghettos and shtetls who landed on Ellis Island—the tired, poor, huddled masses seeking a new kind of life in America. Bernie wasn't introspective and not one to say much about where he came from. However, he once acknowledged that his grandparents, with whom he claimed he had lived for a time as a child, had settled in a "poor and run-down" Lower East Side neighborhood. The master mythmaker also asserted in a magazine article, whether true or not, that "I fought my way out of there. I had to scrape and battle and work really hard."

His younger brother, Peter, who was a trustee of the Lower East Side Tenement Museum, which promotes the experience of immigrant life, was quoted on its web site as saying, "My grandparents ran a Turkish bath in the area that served as a focal point for many new immigrants of different nationalities."

In the early 1940s, the Madoffs moved from a cramped tenement apartment to a modest three-bedroom, one-and-a-half-bath, brick colonial-style home on a postage-stamp-sized plot of grass that was typical of the houses in the quiet, tree-lined, close-knit, predominately Jewish and Italian, middle-class community of Laurelton, Queens. Laurelton was a neighborhood where kids could bicycle and play stickball in the streets, and where their parents didn't have to lock the doors at night.

Compared to the other couples who had settled in Laurelton around the same time, Ralph and Sylvia were older and more mysterious, or so they seemed to Bernie's childhood friends.

Bernie's father, Ralph, told some people he was a plumber, and he certainly fit the stereotype. He was a tough sort of guy, who reminded those who knew him of another Ralph—Ralph Kramden, the blustery New York bus driver played by Jackie Gleason on the popular golden age of television sitcom, *The Honeymooners*. Like the Kramdens' dreary Brooklyn apartment, the Madoff home in Laurelton was poorly furnished and depressing. And like Kramden, the bus driver, Madoff, the plumber, was always looking for a big score—a scheme that would make him lots of money.

"Ralph Madoff was not all sweetness and light. You got the feeling you didn't want to cross him," asserts Joe Kavanau, who became part of Bernie's life during their late teens when Kavanau and his girlfriend and future wife, Jane Silverstein, began double-dating with Bernie and his future wife and Jane's close friend, Ruthie Alpern.

Continues Kavanau:

> Ralph was a tough-looking guy. It was like this guy isn't going to take any shit from anyone. Back then if you had to describe the quintessential tough guy, particularly if he was a Jewish tough guy, he would be Ralph Madoff. You got the impression you didn't want to screw with him. He wasn't somebody one would go out of their way to cross.
>
> He was crude and tough-talking, rough-and-tumble. I could have picked him out of a lineup, and I could probably still pick him out of a lineup.

Kavanau, who then lived a few miles from Laurelton in Jamaica, Queens, and whose family was in the real estate business, says Bernie back then was far different from his father in looks and demeanor.

"Bernie was just the opposite of Ralph," Kavanau points out. "Bernie was pretty smooth, and he was much nicer looking than his father." When Joe married Jane in December 1960 at the Laurelton Jewish Center, Bernie was given the honor of being best man. Photos of him famously—or infamously—grace the Kavanaus' wedding album.

Jay Portnoy also saw Ralph Madoff as a tough guy. For a time, Bernie's father aggressively coached an unofficial football team formed by Bernie and his friends in the fall and winter of 1955–1956, their senior year at Far Rockaway High. The team was called the Long Island Spartans—with Bernie playing defensive end and quarterback. The playing field, located near the Aqueduct Racetrack, was on the grassy strip between the heavily traveled and polluted Belt Parkway and Conduit Boulevard.

Because Portnoy was smaller than the other boys, he was selected to be scorekeeper, and sometimes served as referee and linesman. He used chalk to outline the boundaries of the field, but there were no marked yard lines. Portnoy had poor eyesight, and his parents had not gotten him eyeglasses to correct his myopia; so he was not the best judge of where the pigskin should be placed, which ignited Ralph Madoff's fury.

"In one game Bernie's father started screaming at me for costing the team several downs," recalled Portnoy. "I finally assessed an 'unsportsmanlike behavior' [penalty] against the Spartans, for his outbursts. My actions were instrumental in the Spartans losing that game." Instantly, Portnoy regretted what he had done, because he was depending on Bernie's father to drive him home. On the ride back, Ralph Madoff "cooled off, and was not too nasty to me." But he did bluntly suggest that Portnoy have his eyes examined posthaste.

Looking back, Portnoy's complaint against the senior Madoff was that "he was a rather aggressive, intense individual who put a premium on winning. He was fairly intense, at least during the football games, and he definitely wanted to win. He seemed mildly authoritative—maybe that would be the best word. I don't know if Bernie was intense, because he tended not to seem that way. But it may be a case where he felt he could accomplish more of what his father accomplished in a different way. They both were very obviously success oriented."

Bernie's mother, Sylvia, was a tough cookie herself. As with her husband, Ralph, she always thought about money—how to make it and how to spend it, even when it came down to the least expensive items of apparel for her children.

The popular athletic shoe for boys when Bernie was a kid were sneakers called Keds with black canvas tops and white soles. But for a man who one day would proudly boast of dozens of expensive pairs of imported dress and sports shoes that he compulsively lined up in his luxuriously designed walk-in closet in his penthouse, Bernie was the only kid in his Laurelton crowd who didn't have Keds on his feet. And it embarrassed him no end. As a close friend notes, "His mother would buy his sneakers from a pile at a department store because they were priced cheaper, as opposed to buying him the more expensive Keds, the name brand that everyone wore."

Through the years certain friends who were aware of the Keds story would tease Bernie about it, especially as he became rich and powerful, and displayed the symptoms of what his friends and employees believed to be an obsessive-compulsive disorder.

"Bernie liked things to be done right," observes the close friend. "He liked to look nice. He liked expensive shoes and suits, cars and boats and houses. He liked his home to look just right; he wanted his office to look perfect—everything had to be perfect and in its place. And we used to kid around that he became compulsive about those things because his mother wouldn't buy him Keds when he was a kid like everyone else."

Later on, though, Bernie was determined to show everyone that he could have all the Keds he ever wanted, and lots more.

Bernie was clearly embarrassed by the way his parents lived and acted. Therefore, few of his friends were ever invited into the Madoff home. The place was off-limits and the household had an air of secrecy about it. Social gatherings and parties in which Bernie was involved—and he was thought of by most as a popular, friendly, good-looking kid—were always at the homes of others.

According to Sheila Olin, Elliott's widow, the mother of Bernie's best school friend distrusted and therefore disliked the Madoffs. Sheila Olin, a popular and cute girl who was the president of the social and cliquey sorority Phi Delta Gamma during her junior year of high school, asserts, "My husband's mother never wanted Elliott to be friends with Bernie, because she thought his parents weren't honest people. She did not want them to be friends, and she was not happy about it. She thought Bernie's parents were not owning up to a lot of things they were doing."

In fact, there were a lot of things about the Madoffs that didn't add up. One such source of constant neighborhood speculation was Ralph's and Sylvia's occupations. "It was always a mystery what Ralph and Sylvia did," says longtime Bernie friend Joe Kavanau. "That's absolutely a fact and it's kind of weird."

Ralph told some people he was a plumber, but no one remembers him ever doing any actual plumbing as a way to make a living. Years later he described himself to Bernie's personal messenger, Bill Nasi, as "a plumber in a pin-striped suit."

Moreover, on the Madoffs' 1932 certificate of marriage, the groom mysteriously listed "credit" as his occupation, while his bride put down "none."

Even Ralph Madoff's middle initial—the letter Z—was a fabrication of sorts. He decided it would be classier to have a middle initial, so he just chose to use the last letter of the alphabet.

Elliott Olin's mother especially disliked Ralph Madoff. "She used to say she liked Ralph less than Sylvia," recalls Sheila Olin, whose husband, a lawyer who specialized in workers' compensation, died of leukemia in his mid-50s. "Elliott's mother told him many times, 'I don't want you being in the Madoff house.' Bernie was at Elliott's house much more than Elliott was over at Bernie's. She didn't want Elliott to be friends with Bernie."

But Elliott, whose father was a lawyer, ignored his mother's entreaties, and he and Bernie would remain close friends for a number of years.

To add insult to injury, Bernie and Elliott introduced Sondra Madoff, Bernie's slender and attractive older sister, to Elliott's cousin, Marvin Wiener, a good-looking young man whose family owned a drugstore in Springfield Gardens, a community next to Laurelton.

Sondra and Marvin Wiener, who became a dentist, fell in love and got married.

"Elliott's mother wasn't too happy that her nephew married Sondra, because she didn't like the Madoff family," says Sheila Olin.

Over the years Sondra and Marvin Wiener, like thousands of others, invested their money with Bernie—Sondra having full trust in her brother's financial acumen, and faith that he would never injure her and her family financially. After all, Bernie was blood, a sibling, and a genius in their eyes when it came to making money for people. One of the Wieners' sons, Charles, even went to work at Bernard L. Madoff Investment Securities (BLMIS) in the 1970s, and became the firm's director of administration.

Apparently this mattered little to Bernie, because all of the Wieners would be among the victims in his monstrous Ponzi scheme.

But all of that was still to come.

■ ■ ■

While Sheila Olin notes that Elliott's mother, who died in the late 1960s, never went into detail regarding her ill will and suspicions about Ralph and Sylvia Madoff—"she never said why, how, where"— she believes it had to do with, among other possibilities, a shady stock brokerage operation that the Madoffs were running out of their home, which was located across the street and around the corner from the Olins.

It wasn't until later, in August 1963—with her son already running Bernard L. Madoff Investment Securities, then an over-the-counter and penny stock trading business, and doing quite well for himself at the age of 25—that Bernie's mother tangled with the SEC—a precursor of the problems Bernie would have later. The agency forced the closing of a broker-dealer operation called Gibralter Securities, which was registered to Sylvia Madoff and operated out of the Madoff home. She was one of 48 broker-dealers who, according to SEC records, had "failed to file reports of their financial condition."

The violation resulted in a September 1963 hearing for Sylvia Madoff and the other firms under investigation. In January 1964, the administrative proceeding against Bernie's mother was suddenly dropped. It is believed that she agreed to a deal to get out of the stock business as long as no penalties were leveled against her.

An SEC litigation release stated that the Madoff firm and the others "conceded the violation, but requested withdrawal of their registrations, and in this connection they represented that they are no longer engaged in the securities business and do not owe any cash or securities to customers. The Commission concluded that the public interest would be served by permitting withdrawal, and discontinued its proceedings."

However, suspicions about the Madoff operation lingered. There were those who thought she might have been fronting for her husband in Gibralter Securities—using her name instead of his because Ralph Madoff appeared to have ongoing financial problems and tax troubles. One of Bernie's Far Rockaway High School friends, Edwin Heiberger, who had met Ralph Madoff on a couple of occasions, had gotten the distinct impression from him that he "was a stockbroker." And another high school friend, Peter Zaphiris, clearly remembers Ralph Madoff working alongside Bernie in 1963, several years after Bernie started his firm.

(Years later, the other most important woman in Bernie's life besides his mother—his wife Ruth—would have her name on homes and other assets that sparked suspicion after Bernie was arrested.)

In addition, the Madoff house where Bernie grew up had liens against it for unpaid federal income taxes amounting to $13,245.28— equal to about $100,000 in 2009 dollars. Once again Sylvia Madoff's name, rather than Ralph's, was on all the official paperwork. She was listed as the "grantor/mortgager" for the property, according to Queens borough property records. The taxes were assessed in 1956, the year Bernie graduated from high school, and it wasn't until 1965, when Bernard L. Madoff Investment Securities celebrated its fifth anniversary in business, that the lien was finally paid off and the Madoff house was sold, with Ralph and Sylvia moving to the town of Lynbrook (an anagram for Brooklyn) on Long Island, a short distance from Laurelton.

It was in that sort of troubled and seemingly ethically and morally bankrupt household that Bernie's values, principles, behavior, sense of right and wrong, ideals, and standards were established.

■ ■ ■

Bernie bonded with Elliott Olin—and fell head over heels for Ruthie Alpern—at Public School 156 in Laurelton, where he got his elementary and middle school education.

Located about five blocks from the Madoff home on 228th Street, P.S. 156 was typical of the New York City public schools that were built around the time of the Great Depression—a three-story brick building with a high chain-link-style fence surrounding a playground. Inside the classrooms were too hot in the summer, and too cold in the winter. Mostly everyone wanted to walk home for lunch because of the yucky food served in the cafeteria.

The school, which went from kindergarten through the eighth grade, was located between the Long Island Railroad station and Merrick Road, Laurelton's main drag and commercial center.

Even though it was part of the urban landscape of New York and less than 30 minutes from bustling Times Square, there was a simple, small-town feel to Laurelton in those days—the wartime 1940s and the postwar Ozzie and Harriet 1950s when Bernie Madoff was coming of age. The kids called the local movie theater "the itch" and paid 25 cents on Saturday afternoons for a show of 25 cartoons. They went for ice cream at Raab's, a drugstore with a genuine soda fountain, browsed for yo-yos and gliders and rubber balls for stickball games at Woolworth's, and gathered with their families for Sunday dinners of chow mein and egg rolls at Chung's Chinese restaurant.

Because it was on the train line, Laurelton was a commuter town. Women were homemakers, and most husbands took the train into the city every day. The breadwinners ranged from small, struggling businessmen and New York City cops to accountants and doctors. Like the city itself, Laurelton was a melting pot.

"It was a magical place to grow up," as one former Laureletonian observed a half-century later.

At school Bernie became Elliott Olin's shadow. Elliott was the most popular boy at P.S. 156, handsome with curly blond hair, and was considered a hunk by the girls. Everywhere Elliott went and everything Elliott did, Bernie followed suit. "They were like Martin and Lewis, always together," observes Olin's widow, who from the time she first met Bernie thought of him as "a smooth talker" and "devious."

Jay Portnoy observes that Bernie "was never really that much of a leader, but he was always *with* the leader—Olin." He continues, "Elliott was good-looking, highly intelligent, willing to convince people to do things. Bernie was a follower, and the two of them seemed to work very well together."

So the two became partners in a social enterprise.

In seventh grade, Bernie and Olin started a club called the Ravens, and even had sweaters made with a Raven on them. One had to be considered among the school's elite to be in the club. Jay Portnoy, who became a member, recalls that the club had a "reverse quota system." Because the boys met at the Laurelton Jewish Center, the Ravens "always had to have one more Jew than non-Jew," he said. "If a popular gentile was wanted as a member, they had to search for a usually less popular Jew to invite."

Bernie liked sports, but he wasn't much of a player on the eighth-grade softball team. Portnoy, who kept statistics, recalled that in the season's first three games, Bernie had a batting average of .143, the lowest on the team. When Bernie saw the number, he angrily confronted Portnoy and demanded to know how well Portnoy himself had done at the plate. Portnoy acknowledged he was 0 for 5. When Bernie demanded to know why Portnoy hadn't listed himself as low man, he explained that the statistics covered only those with 10 at-bats.

"This answer did not make him happy," Portnoy noted years later. "He felt that if someone was doing more poorly than he, it should be shown—or, better still, just don't show *anyone* with a batting average under .200. The incident showed that Bernie did not appreciate negative publicity."

Bernie did a bit better on the basketball court. The eighth-grade team on which he played won the school championship. Bernie and Elliott Olin were the best players on the team, according to Portnoy, who supplied the popcorn for the fans.

Because his chum Olin was involved in so many school activities, Bernie joined in, too. He served as a monitor, essentially a crossing guard, and proudly wore a white Sam Brown belt that went across his right shoulder and around his waist. As a monitor he was part of a small group of boys who kept discipline in the schoolyard. Bernie also followed Elliott into the Boy Scouts of America—their troop met at the Jewish War Veterans building in Laurelton—and both stayed in scouting through high school.

Bernie had proudly taken the Boy Scout Oath the day he joined:

"On my honor I will do my best to do my duty to God and my country and to obey the Scout Law; To help other people at all times; To keep myself physically strong, mentally awake, and morally straight."

The first scout law that Bernie pledged to uphold was trustworthiness:

"A scout tells the truth. He keeps his promises. Honesty is part of his code of conduct. People can depend on him."

■ ■ ■

The Alperns—Saul, an accountant who had the demeanor of a college professor, and Sara, trained as a social worker, and their two pretty daughters, Ruth and Joan—moved to Laurelton from Brooklyn when Bernie was starting seventh grade and his future wife was beginning fifth grade.

Ruthie, blonde and green-eyed, had a sweet nature and a keen sense of style even at her young age. Immediately, she bonded with another neighborhood girl, Jane Silverstein, the equally blonde and cute daughter of a men's clothing manufacturer. Jane's father had chosen to move to Laurelton because it was on the train line to Penn Station, which was near his office in the garment district. Jane, whose family had also moved to Laurelton from Brooklyn, was a year older than Ruth and lived two blocks away. The only difference between Jane's cookie-cutter house and Ruth's was that the Alperns had a sunroom in back.

They were two very bright and pretty little girls whose lives would intertwine through the years.

The Silverstein girl, who lived on 227th Street, had gotten to know the Madoff boy, who lived on 228th Street, before Ruthie Alpern had moved to the neighborhood, on 229th Street. "Bernie was a year older," she recalls, "and he came to visit with some boys to see this girl who lived down the block who was his age, and that's when I first met him. He was a popular kid, and he and Elliott Olin were very, very good friends."

Ruth and Jane were good friends from fifth through eighth grade at P.S. 156.

"We were all part of a group. Ruth was a very likable girl who was smart, not bossy, and a good athlete."

She also had a prescient sense of style. Few if any Laurelton girls were decorating their own rooms. But Ruthie Alpern had the ability, the creativity, and the family money to do it.

"Her mother actually gave Ruth a budget and she was allowed to decorate her own room, which was really forward thinking," remembers Jane Silverstein Kavanau, Joe Kavanau's wife of some 50 years. "Ruth picked out nice things. She had very good taste, innate good taste. She always looked good."

(Years later, as Mrs. Bernie Madoff, Ruth would be intimately involved in not only her husband's business affairs, but also in the decorating of their many fabulous properties.)

For several summers, the two girls, Ruthie and Jane, went to an eight-week camp together, and were bunkmates. "I had gone to the camp for many summers and somehow or other Ruth found it interesting because I was so enthusiastic about it," says Jane Kavanau. "She spoke to her mother, and they met with the camp director and her parents decided to send her."

The camp was not inexpensive, but the Alperns could well afford it. Saul Alpern had a knack for making money and generating clients. Down the road, he would become one of Bernie's unofficial first feeder funds.

During Ruth's first summer at coed Camp Adventure, on the shores of Great Pond in bucolic Ridgefield, Connecticut, she set her sights on a boy, but not just any boy. His name was Bobby Dworsky and he was the son of the camp's owners, Bill and Ida Dworsky. Ruth, who would next set her sights on the Madoff boy, knew instinctively back then that it was important to be with a powerful male; in this case it didn't hurt that as the owners' son, Bobby had the run of the place, and Ruth was able to benefit from his perks. Ruth and Bernie—they'd be known that way as a team throughout their lives together—had not yet set each other's hearts aflutter, so the Dworsky boy was Ruth's boyfriend at camp.

The girls' last summer together at camp was in 1954, beginning a slight hiatus in their relationship because Jane left P.S. 156 to commute to a private day school on Long Island called Woodmere Academy, where she'd complete her high school education and meet her future husband. They'd pick up again when both were young marrieds.

Bernie and Ruth, meanwhile, had seen each other around P.S. 156, but being two years younger, she wasn't of much interest to him romantically. He had also gotten to know her because their fathers had become friends—their talk about money and how to make it being one of Saul Alpern's and Ralph Madoff's mutual interests.

Unlike many of the other Jewish and Italian girls at P.S. 156 who possessed stereotypically ethnic features, the Alpern girl had a blonde, WASPy look about her—the flaxen hair, fair skin, and green eyes. In today's world she'd probably be an Abercrombie & Fitch or Ralph Lauren girl, but with one big difference—an identifiable Queens accent. She looked nothing like either of her parents, neither of whom were especially attractive. Ruth's older sister, Joan, was pretty, but not on a par with her sibling.

Jane Kavanau remembers a day when she and Ruthie went to buy some candy at Hamils on Merrick Road, and the proprietor was shocked—*shocked*—to learn she wasn't a gentile because of her goyish look.

"The person who owned the candy store asked her, '*Why* are you wearing *that*?,' pointing to the little gold Star of David she wore on a delicate chain around her neck. So Ruth said, 'What do you mean?' He said, 'Why are you wearing that Jewish star?' And Ruth said, 'Why shouldn't I?' He said, 'But you're *not* Jewish!' But she was of course."

Years later, remembering those days, Kavanau notes that Ruth Alpern "looked like a shiksa. She did, absolutely. I did also but not as extremely shiksa-looking. Ruth and I used to mix our blonde hair together and you couldn't tell whose hair was whose. We used to kid around. We had long hair and we would make ponytails and mix them together and they'd all look the same color."

Ruth had several attributes going for her when she and Bernie started seriously dating when she was a freshman in the class of 1958 at Far Rockaway High School and Bernie was a junior. She had the shiksa look, but was Jewish; she was very social and outgoing, which was the opposite of him; she had a fashionista's sense of style—very preppy; and her father, Saul, was a shrewd and creative accountant who always had his eye on the dollar. Beyond that, Ruth herself was bright, and was a whiz at one particular subject in school. And that subject was math. She knew her numbers and how to work them.

Ruthie Alpern had all the right stuff for a fast-track operator like Bernie Madoff, who had dreams of becoming a Master of the Universe in the gilded canyons of Wall Street.

Chapter 3

Bernie Hobnobs with the Wealthy, Strong-Arms Some Pals, and Courts "Josie College"

ernie Madoff had a choice of two public high schools after graduating from P.S. 156 in June 1952—Andrew Jackson or Far Rockaway, both of which were in the Laurelton district. With his mediocre grades, he never would have made the cut for the elite public secondary schools such as the Bronx High School of Science, or Brooklyn Technical, where his brother, Peter, would be accepted.

Bernie chose Far Rockaway primarily because it attracted a relatively affluent, fast-track crowd. The other option, Andrew Jackson in St. Albans, Queens, was garnering a reputation as a *Blackboard Jungle* sort of school.

As Jay Portnoy, who commuted on the 20-minute train ride to Far Rockaway with Bernie and Elliott Olin, observed, "St. Albans was becoming New York City's first suburban American black area," drawing kids from poor neighborhoods, "which scared many of Laurelton's liberal Jewish parents."

However, many of those same parents, like Ruth's, had low-paid black maids—*schwartzes*, they called them—working either full-time or part-time in their homes.

"They were bringing young girls, young black women up from the South to work in the houses," says former Laureltonian Marion Dickstein Sherman, a doctor's daughter, whose family had a live-in black maid. Sherman, who was a classmate and sorority sister of Ruth's, observes, "Andrew Jackson was getting a little scary. It was low-income, scary black." But she points out that the decision for her to go to Far Rockaway had nothing to do with any form of discrimination, just perceived danger. "That was the feeling."

Bernie's four years at Far Rockaway were for the most part uneventful, except for his social climbing.

Just like he bonded with popular Elliott Olin at P.S. 156, the likable kid from Laurelton began rubbing shoulders in high school with rich kids from the more affluent Rockaway Peninsula oceanfront communities of Neponsit and Belle Harbor. Bernie appeared to have a preternatural ability to move in moneyed circles even in his youth.

Money, and making it, was the gospel he had heard at home from his parents. Their indoctrination had taken hold. Bernie knew that to be a success he needed to move among the affluent.

In that well-to-do Far Rockaway crowd, he became close friends with Cynthia Greenberger and her high school steady and future husband Michael Lieberbaum, an honor student in math. Greenberger's wealthy family would later invest big money with Bernie when he started his company right out of college, and they would lose big money in his Ponzi scheme. At the same time, Lieberbaum's father, who became incredibly wealthy virtually overnight as a stockbroker, would play a key—and very questionable—role in generating business for Bernie in his early days.

At Far Rockaway High, Bernie was laying the groundwork—dotting the i's and crossing the t's, as it were—for his future.

One thing was for certain, though: He wasn't an academic wizard. Bernie's high school performance was unexceptional, and at best he was a C student.

"Bernie was not the brightest bulb," recalls Far Rockaway classmate Mike Gandin, who became an attorney and a Madoff victim.

After Bernie was branded the "Ponzi King" by the tabloids, two other classmates, John Avirom, who was on the swim team with Bernie and became an immigration lawyer, and Peter Zaphiris, who became a businessman, got in touch and reminisced about the Bernie they remembered.

"When the shit hit the fan," says Zaphiris, "I e-mailed Johnny to chuckle about what happened with Bernie, because we'd carry on in school about how he was the dumbest white man we ever met in our lives—excuse me for the pejorative. It's not fair to say he wasn't bright. The guy was a *dummy* in high school. If you said, 'Hey, Bernie, how are you?' his head would tilt to the side—he had a nervous tick—he'd squint, one eye would flutter, and he'd grunt, 'Hello.' He was rather laconic, didn't have much to say, never told a joke or said, 'Look at her—she's some piece of ass,' or anything like that. That was pretty much Bernie. He was just no place."

Or so it seemed.

Fast-forward to one afternoon in the summer of 2008, as Bernie was scrambling to raise big money in a last-ditch effort to avoid getting caught. Zaphiris ran into him strolling in Manhattan's Central Park. "I said, 'Bernie, how're you doing?' And he pulled up his sleeve and he's got two gold Rolexes on his wrist—the same wrist—and I said, 'Bernie, how come you're wearing two watches?' So he still blinks like hell and he leans over and he talks out of the side of his mouth and he says, 'I gotta know what time it is in my London office.' Think about that. He couldn't do the addition and the subtraction" to determine the time difference across the pond.

In the sleek offices of Bernard L. Madoff Investment Securities, where Bernie often boasted of the computerized high technology with which he supplied his traders, he barely knew how to Google, or send and receive e-mail. He thought a BlackBerry was a dessert. It was hard to believe, but true. This was the same self-proclaimed Wall Street wizard who had always claimed he came up with the idea for computerized trading. A former employee who helped co-workers with computer problems set up Bernie's PC as if for a newbie: It was always turned on, it gave him only limited business news that any stay-at-home-mom day trader had access to, and if a minor glitch occurred that a computer-savvy seven-year-old could easily have fixed, Bernie acted as if the World Wide Web had been knocked out by the Taliban. He'd get stressed, and would call for immediate help.

All of which caused friends who thought of Bernie at Far Rockaway High as a "dumb schmuck" to wonder years later how in the world he was able to pull off his amazing fraud all on his own—as he claimed when he pleaded guilty.

"That's what Bernie disdained most. He didn't *want* to be a schmuck, but he really was," observes Cynthia Greenberger Lieberbaum's younger brother, John, who years later as a screenwriter, novelist, and software entrepreneur changed his last name to Maccabee. After Bernie was busted, Maccabee wrote an article for *New York* magazine in hopes, he says, of getting a deal to write a memoir or a novel about his family— an article that angered the Greenbergers and the Lieberbaums because he revealed that the two families clearly had connections to the world's biggest crook.

"Obviously my sister and my brother [Washington, D.C.– based former *Wall Street Journal* Supreme Court reporter Robert Greenberger] are not responding well to the piece," he notes. "They are furious with me. They feel as though I have made something public about their involvement with Bernie. It's rather laughable, but it's wreaking havoc with my family. The Greenbergers believe that there are only three times you should be mentioned in a newspaper—your birth, your marriage, and your death—and that's what they're about. We prided ourselves on being a perfect sort of family, and I guess the article throws some chinks in the works."

The article was entitled: "Mom and Dad and Ruth and Bernie— Our Friend the Swindler."

■ ■ ■

Bernie's extracurricular high school activities consisted of being a locker-room guard and a member of the school's swim team, the Sea Horses— dubbed the Mermen, according to team captain Fletcher Eberle.

Bernie, who joined the team in his sophomore year, "swam butterfly, and I was very often the anchor—freestyle anchor—in the medley relay," says Eberle, who grew up near the Long Island beaches and had joined the Mermen in his freshman year.

Always thinking about ways to make money, Bernie parlayed his swimming ability into a job in his junior or senior years as a lifeguard at the exclusive Silver Point Beach Club in Atlantic Beach, an affluent oceanfront community. Bernie's swimming had impressed the Mermen coach, Richie Sierer, an ex-Marine, who recruited him to work at the club along with others from the team. The pay was about $65 a week. The private club, which had opened in 1938, had some 60 acres of white-sand beachfront, and its well-to-do members rented luxurious oceanfront cabanas for the summer. They were Bernie's kind of people, the kind he would later target.

Eberle considered Bernie "sort of devil-may-care. He didn't take anything overly seriously. When we had a very important meet, we tried to get him hyped up, but he never really cared. But when he had to get in the pool and swim, he did."

Eberle and Bernie had different physiques. Eberle was extraordinarily strong though he stood only five feet five—"everything a swimmer shouldn't be. But I beat out guys who were six feet tall because I had very strong arms, a very strong physique like Johnny Weismuller [an Olympic gold medal swimmer who played Tarzan in the movies]. Bernie never swam the 100-yard breaststroke or butterfly. He always swam the 50-yard event. He was not overly muscular, but muscular enough that he could pull himself out of the water doing the butterfly stroke—a strenuous exercise. Once he got in the water he was pretty driven and ambitious to win."

Indeed, Bernie was a strong swimmer with apparent ice water in his veins. When John (Greenberger) Maccabee was 10 years old he had gone swimming in the Atlantic with Bernie and his future brother-in-law, Mike Lieberbaum, off the Greenberger family's beach in Neponsit. Starting out strong, the Greenberger boy began losing momentum and was near the point of flailing. He looked over at Bernie to signal that he was in possible trouble. But Bernie, eyeing the boy, offered no help. The return swim was even tougher for Maccabee, who recalled

Bernie in his "Noo Yawk accent" telling him, "Take longer strokes. Reach. Trust yourself."

He wondered years later whether that was Bernie's credo.

During Bernie's stint as a Merman, and despite his abilities in the water, his team never won a championship, but did rank in the top three or four among New York's public school swimming teams, according to Eberle. A 1954 issue of the Far Rockaway school newspaper, *The Chat*, reported that the team had a 4–4 record for the season, and stated that the medley team on which Bernie swam had won their first two meets.

Unlike most of the others in Bernie's circle at school, Eberle didn't go to college after graduation, but instead went into the Coast Guard for four years and stayed in the reserves for more than three decades, retiring as a chief warrant officer. He hadn't follow Bernie's career. But when he read about Bernie's arrest, he contacted another classmate, Carol Solomon Marsden. "I said, 'Is that *our* Bernie?' I couldn't believe it. If you told me that guy that I knew in the pool was into all this high finance, let alone major crimes, I wouldn't believe it. I don't have any transcripts to go by, but I know he was not a brain in school. I never thought he was super intelligent."

As a locker-room guard—his only other extracurricular activity— Bernie usually sat around kibbitzing or playing roughneck, macho games such as punch-for-punch, which Bernie felt was idiotic but still participated to avoid being labeled a sissy. The game consisted of one boy slamming his fist into another boy's fist or shoulder.

"We would see Bernie with his knuckles bruised," recalls Jay Portnoy. "He didn't want the others to think he was chicken, or afraid to do it. But he said it was a stupid game, and referred to the other locker guards as 'a bunch of dummies.' He went along because, again, it was a case where [if he didn't participate] he would stand out as some- how not being sufficiently manly, or having enough testosterone."

■ ■ ■

Bernie was always looking for a way to make a fast buck between semesters.

When he heard that two classmates, 15-year-old Eddie Heiberger and Sheldon "Shelley" Fogel, had formed a company called Shedwin—for Shelley and Edwin—and were raking in good money installing sprinkler systems for new homeowners moving from the crowded New York City boroughs to the tract house suburbs of Nassau County on Long Island, Bernie tried to shoulder his way in on their action—with the help of his tough-talking father.

"For kids, we made five or ten grand for the summer," says Heiberger. "Bernie's father wanted him to be involved. His father was very aggressive, and he wanted Bernie to go into partners with myself and Shelley."

The whole lawn sprinkler business would become part of the Bernie Madoff myth. To impress clients years later, he boasted that he bankrolled his 1960 start-up stock and investment business with money saved from installing lawn sprinklers and working as a lifeguard—all of which made for a good story, but was not exactly true. But it honed his image as the quintessential boy from Queens who pulled himself up by his bootstraps and became a multi millionaire and a financial wizard.

At one time lawn sprinkler systems were complicated affairs, requiring expensive copper pipe that had to be cut and fitted and welded; installation was difficult, costly, and labor intensive, and few but the very well-off could afford to buy such systems. But by the early 1950s, when Bernie was in high school, inexpensive sprinkler kits made of flexible polyethylene pipe had become available, along with cheap plastic sprinkler heads.

"As a high school kid I thought installing these things was a good business. Nobody's doing it. We were entrepreneurial," says Heiberger, a lawyer's son, who was in Bernie's class of 1956, and his future wife in Ruth's. "Rockaway," he notes, "had a pretty aggressive group."

A lawn sprinkler kit cost as little as $59, but Heiberger and Fogel charged a homeowner as much as $500 for materials and labor.

"Bernie heard what I was doing installing sprinklers," says Heiberger, "and his father said, 'Go in with Eddie and Shelley—they're raking it in.' Shelley was an entrepreneur like myself hustling a business that made money."

Like the characters in the film *Tin Men*, who used creative tactics to lure customers into buying aluminum siding for their homes, Heiberger and Fogel sometimes used shrewd ploys themselves in order to make a sale.

"It was the beginning of tract homes in Nassau County, on Long Island, and people were putting a lot of money into landscaping, and we were able to convince them not to water their lawns by hand with a hose," says Shelley Fogel. "I'd see a guy watering his lawn, and I'd stop by and start smacking my arms and smacking my legs like mosquitoes were biting me, and I'd show them their shoes were getting all muddy. We'd get them that way. We were getting all these young couples moving to the island from Brooklyn. We gave landscapers stickers with our name and number to hand out to their customers when they mowed lawns, and we'd give them 10 percent of the job."

In order to get cheap labor, he says, they recruited help in black neighborhoods. "They would think we were cops when we walked in," he says. "We used to pay $1.50 an hour when we needed guys."

In the end, Heiberger, who became a successful home builder on Long Island, and Fogel, who went into gaming in Las Vegas, decided against a third partner, which would have reduced their profits. As a result, Bernie went off on his own, a venture he would continue through his college years on a much larger and better-financed scale, and use even more creative tactics to lure customers. However, his brother, Peter, when he was in high school and a student at Queens College, worked for Heiberger and Fogel for a few summers.

"Peter was a good kid," says Fogel. "He had more of a personality than Bernie, and was smarter. Bernie wasn't that bright."

Heiberger had had little or no contact with Bernie after high school.

In November 2008, however, his wife attended the 50th reunion of her Far Rockaway class of 1958, and ran into Ruth Alpern Madoff— who had been voted "Josie College" by her classmates a half-century earlier because of her preppy, peppy, popular persona. She was listed in the Dolphin yearbook as one of the "senior personalities." Another classmate, Barbara Aronson Curreri, also ran into her at the reunion before "all the crap hit the fan," as she put it, referring to Bernie's arrest just weeks after his appearance at the Fort Lee, New Jersey, hotel where the reunion was held. "Ruth looked absolutely stunning," Curreri observes. "She looked in high school exactly the way she looks now, very pretty."

Another member of the class, also a Laureltonian, says Ruth sat at a table at the reunion "with a group she's friendly with because some of her friends from school invested with Bernie. Ruth was a smart girl, not a shrinking violet that follows blindly. Take it from there."

However, Bernie's pal Elliott Olin considered Ruth to be "an airhead," recalls Jay Portnoy, who developed a friendship of sorts with Ruth when the two were students at Queens College. He suggests that possibly "Elliott was a bit envious [because] of being displaced in Bernie's attentions" by the petite, cute blonde who would become Mrs. Madoff in just a few years.

Ruth had been far more popular and involved in extracurricular activities at Far Rockaway than had been Bernie, although her main yearbook photo has her looking rather glum compared to the other graduates, who are pictured smiling. Ruth had been on the staff of the school newspaper, was a member of the Forum Club, was secretary to one of the teachers, and was a representative of the G.O. Council, a link between the students and faculty that sponsored the Kick Off Hop and Barn Dance.

Volunteers from the class of 1958 had turned out a two-inch-thick, colorful, sentimental, and nostalgic book for the reunion that the Heibergers had sitting on a coffee table. In early December 2008 they invited some friends over who were skimming through the book, which featured a color photo of Bernie and Ruth smiling at the camera and looking richly tanned in expensive, preppy sports outfits and chic sunglasses.

Says Heiberger:

When the wife looks at their picture, she says, "Oh, my God, there's Bernie Madoff. He's the hottest broker. So and so invested a lot of money with him! They've been with him for years. He doesn't take all accounts. Bernie's like the guru of investing."

That's how they portrayed him.

A week later Bernie was arrested.

Shelley Fogel jokingly asserts that Bernie "started his own Social Security. Social Security is like a Ponzi scheme," he maintains. "The last ones in pay for the first guys that were in. That's what Bernie did."

After the Madoff scandal broke, Fogel was offered $250 for his Far Rockaway yearbook that had a photo of the internationally infamous fraudster along with his autograph. Bernie had simply written: "To Fogue, Lots of luck in college, Bernie."

In September 1956, Bernie, too, was about to begin his own college career, in the segregated Deep South of all places.

Chapter 4

From Queens to Alabama, Scamming Homeowners and Hustling Stock

When 18-year-old Bernie Madoff arrived at the University of Alabama, on the banks of the Black Warrior River in Tuscaloosa, in September 1956, the school was embroiled in racial ferment.

While the U.S. Supreme Court had ruled in 1954 against segregated schools in the landmark *Brown v. Board of Education* case, Bernie's college of choice was still all-white—and would stridently remain so for some years to come.

Just seven months before his arrival, a 26-year-old black woman by the name of Autherine Juanita Lucy, who had earned a bachelor of arts degree in English at an all-black college in Alabama, was reluctantly accepted by the University of Alabama administration, and with racist hostility from students and the community.

A number of court cases eventually upheld by the Supreme Court, and with the support of civil rights attorney and future Supreme Court Justice Thurgood Marshall, along with activism by the National Association for the Advancement of Colored People (NAACP), resulted in Lucy being admitted on February 3, 1956, as a graduate student in library science. She was "the first Negro" ever permitted to attend a white public school or university in Alabama's long and scandalous history of segregation and racial violence. Though allowed in classrooms, she was barred from dining halls and dormitories; the hope was she would quickly drop out.

But three days into her matriculation, an angry, stick-wielding, confederate flag-waving mob of students and outsiders riled up by the Ku Klux Klan and other hatemongers blocked her from attending classes. A news photograph of the riot scene showed university students standing around a bonfire burning desegregation literature.

If Bernie, who had announced his plan to attend the University of Alabama in his Far Rockaway yearbook, had read the February 7 front page of the *New York Times*—doubtful since he wasn't a reader and cared little about current events—he would have seen the two-column, above-the-fold headline that read: "Negro Co-ed Is Suspended to Curb Alabama Clashes."

According to the report, she was spirited off the campus and Tuscaloosa policemen had to fire tear gas to break up "a midnight anti-Negro demonstration." At one point demonstrators had been "pelting eggs on an elderly Negro" who had driven Autherine Lucy to the campus from Birmingham, the *Times* reported. University officials said she was suspended "for her own safety."

That was the bigoted and rabble-rousing atmosphere that permeated the campus when Bernie arrived in Alabama in the fall of 1956.

The issues of racism and segregation were not of concern to Bernie—Laurelton and Far Rockaway High School had few, if any, blacks, and blacks were sequestered in ghetto neighborhoods in the New York boroughs and on Long Island. Segregation was simply an accepted way of life to him, de facto as it was up North. Bernie was no liberal activist.

After registering, he immediately began pledging for a fraternity. It was called Sigma Alpha Mu, known as "Sammy," and had only Jewish members.

Curiously, while blacks were blocked from the campus, Jews—another group discriminated against in the South back then—were welcomed. Jewish friends of Bernie's, such as Joe Kavanau, then starting at the Ivy League's Columbia College in New York City, were surprised that he would go to school in the South "where they thought Jews had horns and tails."

But as far back as the 1920s the University of Alabama actually encouraged Jewish students to come on down, especially those from the Northeast where many colleges had quotas restricting Jewish enrollment.

George Denny, a university president, had started the cheerleading for the Jewish recruitment—not because he was a flaming liberal, but mainly because the school was financially struggling during his tenure and he needed to fill the coffers with out-of-state tuition money.

William Bradford Huie, the writer, who had attended the University of Alabama in the late 1920s during Denny's tenure, wrote in his autobiographical novel *Mud on the Stars* that those early Jewish students brought a competitive and academic focus to the university. At the same time, those outsiders sparked clashes with the slow-paced, Old South school culture. As a result, the Jews from up North were not welcomed in the traditional fraternities, so they started their own.

By the mid-1950s, when Bernie arrived, there were almost a thousand Jewish students attending Alabama; there were four Jewish fraternities like Sammy, and three Jewish sororities. Most of the members were from the New York City area.

In any case, the Jewish question at Alabama, good or bad, wasn't of concern to Bernie. He decided to matriculate there because he wanted to get away from home, the school had easy entrance requirements, he couldn't get accepted elsewhere, and the tuition was especially low. Moreover, he is believed to have received either a swimming scholarship or a partial U.S. Army Reserve Officer Training Corps (ROTC) scholarship, friends recall, with his pledge that he would stay in the cadet corps for all four years of college, and then serve his country on active duty.

Along with joining Sammy, Bernie became a proud member of Alabama's rifle-toting Crimson Tide Battalion.

"Bernie liked the spit-and-polish. He liked the uniform that had to be crisp and pressed. He even wore it sometimes when he wasn't required to wear it. I guess it sated his obsession with neatness," observes a classmate who had trained with Bernie on campus.

The lineage of the Alabama Corps of Cadets began in 1860, and boasts of having produced half a dozen Alabama governors, hundreds of CEOs and presidents of major companies, a couple of dozen judges, a Congressional Medal of Honor winner, the founder of Habitat for Humanity, and the author of the book that was made into the film *Forrest Gump*, among others.

Cadet Bernie Madoff was in good company.

■ ■ ■

Like his classmates at Far Rockaway, his roommate in the Sammy House, Marty Schrager, from Long Island—another future Madoff investor—was unimpressed with him. The two roomed together not by choice but by chance—a drawing was held to team up the new pledges.

"There was nothing outstanding about Bernie, nothing that would lead anyone to believe that he was a genius or a financial whiz. There was nothing sinister about him. There was *nothing* about him whatsoever," observes Schrager. "Bernie was just an ordinary guy from Queens. This was not a guy I would ever think could, or would, be involved with billions of dollars."

As roommates, Bernie and Schrager "studied together, hung out, went to parties, and pledged Sammy together. It was typical hazing," he recalls. "We were forced to stay up all night, had to wear a burlap sack to class, had our heads shaved, wore beanies, silly things like that."

Asked how it felt to be a Jew in racist Alabama in the mid-1950s, with all that was happening, he claims, "If there was [segregation or anti-Semitism], I never saw anything like that. In terms of blacks, we had black help in the house and they were treated like family. Half of the guys in our fraternity were Southern boys, and the others were Northern boys, not only from New York."

Aside from Schrager, none of the 30 or so Sammy fraternity brothers remembered Bernie being there. Others had vague memories of him: "Nice enough," "low-key," "lacked any personality trait," and "stayed out of trouble" were the typical comments.

One event does stand out, though.

When the fraternity had a big party and dance, Schrager and a few others recall, "a cute little blonde from New York flew down to spend a weekend with Bernie."

His date presumably was Ruth, who would have been a 16-year-old junior at Far Rockaway at the time.

Bernie stayed for just his freshman year. Presumably wanting to be closer to Ruth, who was about to become a senior at Far Rockaway, he left Alabama for the last time in June 1957, and headed home to Laurelton, and his roots.

■ ■ ■

Marty Schrager graduated from Alabama and went into business. But the two former Sammy roommates' paths crossed again in a very curious manner in the late 1970s. By chance, they wound up having the same accountant, Michael Bienes, a man who along with his partner, Frank Avellino, would be a prominent figure in the rise and fall of Bernie Madoff.

"Mike was a jovial guy who didn't seem overly bright, either," says Schrager. "He kept telling me that he had a client who was making all sorts of money for everyone. He was always talking about him, and I never asked for details. But one day I said, 'So, who's this client of yours?' And he said, 'It's Bernard Madoff.' I said, 'You mean you're talking about *Bernie* Madoff?' And he said, 'No, it's Bernard L. Madoff Investment Securities.' And I said, 'Tell Bernie that he still owes me a pair of socks from college.' And Mike laughed at me.

Schrager continues,

Well, the next week I saw him and he was like, "Oh, you really do know Bernie. He was your roommate." Mike, who did the books for me and did the books for Bernie, then impressed upon me to invest money with Bernie's firm. Obviously, Mike made a commission, but I never could understand what was going on. I didn't understand the statements I was getting, so after about a year or so I decided to get out my money.

This was the late 1970s, Jimmy Carter was the president, and banks [because of soaring inflation] were paying interest rates of about 18 percent, and they even gave you a toaster. Then I read later that Bernie was chairman of Nasdaq. I said, "Oh my God, I can't believe this. This is Bernie Madoff? It's like a non sequitur. This is the guy I used to bop around with. Nobody thought he could rise to those heights." My wife said, "You schmuck. You shoulda kept our money in there for 15 more years."

It never dawned on me that Madoff and Company was doing all this business and Bernie had Mike Bienes as his accountant. I guess I was stupid. But everyone was stupid. No one ever questioned that Bernie was doing billions of dollars of business and he's got a two-man accounting firm. It's just like it slipped through the cracks. No one ever bothered to ask about it.

In fact, as it would later be revealed by the SEC, the firm of Avellino & Bienes did more than accounting. They had started in business with Ruth's father, Saul Alpern, and were feeding investors to Bernie early on—and they would become very rich doing it. (In the early 1990s, the SEC would probe their operation, force them to return investors' money, and put them out of business. But they still continued as a feeder fund. The Avellino & Bienes affair would be the first red flag raised and mishandled by the SEC.)

In the mid-1990s or thereabouts, Schrager was invited to attend a business meeting in Boca Raton, Florida, just south of Palm Beach, where Bernie by then had a multimillion-dollar home and a yacht and belonged to the best country clubs. It was there that he was actively working his Ponzi scheme with a slew of the posh resort's wealthy, mostly Jewish elite.

"There were two guys in my friend's office and they were laughing and joking and having a great time," says Schrager. "I was introduced to these two guys, and they had just come off a cruise and they told me that the whole cruise was sponsored by Bernie Madoff, and they were boasting, 'Oh, we're making so much money. It's like crazy.'

"So I said, 'Do you think you could get me an introduction? Maybe I could invest some money in Madoff.'" Schrager was only putting them on, interested in how they would respond. "And one of the guys says, 'Oh, no, no, no! It's closed. He's not taking on any new business.'"

■ ■ ■

In September 1957, Bernie enrolled as a sophomore at Hofstra College, in the town of Hempstead, Long Island. He decided to major in political science, which he had heard was an easy way to skim his way to a bachelor of arts degree. Tuition was inexpensive, and he was able to live at home, thus cutting his expenses. Besides, he and Ruth were now a genuine item.

Back then, before Hofstra expanded and became a full-fledged university in 1963, it was a commuter school. "It was like an extension of high school," says a classmate of Bernie's. Although some big names graduated from there—including director Francis Ford Coppola; actors James Caan, Madeline Kahn, and Christopher Walken; singer Lainie Kazan; and New York Governor David Paterson—the school when Bernie attended was considered to be one of the bottom-feeders of New York City area institutions of higher education.

Just like at P.S. 156, Far Rockaway, and Alabama, Bernie made no impact during his three years at Hofstra. In fact, he didn't even bother to show up for his class's yearbook picture. He was virtually invisible, except for the fact that he continued to serve in ROTC and proudly wore the Army green uniform, drilled weekly, and attended summer training encampments—determined to win the two gold bars of a second lieutenant.

He also knew by this time what he wanted to do with his life. His father and mother, Ralph and Sylvia, who were involved in what was a questionable stock business, and his future father-in-law, Saul Alpern, the creative accountant who would send him some of his earliest investors, had convinced Bernie that Wall Street and the business of trading stocks and managing other people's money was where it was at—where he could make lots and lots of dough.

"Starting a stock brokerage was what Bernie always wanted to do," notes Joe Kavanau. "That was his goal."

■ ■ ■

To make a fast buck during his Hofstra years, Bernie decided to go back into the lawn sprinkler installation business that he first tried in high school. But he needed financial backing. Curiously, he had led some people to believe that his parents were dead and he had no family to give him financial help. Moreover, he had started hustling stocks to friends and fellow classmates at Hofstra, offering them hot tips on penny stocks. He was not a registered stockbroker at the time, and he never told any of his customers with whom he was placing their buys.

To his rescue for financial backing for his sprinkler business came one Sheldon "Shelley" Lieberbaum, a Far Rockaway and Hofstra alumnus and the older brother of Bernie's high school chum, Mike Lieberbaum. Their father, Lou Lieberbaum, had struck it rich in the stock market, bought an expensive seat on the New York Stock Exchange, opened a brokerage—and would help put Bernie on the map by sending him lucrative business a few years hence.

"My husband is the one who put him in the sprinkler system business. Bernie had no money. Shelley loaned him five to ten thousand dollars. I was told he didn't have parents to help him," says Carol Ann Lieberbaum, the widow of Shelley Lieberbaum. A Brooklyn girl, the former Carol Ann Martz first met Bernie in 1958 when she began dating her future husband, and would know him and Ruth for a lifetime.

In fact, as it would turn out, Bernie may have actually used all or part of that loan from Shelley Lieberbaum as capital to fund his start-up brokerage—and he may have been placing his buys for college friends while at Hofstra through Lieberbaum & Company, owned by Shelley and Mike's father.

And down the road Bernie's Ponzi scheme would wipe out Carol Ann and members of her family.

■ ■ ■

Bernie had an interesting marketing ploy when he resumed his lawn sprinkler installation business while a student at Hofstra. Knowing that his potential customers were young couples, including desperate housewives who were home alone in the suburbs all day, he hired good-looking laborers: two fellow students, Mike Gandin and Gordon Ondis, who drew women to them like investors to Madoff.

Gandin had been in Bernie's class at Far Rockaway High and had previous experience installing sprinkler systems for classmates Ed Heiberger and Sheldon Fogel. Ondis, who was a few years older, had just gotten out of the army as a young sergeant, and was married.

Ondis used to hang out at the Hofstra cafeteria table frequented by members of the Epsilon Sigma fraternity, and that was where he first ran into Bernie, who also was a regular there.

Recalls Ondis:

He came up to me one day, and there I am in my army fatigues, and he says, "Hey, good-lookin', how about you wanna job?" Bernie had a shrewd marketing approach. Mike and I were both handsome young gentlemen, and Bernie recruited Mike and me simply on the basis of our physical attributes—there's no doubt about it.

Bernie was the salesman. Mike and I did the labor. Bernie would take us around when he priced jobs. He'd knock on the door and he'd have Mike and me walk around the property talking loud enough for the homeowner to hear about where sprinkler heads were needed. Typically, the homeowner would come out and invariably he would be with his young wife, and she's seeing us—two guys over six feet tall, 185 pounds, lots of hair, and good-looking, both tall, dark, and handsome.

I don't think there's any doubt that the wives saw us and that sealed the deals for Bernie. During the course of those jobs, some of those wives flirted with us and absolutely came on to us. They were always coming out to chat and give us ice tea or sodas.

Agreed the more modest Gandin years later, "The girls liked us."

Ondis, who went on to make a killing and become a multimillionaire investing in inner-city housing, says Bernie was paying him and Gandin, a future lawyer—and Madoff Ponzi scheme victim—two to three dollars an hour.

Typically, Bernie paid $150 for materials and charged $700 or more for an installation. We did this spring, summer, and fall. He was making good money, as much as $2,000 a week. We'd do an installation in a day, and we were working as many as seven days a week.

Bernie's target area was the part of Nassau County, on Long Island, that bordered Queens and was known as the Five Towns—the villages of Cedarhurst and Lawrence, the hamlets of Woodmere and Inwood, and a grouping of communities called the Hewletts, where Shelley Lieberbaum's father, Lou, had a spectacular home on the water in swanky Hewlett Harbor. Years later, Hewlett Harbor was the setting for a fictional television series called *Five Towns* on the HBO series *Entourage*. And the village of Lawrence was where Lorraine Bracco's real-life character, Karen Friedman, lived and became the wife of the real-life mobster Henry Hill in the Mafia movie *Goodfellas*.

Bernie's sprinkler system market area was that kind of place.

Bernie worked quick and he worked dirty—he never got the required building or work permits, didn't always put much thought into his installations, and showed little knowledge about what he was doing. But he still raked in the money.

On one job, he had his workers in a customer's yard dig a well for a sprinkler system. An interested neighbor watching them slaving away came over and asked, "Do you guys have any idea about the water table in this area?" When they said no, he told them that they would have to dig down as much as 100 feet. "That attests to how smart Bernie wasn't," observes Ondis. "He has sold this guy an elaborate sprinkler system, but didn't know how deep we had to dig. We're like two jackasses trying to dig this well. That certainly showed that Bernie was not a whiz when it came to the technical aspects of his business."

Ondis continues, "When the guy came home and Bernie told him that it would cost more money to do the installation than he had estimated, the customer didn't go for it. As a result, Bernie had us abandon all the work and the materials and we just walked away from the job."

Years later Bernie's many dissatisfied sprinkler system customers were still confronting him.

"There'd be times we'd be out having dinner—Jane and I and Bernie and Ruth," recalls Joe Kavanau, "and some guy would come over to Bernie and say, 'You put in my sprinkler system three years ago and I've been trying to find you. It needs to be fixed!' People would come over and shake their fists at him. And that happened on more than one occasion, which was kind of funny."

■ ■ ■

While Bernie was raking in money making suburbanites' lawns wet and pretty, and using questionable tactics to do it, he also was starting to hawk stock tips, and even went so far as to boast to gullible classmates that he had actually bought a seat on the New York Stock Exchange, according to friends from that time.

"I don't think there was any doubt that Bernie was headed for Wall Street," asserts Gordon Ondis. "I don't think there was any doubt that becoming a stockbroker was his focus. I never heard him say, 'That's my life ambition,' but there's no doubt in my mind, or anyone else's mind, that that's where his interest lay at that time. He was *always* talking securities and stocks."

During a sprinkler installation job, Ondis remembers Bernie pitching a stock to co-worker Mike Gandin, who agreed to buy 100 shares. Years later Gandin doesn't actually recall the purchase, but notes, "My whole life I bought crummy stocks, so it's not impossible that I would have spent $300 on a stock tip from Bernie." Ondis recalls that when Gandin agreed on the spot to buy the stock, "Bernie right away went off to make a phone call and place the order."

On another occasion, according to Ondis, they were working on a lawn sprinkler job with a third laborer who was in some way part of the Madoff family. "Bernie was pushing a stock and the guy says 'I'll buy it' right then and there. So Bernie jumped in his car and took off and placed the order. He was selling stock to students at Hofstra because there were a lot of kids there who had money."

Bernie was certainly earning commissions on those trades, or he wouldn't have bothered.

Yet, the question remains with whom Bernie was placing those trades. He never revealed that to anyone taking him up on his tips, but those who knew him well back then believe he was doing business with either his father's Laurelton home-based Gibralter Securities that came under SEC scrutiny, or with the company of his friends' father, Lou Lieberbaum. In any case, Bernie was proving that he had the chutzpah, the drive, the ambition, and the talent to successfully snag investors and make money doing it.

With his business enterprises taking up much of his time, Bernie had little interest in his studies and had a reputation for skipping and missing classes.

To his college pals like Gordon Ondis, Bernie was an enigma.

He was quiet, but he had an assured, authoritarian, unspoken confidence about him. He was not prone to being part of the gang. He was more of a loner. He didn't socialize to the extent that Mike and I did. The thing about Bernie was it was elusive to try to know him. You just *couldn't* know him.

Sharp at business, Bernie couldn't have cared less about being Joe College.

"He was just there at Hofstra to get through it somehow," asserts Ondis. "He was always hustling. *Always*. When he saw me he used to say, 'Hey, *macher*, come to *macher*.' We used to call each other *macher*."

In Yiddish, the word has a number of connotations but essentially the same meaning: A *macher* is a big shot, a mover and shaker, an ambitious schemer.

■ ■ ■

Mike Gandin had lost personal touch with Bernie over the years, but he was aware that friends on Long Island, including "a whole crowd" from the posh Cold Springs Country Club in the North Shore community of Glen Head, had been investing with him.

"I used to joke," says Gandin, "that Bernie was running a scheme."

But when Gandin, a successful lawyer, was struggling and getting nowhere in the stock market of the early to mid-2000s, he decided to give Bernie a shot. Gandin figured it was a no-brainer since his law partner, Arnold Schotsky, was getting returns from Madoff "of 9 percent, 10 percent, 11 percent."

Gandin recalls,

Since I had worked for Bernie back in college, I felt comfortable enough to call and say, "Hey, Bernie, here's the story. I'm not making any money on my own in the market, and if I keep this up I'm going to lose all my money." I said, "Bernie, you gotta take my investment." At that time he required a minimum of $2 million. I said I only had a million dollars, and I told him, "You gotta help me." He said, "All right, all right, I'll let you in."

Gandin gladly sent him a check with seven numbers on it for deposit.

A while later he called Bernie again and told him he had another $500,000 or so, and Bernie told him, "Just send it."

Gandin was thrilled that Bernie had let his old high school and college pal who had installed sprinklers for him into his very exclusive money club.

I wanted to go in and see him and say hello to Ruth, who was a cute, adorable little blonde, and she and Bernie were an item from the get-go in high school, together forever. I called once, and Bernie was hard to get hold of, but it wasn't like he was hiding, and I never got around to seeing them.

Gandin notes that before he turned over his money to Bernie he had done some due diligence in his own "modest way"—talking to friends who had gotten nice returns and who reported getting all their money back when they requested it. "Bernie was," he concluded, "a respected part of the Establishment."

Gandin himself was able without any problem to withdraw $250,000 of his investment in order to purchase a Florida condominium some years before Bernie went bust.

"I felt fortunate. I felt on top of the world. I was gleeful. Every month I'd get 8 percent, 9 percent, sometimes 11 percent on my money, and it was terrific, and other people were struggling with the market."

And then the sky fell in.

A friend called Mike Gandin and told him to turn on CNBC, "and there it was—it was all a Ponzi scheme. My wife and I were shattered, absolutely in shock. Fortunately, we didn't have everything with him, but we've been forced to regroup. From what would have been a very nice retirement, we're hunkering down. All of a sudden I had to come down from this reality where I thought I had $3 million to where it's worth nothing. It's mind-boggling what Bernie got away with.

"The only thing that really bothered me was that I promised my son I would help buy him a house, and then I had to say I couldn't do it, and that hurt. He said to me, 'Dad, if things get tough, come live with me,' and that meant a lot."

Chapter 5

Tying the Knot and Giving Uncle Sam the Business

Bernie Madoff took Ruth Alpern to be his lawfully wedded wife on the eve of a new decade—the Swinging Sixties, one of the most turbulent and radical eras in contemporary American history. But for Bernie the 1960s would be a time of growing success, little turbulence, and no radicalism. It would all be about making money, and whatever it took to make it.

On the Saturday after Thanksgiving 1959—just a few weeks after the Russians sent an unmanned rocket on mankind's first trip to the moon, and a few weeks before John F. Kennedy announced his run for the Democratic presidential nomination—21-year-old Bernie, a senior at Hofstra College, and 19-year-old Ruth, a sophomore at Queens College, were married at the Laurelton Jewish Center.

While it was a Conservative Judaism synagogue, Bernie and Ruth considered themselves "lox and bagel Jews"—neither was religious or observant.

It was a small, quietly elegant, traditional service with the two marrying under a chuppah, and with Bernie smashing a wine glass with the sole of his rented patent leather shoe that went with his rented tuxedo. Ruth wore a simple white wedding dress. There were no special vows. It was Ruth's idea, though, to serve the guests wine and champagne placed on a table in the synagogue's foyer before the ceremony. That night there was a wedding dinner—brisket and all the trimmings—at the Jewish Center.

"There were no special trappings," recalls Jane Kavanau, a guest along with her future husband, Joe, except for the champagne and wine when everyone was mingling before the service. "That was gracious and maybe a little fancier."

There had never been another man, or any serious romance other than Bernie, in Ruth's life. However, Bernie would later seek out female companionship in and out of the office, and Ruth would have to keep him on a tight leash. But that was all still to come.

■ ■ ■

"From the time they started dating when they were in high school, Ruth's life revolved around Bernie," maintains Kavanau, who was a senior at Vassar College at the time of the Madoff-Alpern nuptials. "Ruth would probably have gone away to college as I did [having attended the University of Michigan before Vassar], but she was involved with Bernie, so she wanted to stay close to him. They were definitely head over heels in love."

Ruth was a whiz at mathematics, probably genetically inherited from her numbers-crunching accountant father—the kind of nebbish-appearing but shrewd CPA whose breast pocket was filled with pens and pencils. She had decided to go to Queens College, which was far superior academically to Bernie's Hofstra. Her intention was to major in math. But she ran into problems with physics, and ended up going for a degree in psychology. Later she went back to school to study nutrition "after spending some years in the family business" and earned a master's degree from New York University. (She'd later become embroiled in a brouhaha of her own involving her role in co-authoring a self-promoted, self-published cookbook called *Great Chefs of America Cook Kosher.*)

A couple of days after Bernie and Ruth tied the knot, he went to the SEC office in downtown Manhattan and registered a broker-dealer firm in his name. A financial statement that was added later to the application noted: "Assets: Cash on hand $200. Liabilities: None."

After a short honeymoon, the Madoffs got their first apartment, a one-bedroom in a mid-rise complex called Windsor Park, in Bayside, Queens. The rent was $87.50 a month. They had chosen the building because a girlfriend of Ruth's from Laurelton also lived there.

"They didn't have a lot of money by any means," recalls Kavanau. "They took a very moderately priced apartment, and we would go to visit them. Ruth knew exactly what she wanted decor-wise, and she made it look very nice on a real budget. It was early American. She was always very definite about what she liked, and it always turned out nicely."

■ ■ ■

Seven months after Bernie and Ruth tied the knot, Bernie graduated from Hofstra. By then he already had started his own portfolio, reporting to the SEC one position in a stock, a half-dozen shares in a company called Electronics Capital, worth $300. Within months it would grow to the princely sum in those days of $16,140. It rose because it was supposedly being pumped at his friends' stock brokerage, Lieberbaum & Company, believes Peter Zaphiris, who went to work there.

While Bernie's Hofstra grades and class standing were said to be unexceptional, he had fulfilled one important goal: He had completed four years of ROTC training and received his commission as a second lieutenant in the U.S. Army Reserve.

Others who had been commissioned in his class soon went off to serve their two years of active duty.

But Bernie put off that requirement.

As a senior at Hofstra, he had taken the Law School Admission Test (LSAT) and somehow managed to score enough of a passing grade to be accepted at Brooklyn Law School for the semester starting in September 1960.

Like Hofstra, Brooklyn Law, located on Pearl Street in teeming downtown Brooklyn, had no campus, no dormitories, and no cafeteria. And like Hofstra, its tuition was low, it had both day and night classes, and many of its students were holding down full-time jobs.

As it turned out, Bernie had absolutely no interest in becoming a lawyer.

"Law school for Bernie was clearly a means to stay out of the military," maintains Joe Kavanau, who was at Brooklyn Law with Bernie. "He never had any intention of being an attorney. Back then the 2S deferment kept you out of the military. In Bernie's case he was a commissioned officer, but the 2S had the effect of deferring his active service."

One of the great benefits of Brooklyn Law for Bernie, besides keeping him out of the Army, was that classes were from 9 A.M. to noon. The hours allowed him to actively pursue his stock business, Bernard L. Madoff Investment Securities, which he formally started in 1960. He was then 22 years old.

The law school classes were held in two large rooms, each with about 150 students, and alphabetically divided. One room had students whose last names started with *A* to *K*, and the other with *L* to *Z*. So while Joe Kavanau and his pal, Bernie, were in school at the same time, they were in separate classrooms, though Kavanau's father drove both of them to the Brooklyn-bound subway station in Queens every morning so they could get to class.

A friend of Kavanau's, though, Charles "Chuck" Lubitz, was in Bernie's class, sat next to him, and recalls him with an oft-heard refrain from those days, which was: "There was nothing special about Bernie Madoff."

Bernie, however, was boasting that he already was involved with the stock market and Wall Street, and envisioned himself making it big.

He was a *macher*.

By the end of Bernie's first semester, he'd decided he'd had enough.

To Lubitz, he complained that "the pace was a little too slow" for him. Bernie said he wanted action. "This was not the track he wanted to be on."

Lubitz, however, was unaware that Bernie was only taking up space at Brooklyn Law in order to delay going on active duty.

Years later, as an attorney in Palm Beach, Lubitz crossed paths with his former law school classmate. He had been retained to represent investors who were victims of Bernie's spectacular Ponzi scheme. He says, "Bernie lived a good part of the year in Palm Beach and got around. Most of the people were people who knew him and invested with him directly. I'm trying to get some or all of their money back. This will go on probably beyond my lifetime."

Elliott Olin, Bernie's close friend from Laurelton, was also enrolled at Brooklyn Law. At some point, Bernie approached Olin with an offer he thought his longtime pal couldn't refuse.

"It was their first year of law school, and after six months, Bernie told Elliott, 'I'm getting out of here. I'm going to go full-time into the stock market,' and he asked Elliott to quit law school, too, and go in with him," says Olin's widow, Sheila Olin. "But Elliott told him, 'I'm not going with you,' and Elliott did finish law school, and had a successful practice, and boy, am I happy he didn't go with Bernie." She says Bernie was "annoyed that Elliott wasn't going with him." Sheila believes that this dispute resulted in the end of their friendship, despite the fact that Bernie's sister, Sondra, had married Elliott's cousin, Marvin Wiener, the dentist.

Bernie walked out of Brooklyn Law for the last time in June 1961, having put up with what he felt were boring lectures and required reading about torts and contracts, nothing in which he had a whit of interest.

■ ■ ■

When his 2S deferment ended, the dreaded letter came from Uncle Sam requesting the company of Second Lieutenant Bernard L. Madoff to report for two years of active duty in the Army Reserve. When he

first joined the ROTC at the University of Alabama (and continued it
at Hofstra), he signed a contract committing himself to service to his
country after he got his commission. He had delayed that commitment
for a year by hiding in law school. But now he had to face the march-
ing music. While Bernie liked sporting the Army green and playing
soldier during two weeks of Army Reserve training at Camp Drum
in upstate New York, he didn't see himself spending two whole years
of his life playing soldier on some military base in the sticks, or worse,
being on active duty if a war broke out.

Bernie had money to make.

His call-up came at a most inopportune time, not only because
he wanted to hit the ground running in the world of stocks and high
finance, but also because the world situation was growing hotter. It
was a dangerous time for anyone going into the armed forces. Several
months before Bernie became eligible to serve his country, President
Kennedy increased the number of so-called U.S. Army military advisers
and aid to Southeast Asia, the start of the Vietnam War escalation and
troop buildup, and that year the first U.S. soldier would be killed by the
Viet Cong. Moreover, the Cold War with the Soviets was intensifying:
The Berlin Wall dividing East and West Germany was built, with U.S.
and Soviet tanks facing each other, and the week that shook the world,
the Cuban missile crisis, was at hand.

Bernie was a *macher*, not a fighter, at least not on the battlefield.

With active duty looming, Bernie suddenly suffered a medical mal-
ady that might have been dubbed "nervous from the service."

"He was a commissioned officer. But by the time they got around
to attempting to activate him, Bernie had developed an ulcer and he
got a medical discharge," states Joe Kavanau. "It was perfect. It kept
Bernie, a nervous type, out of the Army. The ulcer was sort of a natural progression [from his facial ticks and twitches]. A couple of guys
who were in ROTC got screwed because they got deferments through
law school and ended up going in. One guy was in the Transportation
Corps and ended up on the docks in Da Nang—not a good place for a
Jewish boy."

Because of an ulcer—real, imagined, or invented—Bernie was a free man. (Due to federal privacy restrictions, it was impossible to secure Bernie's service record, if one even existed, without his permission, which he was in no position to give being locked up in the Metropolitan Correctional Center.)

Unlike Bernie, when Elliott Olin, who had gotten a commission but was deferred through his three years at Brooklyn Law, was called up, he and his wife, Sheila, went to an Army base in Georgia, where Olin respectfully served his required two-year commitment, she says.

For Bernie, who would cheat thousands of investors out of billions and even cheat on his wife, it was no surprise that he would also successfully rob Uncle Sam out of two years of his life.

However, years later Bernie brazenly misled his employees who had actually proudly and bravely served their country. He boasted, or gave the impression, that he had served as a finance officer in the Army for four years. Moreover, he often lorded it over a longtime employee, Tony Teletnick, who had seen combat in Vietnam as an enlisted man.

"The boss would scream at Tony, and Tony would say, 'Boss, you were nothing but a second lieutenant in the peacetime army stationed stateside. When you spend a year in Nam as a grunt like I did, then tell me about hard times,'" recounts the late Teletnick's friend and Bernie's personal messenger, Bill Nasi, who says he and others had no reason to disbelieve Bernie's war stories. "Bernie would say to Tony, 'I'm going to pull rank on you because I own the place and I was a second lieutenant in finance, and you were nothing but a buck sergeant.' And Tony would tell the boss, 'You can't tell me what to do, because you weren't in the infantry.'"

On another occasion, Nasi had heard a news story on the radio reporting that captains of American finance and industry had started out as second lieutenants in the army, and he mentioned it to Bernie. "He had a big smile on his face," recalls Nasi. "He said, 'You're right! Look at me!'"

Bernie even once played out a little military fantasy in the trading room of his company. He was reminiscing one afternoon with Nasi about the old days at Madoff, and noted that his sons, Mark and Andy, and his brother, Peter, now were doing all the hiring, and that he hardly knew any of the young people working at the firm he had built from the ground up. "They're all young kids and I have a feeling they're scared of me," he said. With that, he handed Nasi a clipboard and told him to follow him into the trading room. "Use a pen. Make believe you're taking notes," said Bernie, pretending he was an army officer conducting an inspection of the recruits in his company, with Nasi playing his first sergeant. "As we were walking by these young people, they were getting nervous. We did the five-cent tour. We walked down, did an about-face, and walked out of the trading room, and Bernie's laughing to himself. 'See, what did I tell you?' "

Bernie also seemed to have a fetish about military clothing.

He liked the fact that Nasi mostly wore starched and pressed army fatigues to work. The neatness of the outfit apparently acted as a balm for Bernie's obsession with orderliness, Nasi believes.

At a dinner honoring the future king of Ponzi at the Waldorf–Astoria Hotel in New York City in the early 1990s, Nasi showed up in his best suit, and Bernie came over to say hello. "I pulled up my pant leg and Bernie was impressed because I had on paratrooper boots," recalls Nasi, who himself was never in the military because of poor eyesight. "Bernie says, 'My God, spit-shined boots!' He liked that. He was still pretending he was Mister Military."

Chapter 6

A Borscht Belt Summer Camp Sets the Stage for Bernie's Ponzi Scheme

Bernie had several mentors in the early years of his career. The first were his father and mother, who ran questionable Gibralter Securities out of their Laurelton house. It was from Ralph and Sylvia that Bernie learned some of the ins and outs of the stock buying and trading game.

The second was his new father-in-law, Saul Alpern, who began steering business his way from virtually the moment Bernie slipped the wedding ring on the slender third finger of the accountant's favorite of his two daughters, Ruth—young, pretty, and smart, a chip off the old block, a math whiz.

"The Saul that I knew was the salt of the earth," asserts Joe Kavanau. "The guy was a square—with pens in his shirt pocket. He was just a funny character, a nice man."

At Queens College with Ruth was Jay Portnoy, who sometimes spent time at the Alpern house in Laurelton studying with her. From those visits, he came away with the feeling that "she really adored her father. A couple of times I was in the Alpern home [and met her father] and then afterwards Ruth would say, 'Isn't he brilliant?' or 'Isn't he great looking?' or some such like that. She was very much in awe of her father."

There also would be a third guru for Bernie as time went on, one who would play a role in his early successes, but he was still to come.

Bernie's investment advisory operation that became the Ponzi scheme appears to have begun at a most unlikely place—a low-rent Borscht Belt bungalow colony in the bucolic Catskill Mountains of New York. Called Sunny Oaks, its clientele consisted mainly of elderly Jewish couples, and Saul Alpern was a popular fixture.

The bungalow colony catered to a mostly Brooklyn, Bronx, and Queens middle-brow, middle-class snowbird clientele—a demographic of retired small-time lawyers, teachers, accountants, and merchants, none of them high rollers—who wintered in the Jewish sections of Miami Beach and escaped the blazing Florida summer sun for the cool mountain breezes of the Catskills and Sunny Oaks.

Unlike the famous and flamboyant Catskills resort hotels of that era, such as Grossinger's and The Concord, where big-name entertainers performed for the mostly upscale Jewish guests, Sunny Oaks was an array of simple, rustic cabins attached to a farmhouse that served as the main building. Nestled in the woods of Woodbridge, New York, it was one of the many bungalow colonies that dotted the area. It was a place where everyone was treated like members of the family, or as another observer noted, a "resort of last resorts."

Life at Sunny Oaks was simple and carefree—there were no locks on the doors, no television sets, and no phones in the rooms. The bungalow colony offered yoga, folk dancing, and a place for retired New Yorkers to play cards, read the papers, and kibbitz—all for $300 a week, including room and board.

It was in this picturesque setting, around 1960, that Alpern began advising his close friends, the Sunny Oaks owners, and many of their guests to put their money with his son-in-law. At the time, Bernie, who had just graduated from Hofstra, was said to be sharing office space with Alpern.

As Cynthia Levinson Arenson, the granddaughter of the founders of Sunny Oaks, a classmate of Ruth's at Far Rockaway High, and still later a Madoff victim, observes: "What Ruth Madoff's father did was the start of all this. When you first open a stock market thing like Bernie did, who are you going to get for customers but parents and friends of parents who have a little bit of money to invest? And Bernie started doing very well."

Her stepson, David Arenson, a former journalist, a leukemia patient, and a Madoff victim, notes, "If the Alperns had not been at Sunny Oaks, and if Bernie had never met and married Ruth Alpern, none of us would have invested in Madoff. It was entirely because of family connections."

After Bernie's arrest, Arenson, who had a blog called "CLL Diary" about living with chronic lymphocytic leukemia, headed one of his posts: "Bernie Madoff Screws Leukemia Patient."

He says, "Saul felt comfortable recommending Bernie as a source of investment, and Saul himself was an accountant, so everyone trusted him."

Saul and Sara Alpern were the best friends of Cynthia Arenson's mother and father, Adele and Myles Levinson. Myles Levinson, a lawyer, had inherited Sunny Oaks from his parents. One of Saul Alpern's brothers, Bill, was also a lawyer, and he and his wife, Minette, were part of the close-knit circle that existed at Sunny Oaks. All would invest in Bernie on the suggestion of his father-in-law, and so would many more at Sunny Oaks.

To the Levinsons and Arensons and their guests who put their money and trust in young Bernie, Saul Alpern did not appear to be devious in hawking his son-in-law. They believe he was a *mensch* who just wanted to help his friends make some money, and it was only natural that he would try to help his daughter's groom.

Then in his early 60s, "Saul was very modest, very quiet-spoken, played good bridge, and read the *New York Times*," recalls Cynthia Arenson, who eventually took over the hotel from her parents after they retired and moved to Florida.

■ ■ ■

Saul Alpern was partners with a man named Sherman Heller. Their accounting office, under the name Alpern & Heller, was in midtown Manhattan. However, there's no record of the firm being registered in

New York State's corporate database. The firm expanded when another accountant, fast-talking Michael Bienes, joined the Alpern firm. Later, Bienes teamed up with another accountant, Frank Avellino, and some-time in the 1970s formed the accounting firm of Avellino & Bienes, located at 120 East 56th Street in Manhattan.

It was then that Ruth Madoff's father began referring people at Sunny Oaks and elsewhere to Avellino & Bienes, which essentially took over Alpern & Heller's Sunny Oaks client-investor base when Saul Alpern retired to a condo in North Miami, but still kept on top of things. Bernie wanted Avellino & Bienes to handle those small investors, because he had bigger fish to fry.

Frank Avellino and Michael Bienes took charge of the many modest accounts that had accrued at Sunny Oaks and elsewhere, and at that point their firm became the first official Madoff feeder fund.

Over the years Avellino and Bienes would become hugely wealthy—as would other feeder fund operators—doing nothing but recruiting investors and passing on their money to Madoff, for which they received lucrative commissions and finder fees.

"It was easy money with Bernie," Bienes acknowledged in a TV interview with the program *Frontline* after Bernie was imprisoned. "Easy, easy-peasy money." He thought to himself, he said, "I'm a little too lucky. Why am I so fortunate?"

"All you needed was five thousand dollars to get into Avellino & Bienes," states Cynthia Levinson Arenson, who by then was helping run Sunny Oaks and had started investing on her own, following in the footsteps of her parents, who had earlier put a hefty portion of their money with Bernie.

"Avellino & Bienes started out promising 18 percent," she says. Steady returns were Bernie's modus operandi and one of his lures, and that hefty return continued through good economic times and bad from the early 1960s until the early 1990s.

She asserts that "everyone knew that the money was going to Bernie" even though it was now handed over to Avellino & Bienes.

"Cynthia's mother was just beside herself with just how much money Avellino was paying out," states David Arenson. "She was trying to get everybody [to invest], saying 'Avellino's paid 25 percent last year,' so the people at the hotel were like, 'Oh, my God! How can I get in on this?' I don't think there was a lot of thought as to how they were getting such high returns; it was just that it was being done—because those people were not sophisticated about finances."

Bernie had seen something he liked and trusted in Bienes and begun courting him. The two had quickly become trusted friends and associates in a very lucrative business relationship.

Bienes tells a bizarre story about that courtship—an encounter at an upscale nonsexual private club that permitted members to swim in the nude, according to a story in *Fortune* magazine.

"I once went swimming naked with him," he said after Bernie was in jail awaiting formal sentencing for bilking thousands of investors. Bienes continued, "He invited me to the New York Athletic Club on Central Park South. He asked me to come and meet him and get a rubdown. We didn't discuss anything, really. I think he wanted to get the feel of me, you know, and bring me into his orbit."

The next invitation for Bienes was to a buffet lunch, part of the bar mitzvah celebration for one of Bernie's two sons. "I remember my partner, Frank Avellino, and myself and Bernie meeting in the middle of the dance floor, and we were saying, 'Thanks for having us.' And he said, 'Hey, come on, we're family, aren't we?' And at that moment, he had me. We were family. Oh my God! I was in!"

Unlike others who knew Bernie well, the many from high school on up who considered him "a dummy," "a schmuck," and "a putz," Bienes either was sincerely overwhelmed by what he perceived as Bernie's greatness or he saw money signs flashing like neon on The Strip in Vegas, or a combination of both.

To Bienes, Bernie "had a presence about him, an aura. He really captivated you." Beyond that, he and Avellino jokingly considered Bernie "our boyfriend" because, Bienes later claimed, they thought they were his only client who was feeding him investors. That was an astonishing assertion in light of the fact that they had been doing business with Bernie for decades, and knew there were huge numbers of other investors.

By the mid-1980s, Avellino and Bienes were doing little else but drumming up more and wealthier investors for Bernie, and all were raking in big money—Avellino and Bienes eventually became multi-millionaires, and Bernie's coffers had filled with more than $450 million from about 3,200 investors they had sent his way, which was just the tip of the Madoff iceberg.

■ ■ ■

In 1992, the SEC acted on a tip that incredibly outrageous returns—20 percent or more—were being offered to investors and guaranteed by the Avellino firm. The allegations strongly suggested that a Ponzi scheme was being operated—the very first official red flag raised that appeared to point to Bernard L. Madoff Investment Securities.

As it turned out, the firm of Avellino & Bienes was not registered to trade securities, which the accountants were accused of doing.

When the SEC began its probe of the firm, Bienes acknowledged years later that he and his partner were worried. "We had doubts, and we passed them on to Bernie. . . . Bernie said, 'I know the biggest lawyers on Wall Street. Don't worry." Bienes asserted that Bernie was calling the shots. "I was always captive to him. He owned us."

The investigation came to a quick end when the partners agreed to return all of the money that had passed through them, some $440 million. They were fined $350,000, and their business ordered closed. Their attorney in the matter was one Ira Sorkin, the same Ira Sorkin who 16 years later would represent Bernie when his Ponzi scheme collapsed.

The probe of Avellino & Bienes turned up some interesting evidence, one piece being that while the firm was overseeing almost a half billion dollars of investor money for Madoff, no records were ever kept.

"My experience has taught me to not commit any figures to scrutiny when, as in this case, it [sic] can be construed as 'bible' and subject to criticism," responded Avellino in writing when asked by auditors appointed by the court to prepare a balance sheet. "In this present instance, quite severely, I explained how the profit and loss can be

computed from the records you now hold in your possession that
Bernard L. Madoff and I supplied."

For reasons unknown, Bernie Madoff does not appear on record in
the case—the recipient of the feeder money was described simply
in the SEC complaint as an unnamed broker.

Shut down by the government, Avellino and Bienes continued
to feed investors to Bernie, and Bernie stayed in business unscathed.
Feeder fund operators were instructed to keep Madoff's name a secret.
As time would tell, many of the thousands of investors who claimed
losses in the Ponzi scheme never knew that their money wound up in
his hands.

One of the SEC administrators at the time, Martin Kuperberg, was
quoted in the *Wall Street Journal* as stating, "There's nothing to indicate
fraud."

This would be the first but certainly not the last time the SEC
would seriously fumble the ball when it came to Bernie Madoff.

After the SEC probe ended, Bienes established an accounting firm
called Mayfair Bookkeeping at a time when Bernie had established a
London office in the posh Mayfair district. Like Bernie, who had a villa
in the south of France, Bienes had a fancy residence in London.

Because of the ongoing Bienes-Madoff connection, the once small-
time accountant made so much money that he lived like royalty on an
estate worth almost $7 million. He became a philanthropist and a fig-
ure of respect in the upper echelon of South Florida—a giver of lavish
parties and fund-raisers, and a benefactor of the arts community in Fort
Lauderdale. He and his second wife, Dianne, were even knighted by the
Catholic Archdiocese of Miami, which an observer noted was "not a
small feat for a Jewish kid from New York."

With Bernie behind bars, the 72-year-old Bienes decided to go
public, claiming he, like thousands of others, was a Madoff victim. He
maintained he lost $10 million to Bernie. He gave sometimes inarticu-
late, self-serving, convoluted interviews to *Frontline* and to the *South
Florida Sun-Sentinel* and was quoted in *Fortune* magazine. Asked by the
Frontline reporter how he thought Bernie was able to generate consistent
big returns for his investors—before they lost everything—Bienes
quizzically responded, "I don't know. How do I know? How do [you]

split an atom? I know that you can split them. I don't know how you do it. How does an airplane fly? I don't ask."

Bienes also maintained to the Florida newspaper that he always thought Bernie was legitimate, that he was a genius investor. He swore that he knew nothing about a Ponzi scheme.

> If I did, would I have all my money there? . . . I'm not totally crazy. . . . Doubt Bernie Madoff? Doubt Bernie? No. You doubt God. You can doubt God, but you can't doubt Bernie. . . . Madoff is the enemy. He's a swindler. He's a crook. He stole our money. . . .
>
> My life changed from being a very wealthy man with nothing to look forward to but the rest of my life with ease and charitable giving and all the good things, and just in a second my whole life blew up. I stood there knowing that I was in debt, and I could be forced into bankruptcy.

He also admitted that for years he and Avellino "were the go-between between Madoff" and the many investors.

"He put on an incredible act," observed the business blogger Joe Weisenthal, writing about Bienes' television debut.

■ ■ ■

Avellino, who had remained silent, lived just as high as Bienes— multimillion-dollar homes in Palm Beach and Fort Lauderdale and a $10 million house in Nantucket where he reportedly asked his house-keeper to put her life savings of $124,000 in one of many foundations and partnerships in which he was involved, in her case a "fictitious entity."

She lost it all, according to a lawsuit she filed. Avellino also is alleged to have given her the bad news about her loss and the Ponzi scheme a full 10 days before Bernie was arrested—a strong indication he knew along with Bernie and his closed circle that the ceiling was about to cave in.

In the wake of Bienes' going public, the *Wall Street Journal*, quoting unnamed sources "familiar with the matter," reported in May 2009 that Avellino was among at least eight Madoff investors and associates of the fraudster who were being investigated by federal prosecutors "for signs of complicity." Bienes was not among those named.

The others included two philanthropists—82-year-old Stanley Chais and 67-year-old Jeffry Picower—who had major investments with Madoff, along with one of Bernie's close friends, 96-year-old Carl Shapiro, who parlayed about $20 million into what's been reported to be more than $1 billion through Madoff over the years. Shortly before Bernie was arrested, Shapiro was the one who handed over $250 million to Bernie. Chais's foundation was taken for more than $100 million, and he personally reportedly lost about $400 million.

It was believed by investigators, according to the *Journal*'s sources, that Picower and Chais dictated to Bernie how much return they wanted on their investments. Chais was known to have funneled many California customers to Madoff. After the report appeared, all denied any wrongdoing.

Civil suits were filed by attorney Irving Picard, the trustee overseeing the bankruptcy liquidation of the Madoff firm, who was seeking to recoup billions of dollars to divide among victims. The suit alleged that Chais, a Bronx-born onetime Beverly Hills money manager, and Picower, an accountant and lawyer from Palm Beach and New York City, got exorbitant returns from Madoff—as much as a mind-numbing 950 percent.

Lawsuits alleged that a whopping $6 billion in claimed profits had been withdrawn from Madoff. This was far more than their original investments for various family members and foundations. None of the many thousands of other Madoff investors got anywhere near the returns grabbed by Chais and Picower. In his lawsuit, Picard alleged that the two either knew or should have known that they were "reaping the benefits" of "manipulated purported returns, false documents and fictitious reports." Chais, according to Picard, requested phony losses from Madoff for tax-avoidance reasons. Chais's foundation, which had almost $180 million in assets, was left with a big zero in Bernie's scheme. All denied any wrongdoing and claimed no knowledge of a Ponzi scheme.

Then, on June 22, 2009, just a week before Bernie's scheduled formal sentencing, the SEC filed a bombshell complaint alleging that Chais had "committed fraud by misrepresenting his role in managing the funds' assets and for distributing account statements that he should have known were false."

The complaint, filed in federal court in New York, stated that for the past four decades "Chais has held himself out as an investing wizard who managed hundreds of millions of dollars in investor funds. . . . In reality Chais was an unsophisticated investor who did nothing more than turn all of [his three] funds' assets over to Madoff, while charging the funds more than $250 million in fees for his purported 'services.'

"Although Madoff managed all of the funds' assets, many of the funds' investors had never heard of Madoff before the collapse of his Ponzi scheme, and had not known that Chais invested with Madoff until Chais informed them after Madoff's arrest."

The SEC also alleged that Chais "ignored red flags" that indicated that Bernie's reported results "were false. For example, Chais told Madoff that Chais did not want there to be any losses on any of the funds' trades."

The complaint further alleged that "Madoff did not report a loss on a single equities trade. Chais, however, with the assistance of his accountant, prepared account statements for the funds' investors based upon the Madoff statements, and continued to distribute them to the funds' investors even though he should have known they were false."

Shockingly, according to the SEC, Chais and his family members and "related entities" withdrew more than $500 million more than "they actually invested with Madoff."

The SEC complaint sought injunctions, financial penalties, and court orders requiring Chaise to "disgorge" his "ill-gotten gains," and the SEC said its investigation was ongoing.

Meanwhile, the folks from Sunny Oaks in the Borscht Belt where Bernie's investment advisory business began all fared terribly.

"When Avellino & Bienes was shut down in 1992," says Cynthia Arenson, "Bernie realized that a lot of the people in Avellino were Saul and Sara Alpern's friends, his in-laws' friends, the friends of Ruth Madoff's parents. So out of the kindness of his heart, Bernie said, 'Okay, if you have $50,000 you can go directly with me.' At that point to get into Bernie you needed $500,000. To a certain extent he didn't want to bother. When he had a little account like $50,000 like my son had, he'd just put it into T-bills and he didn't bother trading with it. It wasn't worth it to him. He was looking for big bucks to play with."

Among those small investors Bernie earned the sobriquet "T-bill Bernie."

In the end, Cynthia Levinson acknowledges that while she suffered $750,000 in Ponzi losses, she estimates that she had taken out that amount through the years because of the high returns she was getting.

"In all those years," she says, "I essentially made nothing, but it looked good on paper."

David Arenson and his wife, Marilyn, opened a $10,000 account with Avellino & Bienes around 1990. Because it was such a small amount, he says, it paid a 10 percent return.

"My father and Cynthia always got a higher return than we did because they had a lot more money in Madoff," he says. "I always felt that if you had more in there or if Bernie was sitting in his little office arbitrarily deciding who gets what that he might say, 'Oh, Cynthia has more. I'll give her an extra $5,000 this year.' So it was kind of an arbitrary, weird thing."

As Arenson's health declined with his aggressive form of chronic leukemia that he knew would eventually require a bone marrow transplant and with him facing a possible early death, he decided to withdraw $10,000 to $20,000 in principal every year. In the end, when Bernie admitted his giant fraud, Arenson had lost $65,000.

Says Arenson:

We had been using the money, as opposed to the people we knew who kept reinvesting. Madoff gave you a choice. They could either send you a check every quarter or you could simply have them reinvest. I know people who just had it reinvested and they suddenly found that they had a million dollars [on paper]. But it all turned around to bite them in the butt when they lost everything that they had.

They were going back to the early '90s when Avellino collapsed. After a while they became used to the idea that their money was always waiting for them. It was like the Treasury Department. Madoff was synonymous with bank.

Everybody in my family and this web of friends had almost everything invested in Madoff. People felt comfortable putting more and more money into Madoff, putting all their eggs in that basket. But if that family connection with Saul Alpern hadn't been there, they wouldn't have felt so comfortable. I don't remember anybody in the family—cousins, siblings, anybody—saying, "Oh, God, I'm turning this down. It seems to make sense to everybody else." Nobody expects to be the victim of the world's largest Ponzi scheme, especially after 16 years. I actually took out $10,000 in 2007 to invest in a stock and it was sort of greeted as, "Why would you want to do that? You're taking it out of Madoff to invest in a *stock*?!" They thought it was crazy.

Most, if not all, of Arenson's family were victims of Madoff. His brother, Dan, a helicopter pilot with three children, had an account; and so did their sister, Julie. Arenson's aunt—his mother's sister—left her estate to a daughter. "She inherited money from her family and also put her own money in," Arenson says. "It was in the hundreds of thousands of dollars my guess is."

One of Cynthia Arenson's cousins, Robin Warner, a former producer at Fox News, is said to have lost upwards of $1 million to Madoff after investing a couple of hundred thousand dollars inherited from her parents, who were friends with the Alperns, along with money she had earned and saved.

Saul Alpern had convinced Warner's father to invest in the 1980s. Later, she invested with Madoff through Avellino & Bienes. Initially she thought Madoff "was good as gold." As she told a colleague after the roof fell in, "This was not greed. Why would you want to put your money anywhere else?"

"She was one of those who kept reinvesting, but also living on a 10 percent annual return, or $100,000 a year," says Arenson. "She wasn't spending. She didn't live high on the hog. Now it's all gone. She has nothing."

At first, Warner is said to have told family members that she "wanted to kill" Madoff, but then said she didn't want him dead "because he knows where the money's hidden," and she was hoping to recoup some of her losses.

But Bernie didn't just scam friends; he also scammed family. There was Saul Alpern's sister-in-law, Minette Alpern—Ruth Madoff's aunt. In her mid-90s, Minette was comfortably ensconced in an old age home in Florida, paying her expenses with money that years ago had been invested with Bernie and Avellino on the advice of Bernie's father-in-law. When news of the Ponzi scheme broke, the aged woman was "left bereft," says Arenson. "She said she could live there for a while more and then she won't have any money left. Her daughter lost everything, too. There were so many others from the family and Sunny Oaks who lost everything."

■ ■ ■

After Bernie was arrested and virtually all branches of the Arenson family tree were feeling the pain of their losses, David Arenson came across a curious letter he had received from Bernard L. Madoff Investment Securities. The letter had been sent to investors in the wake of Hurricane Katrina that had devastated New Orleans in the summer of 2005. The letter stated that everyone should rest assured that in case of some major emergency, such as an act of terrorism, a duplicate set of all investors' accounting records had been made and were being kept in a safe place offshore.

"The letter said there was no need to worry about anything," says Arenson. "We had a good laugh over that. It was rich—knowing especially at that point that Madoff was completely a Ponzi scheme."

Arenson speculates that Bernie "was just simply crazy, that at some point he became rather demented, because it's incredible to me that somebody could be that callous, that insensitive, to hurt so many people.

"He acted the role of a philanthropist and a friend to the community. It's possible he had some inner need to screw the system in a grand way that no one had ever done before. It's entirely possible he knew someday his scheme would come out and he was just waiting for his moment in the sun.

"He will go down in history as the greatest Ponzi schemer and thief. I can't think of anybody who's stolen $50 billion from anybody short of one of those dictators in the past—Idi Amin, or the Shah of Iran."

■ ■ ■

When in the mid-1960s Saul and Sara Alpern sold their home in Laurelton, Queens, where Ruth grew up, they bought a condo in a predominately Jewish complex, Point East, in North Miami Beach. But for years, and even as senility set in, they spent their summers at Sunny Oaks.

Despite having a lot of money and being able to afford luxurious accommodations, "They moved into this really disgusting bungalow in the summers," says Cynthia Levinson Arenson. "When they got really old they hired a caregiver to help them."

Ruth Madoff, according to Cynthia and David Arenson, rarely came to visit her aging parents. Her sister, Joan Roman, and her children were seen there more often, and Cynthia Arenson remembers seeing Bernie at Sunny Oaks no more than twice in all those years.

David Arenson, who helped his mother run Sunny Oaks before it finally closed, notes, "It did become a bit of a chore caring for Saul and Sara as time went on. Sara became a little senile. They weren't that self-sufficient."

He said he got the strong impression from Bernie and Ruth that they were happy having the Arensons care for her aging parents during the summer. "Bernie would say, 'Well, you guys take such good care of Saul and Sara.'"

By all accounts, Saul Alpern was frugal and fiscally conservative even though he became a multimillionaire through his close business ties with his son-in-law. In fact, he was so tightfisted, especially as he grew old, that he rarely bought new clothes for himself. He continued to wear the same suit, which had grown shiny and frayed with age. For his 80th birthday, Cynthia Arenson recalls, "My parents' friends had to chip in and they bought him a suit of clothes."

Sara Alpern died in 1996 in Florida, leaving more than $2 million in three trusts at Bernie's firm, according to her will. She bequeathed the money to her husband, who was then 92 years old. Under the will's terms, Ruth and her sister, Joan Roman, married to insurance agent Bob Roman, who for a long time handled all of the Madoff firm's insurance, were to inherit more than $1 million after their father's death. Saul Alpern died at the age of 95 in December 1999, when his son-in-law's Ponzi scheme was at full throttle. After Bernie's arrest, Ruth claimed she had inherited millions from her father's estate.

In Saul Alpern's brief death notice in the *New York Times* on December 9, 1999, the "Yeshiva University family" mourned his passing, noting that Bernie's father-in-law was "a well-respected member of the Jewish community." The university's president and the chairman of its board of trustees said of his survivors, "May they be comforted among the mourners of Zion and Jerusalem."

■ ■ ■

Bernie sat on Yeshiva's board of trustees, was in fact its treasurer, and was one of the founders and chairman of the university's Sy Syms School of Business, named in honor of the discount clothing chain founder.

In Bernie's massive swindle, Yeshiva University was one of many Jewish nonprofits that had invested with him. The day after Bernie was arrested, the university's media relations director, Hedy Shulman, told the *Jewish Journal*, "We are shocked at this revelation. Our lawyers and accountants are investigating all aspects of his relationship to the university."

And Bernie's name quickly vanished from the university's web site.

But in 2001, when Madoff and Yeshiva were as close as pastrami on rye, the university had awarded the Hofstra College nobody and Brooklyn Law School dropout an honorary degree, and a year later its trustees made him treasurer.

Initial accounts had stated that Yeshiva, located in Manhattan, with a student body of some 7,000, and home to an Orthodox rabbi seminary, had lost a whopping $110 million, but that estimate was soon lowered to $14.5 million because "fictitious" numbers allegedly had been given to the university by the head of one of Bernie's biggest feeder funds, J. Ezra Merkin, who had been chairman of Yeshiva's investment committee. Even though the loss was far less than had been estimated, the university didn't have the larger sum that its administrators had thought was available.

The school also faced the problem of governance—a question raised by Moody's Investors Service: How and why was such a thief as Bernard Madoff appointed to such a sensitive position at the university?

There was much to atone for.

Chapter 7

Moving On Up

One of Bernie Madoff's first offices—a $50-a-month hole-in-the-wall that he shared on and off with his father—was in the 20-story edifice at 40 Exchange Place known as the Lords Court Building that was built in 1893 and was located about a block from the center of American capitalism, the New York Stock Exchange, at 11 Wall Street.

It was in the Exchange Place office that Bernie scored one of his first lucrative stock underwriting clients in March 1962, a month before he turned 24. Along with the investment clients he was getting through Ruth's father at Sunny Oaks, a Queens company had retained him to help it go public with 100,000 shares of common stock. He was handling the offering "on a best efforts all or none basis," according to an *SEC News Digest*, dated March 30, 1962.

The principals of A.L.S. Steel Corporation, Abe Eisenberg, Herman Loonin, and Gabriel Sobel, may have been connected to either Ralph Madoff or Saul Alpern since Bernie was getting his early business from family and friends.

A.L.S., on Northern Boulevard in the Corona section of Queens—Bernie's old stomping grounds—was involved in the sale of "processed flat rolled strip steel to a customer's specifications and requirement," the SEC announcement stated.

For Bernie, it was an esoteric product that could have been made on Mars, but the fees that were part of his underwriter deal—if he was able to pull it off—were, in fact, out of this world.

On each of the 100,000 shares offered for public sale at $4.50 per share—common, over-the-counter stock—Bernie as the underwriter was set to receive 45 cents, or $45,000 if all shares were sold at the offering price. Beyond that, he was to receive a whopping $15,000 for "expenses," which were never explained. All told, the full $60,000 would be equal to more than $420,000 adjusted for inflation in 2009 dollars.

Above and beyond that, the company sold Bernie "6,000 outstanding shares . . . at ten cents per share" and "at one-cent each five-year options to purchase 10,000 shares at $4.50 per share."

With that deal, if in fact it was ever fulfilled, and along with the business he was scoring from his elderly Borscht Belt clientele, Bernie was generating enough money for him and Ruth to move from their little apartment in Bayside, Queens, to a rental in the more affluent village of Great Neck, on Long Island's North Shore, a 45-minute train and subway commute to the Wall Street area.

"The new apartment was definitely more upscale," says Jane Kavanau. "Ruth had been working for somebody on Wall Street doing some sort of bookkeeping and accounting, and then she went to work for Bernie."

Bernie and Ruth in those days weren't all about business all the time. They were young and a bit carefree, and spent time socializing with their young friends, such as the Kavanaus. Several times a month, the two couples went out for fun dinners, mostly to simple restaurants on Long Island, rather than to pricey and extravagant Manhattan eateries. In the winter, they spent weekends together skiing at Bel Air and Hunter Mountain in upstate New York, a far different milieu from the high-flying Aspen lifestyle the Madoffs would later enjoy and profit from as they made the rounds of chic resorts, entertaining and rubbing shoulders with the wealthy who would entrust their money to Madoff.

Recalls Joe Kavanau:

One weekend when we were all married but before we had children, Jane and I, and Bernie and Ruth checked into a motel because we were staying over Saturday night—I think we were skiing that weekend, and Ruth and Bernie had a dog, and they would take that dog everyplace.

Bernie snuck the dog, Muffin, a female schnauzer, a very sweet dog, into the motel, and the motel owner caught him, and so we had to leave.

Bernie gave the place a name, which was not a very nice name. He called it the "Fuck You Motel."

After they had kids, Muffin was around for quite a few years. She was definitely part of the family. They had one or two cats, and one of them, I think an angora, got sick. Bernie took the cat to the vet, and I remember Bernie told the vet, "I don't care how much it costs—you gotta take care of it, make it well."

The man who years later admitted to taking the lifeblood from thousands of investors was once a pussycat who fawned over his pets.

■ ■ ■

Generating enough income in the early 1960s, Bernie and Ruth fulfilled the American dream by buying a new home in the incorporated village of Roslyn Estates. Their house was in one of the many developments springing up in the 1960s on former Long Island farmland, housing tracts that were bedroom communities for New York City commuters. It was during this time that they also welcomed their first son, Mark, into the world—the beginning of what would become the infamous Madoff dynasty.

The Madoffs' purchase at such a young age and so early in their marriage tended to raise eyebrows among other young couples in their circle—friends from Laurelton, and pals like Elliott Olin and his wife, from high school and college, many of whom were still struggling to make ends meet.

Recalls Olin's widow, Sheila, "I said to Elliott, 'I want to ask you something. How in the world after a year or two of working, how could Bernie buy a house there?' Elliott, who was finishing law school, just pushed off the question, but I just had bad feelings about what Bernie was doing. I thought he was doing something wrong, because how could he have so much money to buy a new home? Everyone else was still struggling. I was making $115 a week and we were barely paying our rent, and Bernie has suddenly become so successful."

Jay Portnoy, Bernie's friend from Laurelton who had gone to college with Ruth, was hearing through the years about his childhood pal's growing success from his mother, who had remained friends with Sylvia Madoff and Sara Alpern.

He recalled Mrs. Portnoy telling him:

> "Mrs. M. says Bernie is doing very well." "Mrs. A. says Bernie is doing very, very well on Wall Street." And still later: "Mrs. M. says Bernie is a millionaire." "Mrs. A says Bernie is a multimillionaire."

The Madoff home on Diana's Trail, on the southern border of Roslyn Estates, was typical of the type of suburban development-style houses that were being built at the time on Long Island: It was a raised ranch with four bedrooms, two and a half baths, and an above-ground finished basement. Nothing was extraordinary about the architecture or construction or curb appeal, but Ruth decorated it to the nines and visitors were impressed. Not long after she and Bernie moved in they had their second son and last child, Andy.

The Madoff house was far different from the 480-acre estate once owned by Roslyn philanthropist Clarence Mackey, who inherited a silver mining fortune, and entertained the likes of the Duke of Windsor and the aviator Charles Lindbergh after he returned from his solo Long Island-to-Paris flight.

"The Madoff house was definitely *not* a mansion," observes Jane Kavanau. "They stayed in that house for many, many years and raised

Mark and Andrew there. They could probably have afforded a mansion after a while, but they just stayed in that house." They'd later move on up: the stylish East Side penthouse, the chic Hamptons beach house, the gated Palm Beach mansion, and the luxurious getaway in the south of France.

■ ■ ■

Charles Lubitz, Bernie's Brooklyn Law School classmate, who would later represent Palm Beach clients ripped off by Bernie, also moved into a home nearby, in an area known as Roslyn Heights. He and his wife saw the Madoffs on and off back in those days, and were part of a circle of young couples that included the Kavanaus—Lubitz's wife had gone to Vassar with Jane Kavanau. Lubitz remembers Bernie and Ruth back then as "a lovely couple. Bernie was a nice guy. We spent social evenings together. Bernie was, of course, much more successful early on than most people of our age." But he recalls that the Madoff house was nothing fancy, "although it was a step above that which others of us had."

In that same time frame, Bernie and Ruth joined the first of many fancy country clubs with well-to-do, predominately Jewish members who would put their money in Madoff, and subsequently get Ponzied by Bernie—clubs from Long Island's Gold Coast to the platinum links of Palm Beach.

Chuck Lubitz recalls how Bernie boasted about being one of the youngest members of the prestigious Fresh Meadow Country Club in Great Neck, which had rich members and a spectacular golf course designed in the early 1920s by A. W. Tillinghast. "From the beginning, Fresh Meadow traveled first class," according to its history. "The members wanted their course to be one of the country's great examinations of golf."

Now, in the early 1960s, its membership included the hustler from Queens.

"He was basically a kid like I was, and he told me that one time at Fresh Meadow he was standing outside waiting for his car and he had on a pair of jeans and a leather jacket, and one of the ladies from the club came up to him and handed him her ticket to retrieve her car, and asked him would he please hurry," says Lubitz, recalling Bernie's glib recitation of the event. "Bernie said, 'Oh, absolutely, Madam.' And he went through the whole routine—went running for her car and got it. He even pocketed her tip.

"He was so young to be a member that she thought he was the valet. He was very amused by it and got a good chuckle out of telling the story. Most of the members were wealthy, graying, Jewish overachievers of a senior age. Bernie would have stuck out like a sore thumb."

Bernie and Ruth remained members of Fresh Meadow for years. Some people have long referred to it as "the Madoff country club" because they had such close ties to the club. Major family events took place there such as the "small, understated, not particularly religious" wedding of son Mark Madoff and the first of his two wives.

Later, Fresh Meadow's membership, like so many other elite clubs to which Bernie belonged, was hit by the nuclear blast of his fraud. One such member and victim was a longtime Madoff acquaintance, Sherry Fabrikant, and her son, Andrew. From a wealthy family in the New York City diamond trade, Sherry, who became a noted collector of contemporary art, had gotten to know Bernie and Ruth when they lived in Roslyn Estates and she in Great Neck, and as members of the club. Beyond that, her niece was friendly with Mark and Andy, whom Fabrikant considered "morons." In any case, the two families had a comfortable comradeship.

Looking back, Fabrikant found the Madoffs an interesting study.

Bernie never showed up for any of the events, and anytime I saw him there he was very low-key, very reserved.

Ruth used to come in the spring and in the fall by herself. They did not lead the life of those crazy socialite people. He wasn't a social climber, not at all. I thought it was sincere. He never went to any of the stupid things that all the other totally dumb people went to—all those parties. He didn't have Ruth dressed up in some stupid gown. I didn't find him good-looking, and that smirk that he has—that's not a smirk, that's how his face is formed. He has funny-looking cheeks.

Despite how he looked and how he and Ruth acted, or at least as she perceived it, one thing was clear to Fabrikant: Bernie was making money for her friends. A doctor and his wife whom she'd known for more than four decades had invested millions with Madoff. "Year in and year out she always said to me, 'You'd better invest with Bernie.' For all of those years they talked about him and how they had done very, very, very well with him."

Finally, Fabrikant decided around 2004—when the Ponzi operation was going full blast—to join the ecstatic and beholden. "My guys in the stock market were doing lousy," she says, "and I thought, okay, go with Madoff."

Recounts Fabrikant:

I called Bernie personally. I knew him for 30 years. I said, "Andrew and I want to invest with you; is that okay?" He said, "I need a certain amount of money from you," but he didn't say how much. I said, "Well, we can't do that." And then he said, "Well, whatever you want. Okay, Sherry, come up."

She did, handing over $3 million to $4 million.

We did not give him all our money, thank God.

She says she began getting a return of 8 to 9 percent—on paper, because whenever she did need money she usually took it out of her stock brokerage account, but periodically took some out of Madoff.

Whenever I wanted money I called him. I said, "I need ten dollars," whatever. The check was in the mail the next day. To me it looked legit. You should see his statements—they're *gorgeous*!

My accountants said, "Don't take it out of Madoff, because he's doing so nicely." Not that he was making me a fortune. It was nothing so outstanding that I would call him a genius.

But when he thought the market was going down he said he invested in T-bills, which we thought was brilliant. We thought it was a decent, safe investment.

Then we lost everything. It was a big shock to me. I'm not as rich as the people who lost $20 million—except for my art collection, which is worth a fortune because luckily I have put most of my money on my walls.

She says that some other members of Fresh Meadow lost so much money in the Ponzi scheme that they "went bankrupt" and other members were going to support them financially. "It's an older club with people who are much more like family, much more into each other."

■ ■ ■

Not only did Bernie cheat his friends, family members, and other investors by offering questionably high and steady returns in good economic times and bad, but he also scammed in another way by possibly misrepresenting himself on the golf course.

Bernie had started playing golf when he was in high school, driving balls down the median strips of highways, and then playing at public courses. Later, when he belonged to clubs like Fresh Meadow and the Palm Beach Country Club, whose members were also ravaged by him, his golf scores were suspiciously and eerily as consistent as the returns he was promising.

For instance, he never went below 80 or above 89 in 20 rounds during the period 1998 to 2000, scores that surfaced after his arrest.

As golf pro Michael Hebron observed, "Consistency this high is very unusual. And that's even before I knew who they [the scores] belonged to."

Chapter 8

The Bagel Baker Becomes a Financial Guru, and the Mob Boys from Rockford Pay a Visit

"I've known of Bernie my whole life in a messiah kind of way," states Jonny Lieberbaum. "My family regarded Bernie like as a messiah. He was spoken of as if godlike."

All of those intense and respectful feelings evaporated in anger and hate after Jonny Lieberbaum's mother, Carol Ann Lieberbaum, lost most if not all of the millions she and her late husband, Shelley, had invested through the years in Bernard L. Madoff Investment Securities.

Other family victims in Madoff, according to the list made publicly available after Bernie was arrested, included Shelley's brother and sister-in-law, Mike and Cynthia Greenberger Lieberbaum, and her two brothers, John Maccabee, the writer of the *New York* magazine piece about Bernie, and Robert Greenberger, the former *Wall*

Street Journal reporter. Greenberger's wife, the former Phyllis Eileen Morel, a Brooklyn girl and the first president and CEO of the Society for Women's Health Research, was named one of "The 100 Most Powerful Women" alongside then Senator Hillary Clinton and then Secretary of State Condoleezza Rice in 2006 by *Washington* magazine. One of their sons and a daughter-in-law had been on the staff of the *Boston Globe*.

As related earlier, Bernie's lifelong close relationship with Mike and Cynthia Lieberbaum started when they became friends at Far Rockaway High School and graduated together. Mike Lieberbaum also was a student at Hofstra. And Shelley Lieberbaum helped finance Bernie's lawn sprinkler business when he was at Hofstra.

After Bernie was arrested, maintains Carol Lieberbaum, "I was wiped out, basically. I lost 90 to 95 percent of what we had in Madoff"—investments that began around the time Bernie started his now-infamous company.

"We all helped Bernie get off the ground by investing with him," she says regretfully.

However, in exchange, she and her husband (and some other family members) had many, many years of what Lieberbaum describes as spectacular returns. She says the Lieberbaum and Greenberger families "definitely believed" that Bernie had given them "special consideration" with higher returns because of their long friendship, and what family members had done for him in the early years.

Lieberbaum asserts:

You don't question when the going is good.

What were we going to do—call up Bernie and tell him, "God, I'm making too much money. What's going on?" We made a lot of money with him. Nobody made more money than people with Madoff. It was absurd the amount of the returns—they were *amazing*.

We had friends who would have done anything—they would have *killed* to have gotten in Madoff, and Bernie turned them down. For whatever reasons, he said no. We had friends of *tremendous* wealth who couldn't get in, but that was part of Bernie's allure. He made it absolutely intoxicating and exclusive.

When the news broke of the Madoff Ponzi scheme and Bernie's arrest, Lieberbaum couldn't believe it. She had last talked to Bernie several months before he was arrested to "just say hi" and to say she was getting ready to take a trip to Mexico.

> I thought there was a misunderstanding. I was in utter shock and disbelief. Bernie and Ruth were the nicest couple you can ever imagine—kind, generous, warm. They were phenomenal, terrific, very devoted. I knew them for 50 years—or thought I did.

She immediately called the Madoffs' penthouse hoping to talk to Ruth, who she knew "had kept the books" for Bernie at one time and presumably was aware of everything that was going on. She and Ruth had close ties. For years Ruth's parents rented a Manhattan apartment from the Lieberbaums that the Alperns used as a pied-à-terre. Over the years, she says, she came to the conclusion that Ruth was "definitely classier" than Bernie. "She was refined. He acquired as much as he could, if you can say you can *buy* class. But he wasn't showy. He was not ostentatious. He was humble. It sounds ludicrous to say that today, but I mean he was a good guy. He was low-key wealth—enormous wealth. That's how it looked."

No one picked up the phone at the Madoffs', and Lieberbaum left a message on their voice mail.

"I told Ruth, 'I can't believe what's going on. This is all a terrible, terrible mistake, right? I hope everyone will be all right. My prayers are with you. Call me.'"

She never heard back.

"Now I'd like to put a bullet in both their heads."

■ ■ ■

Carol Lieberbaum's sister-in-law, Cynthia Greenberger Lieberbaum, came from an immensely wealthy family. "I know Cynthia's parents had a lot of money with Bernie from the very beginning," says Carol Lieberbaum.

The patriarch, Sidney S. Greenberger, who died of heart disease in 1964, made his fortune as founder of the Graphic Paper Corporation in New York. Before joining the *Wall Street Journal*, one of his sons, Robert Greenberger, was listed as secretary-treasurer of Graphic Paper.

Robert and Cynthia's brother, John (Greenberger) Maccabee, says their late mother, Ruth, who died in March 2004, "would have killed" Bernie had she lived to see how he stole the family's investment in his Ponzi scheme—an investment that began in 1961, a year after Bernie started his company.

When Ruth Greenberger's funeral was held in Queens, Bernie and Ruth Madoff were two of the few nonfamily members who were among the mourners. At the time, Bernie's Ponzi scheme had been in operation for years without the Greenbergers' knowledge.

Maccabee recalled that as he was leaving the cemetery following the interment Bernie approached him and discreetly told him that "the deal" he had had with the Greenberger family was over now that the matriarch, whom he always called "Mrs. G.," was gone.

Maccabee says that Bernie "was able to get away with this kind of dark humor," but he meant what he said.

> He's tainted so many people. He's corrupted us all by his very presence, and by having been welcomed into our house and our family. It's *so* fucked up. Somebody asked me if I'm angry and I'm not. I'm *amazed* by the complexity, the lunacy, the absolute pathological lunacy. The thing about Bernie is—he's crazy.

When Maccabee learned that he and his wife, Sherry, and their two sons had lost their invested money in Madoff, he said:

> I felt punched in the stomach. I said to myself, or I said to my wife, "Well, if this motherfucker made it his business to steal my money, then I'm going to make it my business to make some money with him."

He decided to write the magazine piece about Bernie, and planned to write a book about the Greenberger family, and the impact that Bernie had on it through the years.

> He fucked everybody—his own sister; Elie fucking Weisel. How do you fuck over Elie Weisel? How do you do that? Bernie was giving to Yeshiva University and then stealing their money on the other end. It's just amazing.

Yet, Maccabee did not always feel this way about the former "messiah." At one point in his life, acknowledges Maccabee, "I was proud of Bernie, actually. There was something about him that he engendered that made you want to take care of him as well as be taken care of by him. I did like Bernie and Ruth, and we had a long and complicated relationship. There were a great many people who revered Bernie for what he made of himself. He was a legend. A lot of people felt that way about him."

A 1963 graduate of Far Rockaway High School, Maccabee characterized his parents as Bernie's "angel investors"—meaning they had been in business with Bernie from the very beginning, just like the Lieberbaums. He recalled that when Bernie first approached his parents to invest, he whipped out a recent bank statement that showed he had invested $5,000 of his own money in his fledgling business—proof that he believed enough in himself and his abilities to make money for Bernie Madoff and for other people. Later, he convinced Mrs. Greenberger, after she became a widow, to invest another $300,000.

Yet, the Greenbergers were tough angels who demanded and received returns on their money every quarter in the form of a "golden-yellow" check from the Madoff company—along with a detailed accounting.

Maccabee's mother, who had knowledge of bookkeeping, and had been his father's secretary at Graphic Paper, would sometimes catch an error in the Madoff accounting and immediately call Bernie, usually speaking to his assistant, believed to be Annette Bongiorno. She would come under suspicion as a participant in Bernie's fraud for allegedly ordering the creation of fake trading tickets, and for feeding Bernie investors from her Queens neighborhood, according to reports.

Bernie usually returned Mrs. Greenberger's call to say that the error was minor. Maccabee quoted Bernie in his *New York* magazine piece as telling her, "Give me a break, Mrs. G. Don't worry, I'll make up the $17 to you next quarter." He said his mother actually wanted the *full* amount that she was shortchanged—"17 dollars and 63 cents."

Bernie's response, in his Queens accent, was: "Mrs. G., ya killing me."

His mother ended the conversation by saying, "On the contrary, Bernie. I pray for your health daily."

And then Bernie would often flatter her, probably in hopes of softening her up for more money. He used niceties like, "I've got a lot to learn from you, Mrs. G."

However, he was incredibly mean-spirited with Maccabee's sister, Cynthia, with whom he had bonded in high school, and who married his pal, Mike Lieberbaum. Maccabee quoted Bernie as once telling his sister: "If you think you're any prize, and that your husband should kiss your ass for the measly couple of million bucks you stand to inherit, you are fuckin' delusional."

Despite their close ties, Bernie felt no qualms in laying into his longtime friend. That was Bernie, they all thought. Don't take him too seriously. After all, look at those golden returns. But with friends like Bernie, who needed enemies?

■ ■ ■

If Bernie ever had a Wall Street guru and someone he hoped to emulate, it was Mike Lieberbaum's father, Lou Lieberbaum, who would serve as Bernie's third mentor on his journey to fraud, deception, and deceit.

Originally from Brooklyn, Lieberbaum had moved his family to Belle Harbor, one of the fancy communities on the Rockaway peninsula of Queens, up the road from the wealthy Greenbergers in Neponsit. But in the beginning he was considered the neighborhood schlepper.

Surrounded by mostly affluent Jewish families, the Lieberbaums had moved into a small two-family house about a block and a half from the ocean. In order to put food on the table and pay the rent, the patriarch worked as a milkman in Belle Harbor and, his daughter-in-law Carol says, a bagel baker in Brooklyn.

But like Bernie, who would become a partner of sorts, Lieberbaum was a shrewd, street-smart hustler who had an interest in the stock market.

Bernie could have been his son.

The stock that would make Lieberbaum very, very wealthy was Polaroid.

In the mid-1950s, he is said to have switched from delivering milk to selling mutual funds and stock for a relatively new firm, Dreyfus and Company, one of the first on Wall Street to aggressively hawk mutual funds to the public through its Dreyfus Fund. Lou's son, Shelley, four years older than Bernie, also worked for Dreyfus for several years in the late 1950s. The founder, Jack Dreyfus, considered one of Wall Street's most successful investors in the 1950s and 1960s, was a onetime candy salesman who started his company on the advice of a gin rummy partner. These were the kind of wheeler-dealers who ran the Street long before the MBAs came along.

The former candy salesman is said to have taken a liking to the former bagel baker.

Lieberbaum started making decent money hustling everyone he knew to buy into Dreyfus, targeting among others the well-to-do in Belle Harbor and Neponsit who had been on his milk route. It wasn't a difficult sell. The Dreyfus Fund was a gold mine. For the period from the mid-1950s to the mid-1960s, the fund had a return of a whopping 604 percent while the Dow Jones Industrial Average showed a measly 346 percent return.

In 1957, when Bernie was still a Sammy fraternity boy at Alabama, Jack Dreyfus, who by coincidence was born in Alabama, invited his protégé Lieberbaum to take a tour of the Polaroid factory. Still a privately held company, Polaroid a year earlier had sold its one-millionth camera, and was about to go public. After the tour, Dreyfus gave the former bagel baker a piece of advice: He said, "Lou, if I were you I'd run up and down the street trying to sell everyone Polaroid," according to people who knew Lou Lieberbaum and his legendary rags-to-riches story.

A fast learner, Lieberbaum didn't have to be told twice. "My father-in-law was extremely self-taught. He was brilliant," observes Carol Lieberbaum.

"Lou became enamored with Polaroid when it was down at a new issue price, and he told everybody and his brother, 'Buy Polaroid! This stock's gonna fly!' And voilà, the stock *flew*," says Bernie's high school classmate Peter Zaphiris, who later worked for Lieberbaum. "Lou, along with a whole bunch of other people, made quite a bit of money, and better than that, Lou was smart enough to understand that he now had a *following*, people who loved him, trusted him, and would invest their money with him."

It was just like the kind of following Bernie would develop and captivate.

While Lou Lieberbaum never made it as big or became as famous as his mentor, Jack Dreyfus—who was a bridge expert, won many amateur golf championships, owned thoroughbred racehorses, served as chairman of the New York Racing Association, and lived like royalty, according to his obituary in the *New York Times*—Lieberbaum did quite well for himself.

Not only did he make millions on Polaroid as the stock soared, but he bought a seat on the New York Stock Exchange. With his following of avid investors, he also opened his own brokerage, Lieberbaum & Company, sometime in the late 1950s or early 1960s, with the blessing of his mentor, Jack Dreyfus, who died at the age of 95 in March 2009, as the Bernard Madoff scandal raged.

Lieberbaum would become one of Bernie's mentors.

■ ■ ■

Flush with riches, Lieberbaum bought a spectacular home in Hewlett Harbor. In order to let guests know where all his money came from, he is said to have had the Polaroid logo etched on a big mirror "like it was a Picasso" in the expensively and overly decorated living room of his mansion. The ex-milkman and his wife, Lillian, staffed the huge home with servants, had chauffeurs to drive their fleet of Cadillacs, and oversaw a small flotilla of boats moored at their dock.

The Lieberbaum brothers, Mike and Shelley, were weight lifters and because Shelley was especially buff, his proud and newly wealthy father commissioned a sculptor to fashion a bronze statue of him in a muscleman pose.

On one memorable occasion Lieberbaum invited some pals to the house to show off a gift he'd bought for his wife.

"We were having bagels and coffee in the kitchen at Hewlett Harbor, and he says, 'What do you think of this? I just bought this for Lillian,'" recalls Zaphiris, who was present.

> He opens up this flat case that must have had a thousand diamonds in it. The gift was like a cluster diamond necklace. Forget about the diamonds—the case looked like it cost a fortune. The necklace that I saw, and again that was 50 years ago, cost $600,000. God, it was spectacular.
>
> Later, someone told me Lou was full of shit, that he takes this stuff out on consignment. They give it to him because supposedly he's going to buy it, but he'd never bought anything like that necklace. Lou had the ability to paint pictures in the sky—just like Bernie did.

Carol Lieberbaum doesn't dispute her father-in-law's ostentatiousness. "He was flashy. He was nouveau, and definitely showy," she says, but with love. She adds:

> He never had and all of a sudden he got and he just flaunted it—big homes, big parties, drivers, cooks, the magnificent place on the water in Hewlett Harbor with tennis courts, swimming pools, spas, a gym. It was amazing. And because of that Polaroid money, Shelley was able to loan that money to Bernie for his

sprinkler business. Shelley, Michael, and my father-in-law had money. Bernie didn't have anything.

He also brought his two sons, Mike and Shelley, Bernie's pals, into the business. Shelley served as an officer of the company from 1960 to 1971.

Lieberbaum & Company was a family affair, just like Bernard L. Madoff Investment Securities became when Bernie brought his two sons, Mark and Andy, into the business, along with their mother, Ruth, and Bernie's brother, Peter, among others.

Not long after Lieberbaum & Company got rolling, Bernie Madoff entered the picture.

Around 1962, he moved from his small office on Exchange Place to a small suite at 39 Broadway.

Recalls Bill Nasi, who worked there as Bernie's runner:

It had a tiny reception room the size of maybe three large closets, a back office that was the size of three closets, and a trading room with an oversize blackboard. Bernie had a girl standing on a three-foot-high carpeted bench, and as the stock prices would change she would erase the old quotes and put in the new ones with a piece of chalk.

The layout, though, wasn't as important as the location. Bernie was now directly across the street from 50 Broadway, the headquarters of Lieberbaum & Company.

And instantly, new and bigger business was flowing his way courtesy of the Lieberbaums.

Whereas Lieberbaum & Company was known as a New York Stock Exchange–registered brokerage house, Bernard L. Madoff Investment Securities was not. According to Zaphiris, who worked at Lieberbaum at the time, an arrangement appeared to have been worked out between Bernie and Lieberbaum whereby all orders given to Lieberbaum for over-the-counter stocks were "walked across the street" for Bernie to handle.

Zaphiris, who worked at Lieberbaum as a 25-year-old broker trainee in 1963 after being recruited by Eddie Rochelle, another Far Rockaway graduate from Bernie's class of 1956, continues:

The over-the-counter trades were all spooned to Bernie. He was handling *all* of that Lieberbaum over-the-counter business so far as I knew. That was the way Bernie made his living at the time. About 95 percent of his over-the-counter business was coming from Lieberbaum.

Lieberbaum had 50 brokers churning out orders and talking to customers. I don't know how much volume they produced in over-the-counter, but it had to be significant and every drop of it was going to Bernie.

Each side made out on the deal.

Bernie made a commission for making the actual buy or sell, and Lieberbaum marked up the trade "an eighth or a sixteenth" above and beyond its usual commission (commissions back then were significant, much more than they later became). The customer was never the wiser, thinking he or she was doing business strictly with Lieberbaum when, in fact, it was all being funneled to Bernie.

Looking back, Zaphiris says he "thought" what was going on was "unethical. I don't know if it was illegal."

Carol Lieberbaum asserts she didn't get involved in the family business, and says she "can't remember" whether Bernie ever worked with the family brokerage. "I don't *think* Bernie and Shelley and my father-in-law were ever in business together, but of course they all were in the *same* business. I don't know the business aspects of their connection."

But Zaphiris emphasizes:

Bernie was like another facet of the Lieberbaum business. They definitely were in business together, whether it was official or unofficial. If a customer bought a stock that was not listed, and the customer bought it from Lieberbaum, the customer had no idea that Bernie was involved in any way, shape, or form.

Michael Lieberbaum, the only surviving member of the family troika that ran Lieberbaum & Company before its demise, declined requests by the author for an interview through his wife, the former Cynthia Greenberger.

"The Lieberbaum thing was the genesis of Bernie's career," Zaphiris believes.

Yet, it should be noted that at the same time, Bernie's investment advisory business—which was helped along by his father-in-law—was going strong, too.

That being said, the arrangement between Lieberbaum and Madoff back in the 1960s appears to have been a prototype for the future of how much of Bernie's investment advisory business-cum-Ponzi scheme operated: So-called feeder funds recruited investors for Bernie and fed billions of their dollars to him. The investors were unaware that their money was actually being passed on to Bernie. In exchange, Bernie gave the feeder fund operators hundreds of millions of dollars in commissions, simply for being middlemen. It was only after Bernie was arrested and his scheme revealed that many investors first heard the Madoff name, and by then it was too late.

■ ■ ■

The Lieberbaums and the Madoffs were a close-knit group, almost like family. As young couples, the Lieberbaums and the Madoffs often socialized, and had playdates for one another's children. Mike and Cynthia Lieberbaum lived in Roslyn Heights, near Bernie and Ruth, and Shelley and Carol Lieberbaum lived in nearby Woodmere.

Because of their friendship—and because he was handling all of Lieberbaum & Company's over-the-counter trades—Bernie was a constant presence in the Lieberbaum offices, "bullshitting with Shelley, Mike, and Louie," recalls Zaphiris. "Bernie and the Lieberbaums were *really, really, really* tight together, and they did a lot of business together. The Lieberbaums at that time were kingpins. Across the street Bernie had a little dinky office with a couple of machines and a girl working for him."

Working together with him at that time was his father, Ralph Madoff, with the fake middle initial Z. This was in the same time frame that Bernie's mother, Sylvia, got into trouble with the SEC for operating questionable Gibralter Securities out of the family home in Laurelton, and was suspected of fronting for her husband.

■ ■ ■

During the time Peter Zaphiris worked at Lieberbaum & Company, he noticed other curious activity along with the firm's close Bernie connection and the shuttling of over-the-counter trades to him. This included clients who were "clearly gangsters" and were believed to be from the Rockford, Illinois, family of La Cosa Nostra, which was a faction of the Chicago mob.

"The boys from Rockford were calling all the time, and I suspected that there was some sort of money laundering going on, something crazy going on," says Zaphiris. "There was a broker who was trading a company for these guys. He'd get a phone call before the close and they would tell him what to close it at and he would buy 30,000 shares and sell 30,000 shares. They would manipulate the stock like crazy, and that was one of about 300 deals going on, and they were all pretty much the same bullshit."

One day word spread through the office to expect visitors. The Rockford boys were coming to town to pay a visit. Remembers Zaphiris:

> Three guys came into the office and they were like five by five, the guys that wear expensive Italian suits, and they look cheap.
>
> A couple of my acquaintances in the office—the guys who did business with them and who were in the hierarchy of the 50 or 60 brokers working at Lieberbaum—were literally shaking. They weren't looking forward to this visit because they had either just lost a great deal of money for them, or they had put them in some sort of situation they didn't want to be in.

A private meeting was held between the mobsters and the brokers in a conference room. "It was a poof," says Zaphiris. No shots were fired.

No horse's head was left behind, and after a couple of hours the boys left and everyone was relieved.

But the fact that mobsters did business with the firm to which Bernie had close connections raised a red flag. However, during the time Zaphiris he worked there he never was aware of any questions of illegalities being raised or investigated by the SEC, the agency that years later gave Bernie a free parking card when presented with hard facts that he was running a Ponzi operation.

"We weren't dealing with customers coming in and bringing in presents from Tiffany's," he observes. "Most of the people who showed up were *screaming* at the brokers. They were people who were really wounded."

Zaphiris believes the wounding occurred because of what he suspected or witnessed—stocks that were being pumped and dumped and manipulated. "They ran one stock from seven bucks up to around $140 and they manipulated it. They put all sorts of people in it, and then they dumped it out. Most of the brokers there were fast and loose. They scoffed at the investors. They thought they were idiots."

On another pump-and-dump stock, Canadian Javelin, two brokers who acted as partners within Lieberbaum had a deal under which they received one dollar in cash for every share that they placed. The SEC eventually halted trading by all brokers in the stock, and the case went to the U.S. Supreme Court to decide on the agency's action. It became a landmark securities case, and existing certificates of the stock later became collector's items.

After the two brokers left Lieberbaum, they were caught in a stock scheme. Federal court papers called them "New York stock manipulators," and one of them pleaded guilty to a conspiracy count. One of the federal prosecutors in the case was Ira Lee Sorkin—Bernie's attorney. One of the two former Lieberbaum brokers later was involved in another fraudulent scheme involving the writing of a questionable newsletter promoting the stock of a California firm. The ex-Lieberbaum broker was sentenced to six months in prison. One of the big-name investors in the company was then New Hampshire congressman and later the state's U.S. senator, John E. Sununu, son of John H. Sununu, former chief of staff in the George H.W. Bush White House.

Besides the mob boys, loan sharks appeared one day to deal with another Lieberbaum broker who was a compulsive gambler, an East Side playboy who was an heir to a fortune that he wouldn't inherit for a few years, and who had been hired at Lieberbaum mainly to bring in rich friends and family as clients. He was betting as much as $5,000 a day from his trading floor desk, studying the *Racing News* rather than the *Wall Street Journal*.

Says Zaphiris:

> One time these torpedoes came up and they threw him over the desk backwards in the Lieberbaum office.
>
> They were sitting on him and saying, "You pay up or we're gonna break your fuckin' legs." He said, "If you break my legs you're not going to get the money any faster. Your boss knows I'm good for it." So they pushed him around and they actually pushed him over his freaking desk and his ass hit the back of the desk and he went overboard. It was frightening.

Prospective Lieberbaum clients with big money were usually given the grand tour of the offices by either Shelley or Lou Lieberbaum himself—a short, unassuming man who dressed to the nines, rarely talked to his brokers, and didn't spend a lot of time in the office—much the way Bernie operated when he got into the big time.

Visitors to Lieberbaum & Company saw brokers busy working the phones, ticker tape machines spewing buys and sells, world time zone clocks ticking away—it all looked very official and heady.

"When you walked in there," recalls Zaphiris, "it looked like the place was popping. Today they call it a boiler room, but it was only nicer."

Lou Lieberbaum always saved his tour's big Hollywood ending for last, literally and figuratively. Shelley would call Bernie at his office across the street and he'd come running over to watch the maestro's closing act, the pièce de résistance.

"And now," he'd proclaim as if to a drumroll, "How would you like to meet . . . ta-da . . . *Buster Crabbe*?!"

Seated right up front, handsome as ever, dressed like a movie star-turned-stockbroker in a pin-striped suit, starched white shirt, and subdued tie, was one of Hollywood's one-time biggest box office attractions—the actor who thrilled millions of kids playing comic strip heroes like Tarzan, Flash Gordon, Billy the Kid, and Buck Rogers on the big screen in films and in serials, and who later starred in television.

Then in his mid-50s, Crabbe was hustling stocks for Lou Lieberbaum. Like Bernie, Crabbe also was a swimmer—but big-time, winning a bronze medal in the 1928 Olympic Games and a gold medal in 1932. When his Hollywood career waned, he became a stockbroker and a businessman—hawking Buster Crabbe swimming pools for a New Jersey company. And like Bernie, he was swimming with sharks in the frenzied waters of Wall Street.

"Buster was a nice guy," says Zaphiris, who sat in the trading room near him. "He was handsome as hell and dressed like Douglas Fairbanks. Everybody who was coming into Lieberbaum knew who Buster Crabbe was. He was Tarzan *and* Flash Gordon."

In 1983, at the age of 75, Crabbe suffered a fatal heart attack.

After less than a year, Peter Zaphiris decided to leave Lieberbaum & Company. He had seen enough.

I don't want to make myself sound like I'm some kind of an angel, which I'm not. I couldn't see it. There was nothing in that business that I would have been happy doing, because it was a bunch of manipulation.

I didn't go there and find out how to research a stock, or how you develop clients, or how you recommend a portfolio to them. I never learned any of that. I learned—how do you find a guy and churn him. Part of my training was to tell half of the customers to buy and half to sell. Then 50 percent of your customers love you. They think you're a genius. It was definitely *not* for me.

I can't say that Louie was a crook. I know that a lot of people praised him up and down. He made a lot of money for people and he also ruined a lot of people—exactly the same as Bernie, but in Lou's case it wasn't a Ponzi scheme. They were putting customers into stock and taking them out of stock. They were doing crazy shit.

■ ■ ■

Lou Lieberbaum retired to "God's waiting room," Pompano Beach, Florida, where the state bird is jokingly referred to as "the early bird," and a home bordering the exclusive Palm-Aire Country Club. He died in the 1980s of a type of leukemia, his daughter-in-law says.

In 1985, Carol and Shelley got divorced.

Mike Lieberbaum had gone off on his own, settling in Westport, Connecticut, and Sarasota, Florida, where his in-laws, the Greenbergers, had a home. But Mike and his wife, Cynthia, continued a "very close relationship" with Bernie and Ruth, and lived the good life like them. In a June 2003 letter to the *New York Times*, Cynthia Lieberbaum wrote about how she and her family vacationed in Positano, Italy, every year for more than three decades "and finding no travel experience more rewarding than being welcomed with open arms . . . by people who have known us since we were in our early 30's."

By the 1990s, as Bernie was in full Ponzi mode, his close friend and investor, Shelley Lieberbaum, began getting into some serious trouble himself.

The National Association of Securities Dealers (NASD) alleged that he and some others "engaged in market manipulation, inaccurately maintained books and records and failed to adequately supervise the activities of employees" in connection with a public offering of a stock, according to SEC records. In 1995, Lieberbaum and the others "voluntarily entered into a Letter of Acceptance, Waiver and Consent" with the NASD. He was censured and fined by the association, agreed to pay with the others restitution to customers, and was suspended from associating with any NASD member for a month.

That same year, after a decade-long divorce, Shelley and Carol Lieberbaum remarried.

By then the original Lieberbaum & Company, founded by Shelley's father, had morphed in 1990 into one called Lew Lieberbaum & Co., a stock brokerage headquartered in Garden City, on Long Island, with an office in lower Manhattan. It had a customer base made up of thousands of affluent people in five states.

Starting in 1992, the new Lieberbaum company, with more than 200 employees and over $20 million in revenue, had been censured by the NASD four times, and ordered to pay fines and restitution to customers of more than $1.2 million. But none of the principals ever admitted guilt.

Now money and sex and racism seemed intermingled.

Shelley Lieberbaum became a key figure in a full-blown, headline-making case in the mid-1990s—a sensational sexual and racial harassment scandal in which his company became a "brokerage firm-turned-animal house," as the *New York Daily News* called it, where top executives were accused of groping women, holding lesbian stripper parties, and mistreating minorities.

All of it was revealed in shocking lawsuits against Lew Lieberbaum & Co., of which Shelley was one of the founders, filed by three former white female employees and the U.S. Equal Employment Opportunity Commission (EEOC). The probe began in April 1996, when the women complained of widespread and routine sexual harassment in a $100 million lawsuit against the company and nine executives, including Shelley Lieberbaum.

One young woman claimed that two Lieberbaum executives demanded oral sex from her. "I felt like nothing but a shell when I left," she was quoted in a press report as saying. Another said she was forced to give an executive back rubs, watch lesbian strippers perform, and "run a gauntlet" in the trading room, known as "The Pit." Relevant evidence in their case included photos of a Lieberbaum executive celebrating his birthday at the office with his face between a stripper's bare breasts, with his head between her legs, holding a banana near her crotch.

Several months later the charges of racial discrimination were added by the EEOC involving at least nine women. About 40 percent of Lieberbaum's employees were female.

One of the women, identified as Keiser L. Williams, who had worked as a receptionist in the New York office of Lieberbaum, maintained she was "sickened" by the behavior, pointing directly at Shelley Lieberbaum. She alleged that he made racist slurs and told jokes of a racial and sexual nature. Mark Lew, the company's chief executive—the Lew in Lew Lieberbaum—consistently denied all the charges. He was quoted in the *New York Times* as saying that Shelley "was known for telling such jokes" and that Williams had "encouraged" him to do so. Lew said the allegations of racial discrimination were "outrageously untrue."

In April 1998, however, without admitting any guilt, the Lieberbaum firm agreed to pay $1.75 million in an out-of-court settlement with the EEOC—the second largest settlement ever reached by the commission in a case of harassment. By then the company, facing a sharp drop in revenue because of the publicity surrounding the case, had changed its name to First Asset Management, and Mark Lew had changed his last name to Lev. Four months after the settlement, Lew Lieberbaum & Co. went out of business.

Carol Lieberbaum maintains that Shelley had gotten involved with "bad guys" and was "really devastated" by the scandal. "Shelley was a very classy guy, very quiet and refined, everything that his new partners were not. Shelley was just a very aboveboard guy, and my recollection of the others was that they were not."

Shelley Lieberbaum died in March 2007 at the age of 72, having suffered from Parkinson's disease and dementia, she says.

Bernie and Ruth, loyal to the end—except for the fact that he was stealing the Lieberbaum-Greenberger money in his Ponzi scheme—attended the funeral service in Fort Lauderdale.

Lieberbaum's death notice in the *New York Times* was filled with love and respect, and described him as "A true *mensch* who was loved by his friends, family and fine doggies and who loved him [*sic*] back in double doses. Master of the one-liner, author of epic comedic poems, victor over countless landlocked salmon, tennis player whose game was feared from Boro Park [Brooklyn] to Emerald Hills [an exclusive club in Hollywood, Florida]. He will be lovingly remembered."

Speaking of her late husband, who was instrumental in many ways in Bernie's early successes, Carol Lieberbaum declares:

Shelley would die a second time. He had the utmost respect and admiration for Bernie all through the years. He would have put everything he owned on the fact that Bernie was legit, that he was an upstanding citizen of the world.

I guess he was wrong.

At Far Rockaway High School in Queens, class of June '56 graduate Bernie Madoff was considered a "dummy" by some classmates, but he also established bonds with wealthy school chums who later invested and lost in his Ponzi scheme.

Source: University of Alabama Corolla yearbook.

A far different Bernie as he poses emotionless for his U.S. Justice Department mug shot after he admitted in December 2008 that he was running history's most massive fraud, bilking thousands out of billions of dollars.

Source: U.S. Dept. of Justice.

COURTESY: U.S. DEPT. OF JUSTICE

Bernie's Ponzi scheme was named after Charles Ponzi, an arrogant, dapper con artist for whom the fraud—using later investors to pay early investors—was named.

Source: Bettmann/Corbis.

Bernie and the former Ruth Alpern became an item in high school, married young, and were considered a team for half a century. But after Bernie was sentenced to spend the rest of his life in prison, she distanced herself from him, and reportedly reverted to her maiden name.

Source: Rex USA, May 2008.

Bernie and Ruth socialized in chic places from Palm Beach to the French Riviera where investors—wealthy and middle class alike, thousands of them—invested in Bernard L. Madoff Investment Securities and were taken to the cleaners by the con man.

The couple is shown here at the September 2007 wedding of niece Shana Madoff to Eric Swanson at the Bowery Hotel in New York.

Source: Rex USA.

Peter Madoff, Bernie's younger brother, was his second in command, and was considered brighter than his sibling but was dominated by him because it was Bernie's name on the door of the firm. As former Chief Compliance Officer of Bernard Madoff Investment Securities LCC, he is shown here arriving at Mineola State Supreme Court, April 3, 2009, in New York.

Source: AP Photo/Louis Lanzano.

Peter's daughter, Shana, in charge of compliance at Madoff, with her second husband, Eric Swanson, a former SEC official. Their nuptials sparked federal prosecutors' interest. Bernie once said his niece had married "the enemy."

Source: JP Pullos/PatrickMcMullan.com.

Ponzi central—the high-tech Lipstick Building in Manhattan where Bernie had his firm's offices on the 17th, 18th and 19th floors. On 17 was where he ran his secret investment advisory business, and from where bogus statements were sent to bilked clients.

Source: AP Photo/Diane Bondareff.

The posh Upper East Side Manhattan co-op building where Bernie and Ruth lived in royal splendor in their $7.5 million duplex penthouse. For a time Bernie was under house-arrest there, infuriating investors who had lost everything. The Madoff apartment was later ordered sold along with other assets.

Source: AP Photo/Brian McDermott. Photo taken in December 2008.

Among the luxuries owned by the one-time poor boy from Queens were several boats and yachts, all with the name 'Bull.' While many thought the name had to do with bull markets, insiders believed it had to do with "the bull" Bernie was feeding investors. Like the Madoff penthouse, the boats also were seized and ordered sold.

Source: AP Photo/Lionel Cironneau.

Madoff was a great place to work until the roof caved in. Every summer the firm's employees were invited to the firm's summer bash at Montauk, in the chic Hamptons, where Bernie and Ruth's fabulous ocean-front house was located. Like their other treasures, it also was seized to help pay back swindled investors.

Source: AP Photo/John Dunn.

After his arrest, but before he was ordered confined to his penthouse and later sent to jail, the most reviled crook in America had the freedom to walk the streets, with an enigmatic trademark smirk on his face. He is seen here walking down Lexington Avenue to return to his Manhattan apartment.

Source: AP Photo/Jason DeCrow.

Bernard Madoff leaves U.S. District Court in Manhattan escorted by U.S. Marshals after a bail hearing in New York, January 5, 2009. Under that black raincoat and suit jacket is a bulletproof vest because prosecutors and his lawyers feared Bernie might be the target of a furious, deranged investor as he leaves court after pleading guilty to eleven criminal counts, and claiming he pulled off his mind-boggling fraud alone, which no one believed was possible.

Source: AP Photo/Kathy Willens.

The dapper tight-lipped swindler lost in thought before he went to jail to spend the rest of his natural born days. The 150 years to which he was sentenced was symbolic, since at 71 he was believed to have about a dozen years left to live.

Source: Justin Lane/epa/Corbis.

Chapter 9

"Whatever You Do, Kid, Never Invest a Penny in the Stock Market, Because It's Run by Crooks and Sons of Bitches"

B y the mid-to-late 1960s, Bernard L. Madoff Investment Securities was making good money—from Bernie's take of the business being fed to him by his friends at Lieberbaum & Company, from positions he was personally holding and selling in over-the-counter and penny stocks that were possibly if not probably manipulated, and from fees and commissions related to the business he got from his growing private investment group that would eventually turn into his massive Ponzi operation.

Life was good at 39 Broadway, although Bernie was starting to act weird—and Bernie's world would become even more bizarre as time went on. His obsessive-compulsive tendency was beginning to manifest itself so that others who worked with him saw his odd behavior for the first time, such as when he personally began vacuuming the office floors on a daily basis, even though the building had a cleaning crew to do that every night.

Ruth, a mother of two, would stop in every so often from the Long Island suburbs to see how things were going, and she'd be there especially around the holidays to help Bernie dispense gifts. In exchange for probably getting stock tips and business from other brokerage houses, he was giving away bottles of expensive Chivas Regal scotch whiskey.

"At Christmastime the office was awash with cases of Chivas," says Bill Nasi, Bernie's longtime trusted messenger, who spent some 20 years at Madoff during two separate stints, and was there when the Ponzi scheme came crashing down, ruining his life and the lives of so many others.

He continues:

> I was running the bottles with little cards that said "Thank You!" to stock traders at other companies within the financial district. They were guys feeding him business. He sure wasn't sending bottles of Chivas to people who had no connection with him. I'd get there and they'd stand up and say, "Hey, look what's here from Madoff!" I usually got a five-dollar tip from each. I was making more on tip money delivering whiskey from Bernie than on my regular salary.

It was during one such frenetic holiday time in the late 1960s that Nasi witnessed a most curious tableau in the office involving Ruth, then in her late 20s, ministering to Bernie, who was nearing 30, one that in a strange, indecipherable way seemed to underscore their close bond.

Recalls Nasi:

> Bernie's holding a glass in one hand and Ruth's pouring Chivas into it on the rocks, and Bernie takes a sip and puts it down as Ruth pours another shot into it.

In his other hand Bernie has another glass without ice, and Ruth's pouring Milk of Magnesia [an antacid and laxative] into it and Bernie's drinking that as a chaser.

I said to Bernie, "What's going on? What are you getting ready for?" because he's drinking this weird mix—whiskey, and taking this other stuff to calm his stomach—and all he says is, "I'm getting ready to do battle. I'm getting ready to make a decision." That's all he said. It sounds nuts, but it's more like the bizarre world of Madoff.

■ ■ ■

It was at 39 Broadway that Bernie began hiring devoted employees like Nasi who would work for him their entire lives. Unlike Nasi, who went on to college later in life, the others for the most part were barely educated 'dem' and 'dose' bridge and tunnel people— from Queens, Staten Island, and Brooklyn—who spoke Bernie's Noo Yawk-ese.

"They had minimum training and learned on the job," says Nasi. Through the years entire families—brothers, sisters, cousins—worked at Madoff, and a number were there until the very end when the FBI and SEC took over, some losing their life savings in the boss's scheme. Those employees ranged from Charlie Wiener, Bernie's sister Sondra's son, who was given the post of office administrator—both of whom lost their savings—to Frank DiPascali Jr., his reputed right-hand man, who Nasi believes may have started as a driver for Bernie at 39 Broadway.

"There was a lot of nepotism. It was almost like tribes working there," says Nasi, who between stints at Madoff worked for several years at a Times Square porn emporium called Peepland, where he collected the quarters and mopped the floors. After having toiled in the sleazy 42nd Street hellhole and at Bernard L. Madoff Investment Securities, Nasi saw a metaphysical connection between the two. "They were basically the same type of cultural atmosphere," he observes. "If you had money in your pocket you'd go in one and get a sexual thrill, or you'd go up to Bernie and make money and get a thrill."

One of those who fit Bernie's hiring profile in those early days was Annette Bongiorno, who worked in his 17th-floor office and whose role in his investment advisory business was being scrutinized by prosecutors, as were a number of others.

Bongiorno, the wife of a retired New York City Department of Transportation electrician, was reportedly Frank DiPascali's neighbor growing up. She liked to tell the story around the Madoff office of how she was a poor Italian-American girl who grew up in a "lower-middle-class neighborhood in Howard Beach, in Queens" and ended up "getting this great job of just answering the phone in an office, not working in a factory." She'd boast about how she was "making $95 a week at the start, and how Bernie treated me nice," and how she kept getting promotions and making more and more money, and how her "parents were proud of me, and that a Jewish guy pulled me up and out."

Next to DiPascali, among non-Madoff family members, Bongiorno became one of Bernie's closest in-house associates, earning as much as seven figures a year. The Bongiornos, at the time of Bernie's arrest, had come far courtesy of Bernie—with homes valued at as much as $2.6 million in the exclusive towns of Manhasset, on Long Island, and Boca Raton, Florida, and with three Mercedes-Benzes to choose from.

Another Madoff recruit showed up with long, unkempt hair, unshaven and smoking marijuana. Bernie hired him. He cleaned himself up and rose to second in command of one of the Madoff departments.

According to a veteran Madoff worker:

In the early days when those employees were hired they were literally sleeping in the office because Bernie was trying to get his business off the ground, and everyone liked him, and he told them, "I promise if you take care of me now, I'll take care of you later." People worked all night, slept in the office, and went home to shower and get clothes, and came back. For a while that's how he treated them.

No one intimately familiar with the way Bernie operated believes for a second, however, that he was the patron saint of hiring the underprivileged.

As one veteran Madoff insider asserts, "Bernie made it a point to hire people who weren't that smart so they wouldn't trip over anything incriminating. You could have a great job at Madoff even if you were a semimoron, because you were well-trained on the job and paid far better than anyone on Wall Street, and didn't ask too many questions."

■ ■ ■

Bernie's father, Ralph, was in the 39 Broadway office on a day-to-day basis, says Nasi, who had bonded with him.

"Ralph would just show up, come in, and talk and listen. He was a real outgoing guy. He was a blustery, tough Brooklyn type who sounded like he grew up next to the Brooklyn Navy Yard. He was street-smart, the type of guy who feels Brooklyn's the center of the universe—'I can get anything accomplished even if I have to fix broken toilets for 30 years.'"

Ralph Madoff took a liking to Nasi, and the two together would ride the R train, the subway that rumbled between Brooklyn and Queens. On one of those jaunts, the Madoff patriarch turned to Nasi with a bit of startling advice.

He told him: "Whatever you do, kid, never invest a penny in the stock market, because it's run by crooks and sons of bitches."

Nasi was dumbfounded. Here was the father of a young man whose entire life revolved around Wall Street every waking hour warning him to stay away from his son's world, one that the patriarch himself had had a questionable role in.

Years later, not long before Bernie's crooked world came apart, Nasi mentioned the conversation to his boss, who, at the time, was "up to his neck in this goddamn fucking Ponzi scheme," unbeknownst to Nasi.

"Bernie starts laughing and says, 'My, God, if everyone thought like my father, where would I be today?'"

■ ■ ■

One of Bernie's young colleagues on Wall Street back then was a fellow by the name of Andy Monness, who had a small boutique firm at 120 Broadway called Monness, Williams & Sidel. Monness lived out on Long Island, too, near Bernie's home in Roslyn Estates, and he often picked him up at the house and the two drove into the city together.

On one sunny spring morning as Monness was thinking how great it was to be young and that both of them had money-making businesses, Bernie got in the car and the first thing he said was, "The best fucking thing about today is that I have one less day to live."

Many years later, after Bernie's arrest, Monness clearly remembers the moment as if it had just happened.

"Bernie was sort of joking," Monness believes, looking back, "but I think there was a note of something in what he said. I think it was more insightful than what I thought it was at the time."

Through the years Monness would run into Bernie at United Jewish Appeal dinners and later at the Palm Beach Country Club. While Monness watched him become "almost a living legend" on Wall Street, "we [the Monness firm] were in the camp that were really suspicious about Bernie's record. No one's performance was ever like that. I never saw anyone remove the unpredictability of the market. I've seen guys not have good months, and I've seen guys have very few bad months, but never like Bernie. It's almost comical. I thought, 'How could this be that no one's skeptical?' That's a little beyond my beliefs."

But, the question remains: How did Bernie garner all of the business of all these wealthy investors? As his victims have said, they trusted him. They trusted him because they had no reason to distrust him. He was making money for them. His returns were extraordinary. His credentials got better and better, such as becoming chairman of Nasdaq. If there were red flags, few knew about them. As Carol Ann Lieberbaum observed, why question a good thing? Even investors in

Madoff with real financial acumen kept putting money in without doing any real due diligence. The promise of good returns (or greed, it appears) took many forms when it came to investing with Bernie Madoff.

Yet, Monness suggests otherwise. He believes that a good part of Bernie's success in pulling off the biggest Ponzi scam in history was the fact that "he was not *so* conspicuous. He was not *so* flamboyant. He didn't have the nicest house. He didn't have the nicest car. He didn't have the biggest plane. He had *all* the trappings, but none of them crossed the line. I think that was his skill."

Still, he was shocked like everyone else when the news broke and the details of the fraud emerged. Months after Bernie's arrest, Monness wonders what the thief's "end game" was. The problem, he fears, is that it will never be discovered because "I don't think anyone can possibly get into his mind. I think it's so distorted. I'm not a religious man. I don't believe in an afterlife. But I wouldn't want to die and leave my family or my reputation in such shambles."

While he feels sorry for the little old ladies who lost their money in the feeder funds, people who had never heard of Bernard Madoff, he questions the big institutions and especially charities that got taken for hundreds of millions, if not billions.

"They were investing *so* aggressively. I didn't realize they were in the business of *making* money," he observes wryly. "I thought they were in the business of *giving out* money."

Nonprofits, however, needed to raise money, too. Most if not all of those that got taken in the Madoff mess had invested in feeder funds, so they were completely unaware of Bernie's name until it was too late. At the same time, Bernie connected socially with people. As documented, he was even named to the board of Yeshiva University, and was prominent in other organizations. Again, he was a trusted friend, and a philanthropist (with other people's money, as it later turned out). "The nonprofits weren't going out and buying houses in Palm Beach, but using the money made in Madoff for good causes," says a developmental executive with one such organization. "Through [these investments] all the nonprofits probably did more good for their causes than through routine fund-raising. That is, until the roof caved in. Now many charities don't have a dime to spare."

Back when Monness's firm and Bernie's firm were young upstarts, Monness was a bit of a wild man himself. His partner, Kenny Sidel, once boasted to the author, "We were kicking the shit out of the staid, white-shoe, alcohol-drinking jackasses on Wall Street. The competition had become fat and stupid, and we went in and took the business away from them."

Monness liked to hire brokers who were a bit offbeat. As detailed in the author's biography of Martha Stewart, *Just Desserts*, one of his firm's crackerjack salesmen back then was a big, good-looking Irishman from Brooklyn who had been driving a meat truck by day and acting in amateur theatrical productions on Long Island by night. His name was Brian Dennehy.

Monness started bright, aggressive, and leggy former model Martha Kostyra Stewart, a Jersey girl, at a salary of $100 a week, plus her share of a commission pool. Before long she was making as much as $250,000 a year, according to Monness, and was running in a circle that included the likes of Ross Perot and financier Saul Steinberg.

Years later, as the world knows, the domestic diva, like Bernie Madoff, wound up behind bars, in her case for conspiring to cover up a government insider-trading investigation of a personal stock sale. Unlike Bernie, who presumably will die in prison, Stewart spent five months in the slammer, served five months of home detention in her mansion, and paid a fine—the lightest possible sentence under federal guidelines.

"If Martha did five months," says her onetime boss, Monness, "then Bernie should get 140 years. There's no similarity. I felt what they got Martha on was so silly when you think of things done not only by Bernie, but by others in Wall Street in the last decade."

■ ■ ■

In the mid-1960s, Bernie began sharing office space at 39 Broadway with another broker also relatively new to the business—Marty

Joel Jr. A dozen years Bernie's senior, Marty was the founder of Martin J. Joel & Company and was determined to make a bundle selling stocks rather than working a slide rule as an engineer. Like Bernie, Joel started with over-the-counter and penny stocks, and the two did business together and apart, but were never formal partners back then.

Socially, the Madoffs and the Joels became close friends. One of Joel's daughters, Patty, babysat for Mark and Andy Madoff; and her sister, Amy, would spend some 20 years in management at Madoff. After the death of his first wife, Marty Joel went to work for Bernie as what his daughter, Amy, calls a "star broker." He put all of his trust and faith in Bernie, and millions in Madoff.

Looking back now, that was a big—and costly—mistake.

Like so many other cases where Bernie had close family ties, virtually every member of the late Marty Joel's family would be financially ruined in the Ponzi operation.

In total, they lost a whopping $23 million, according to Amy Joel.

Among the family victims was Patty and Amy's 82-year-old stepmother "who's left with nothing," says Patty Joel Samuels.

> As recently as a few days before Bernie was arrested my stepmother was with Bernie and Ruth. When she heard about the Ponzi scheme she didn't believe it. She said, "He would never do that to us. We're not affected." And I had to convince her that we were. My father left all her money in Madoff [for Bernie] to take care of. Every cent he ever earned was put in Bernie. There was never a reason to even worry about all of our money. It's just really a case of misplaced trust. I'm glad my father wasn't around to see what happened. He wouldn't believe it.

Her husband's elderly mother also was wiped out, and had to revert to driving other old folks around in Florida to supplement her Social Security.

But all of that was far down the road, long after Marty Joel himself had big-time legal problems when he was sharing office space with Bernie at 39 Broadway.

In October 1967, Martin J. Joel & Company was sued in federal court in New York City along with two other brokerages, two officers of one of the firms, and the president of Liquidonix Industries, Inc., for allegedly manipulating the price of Liquidonix stock, an over-the-counter offering, which rose from $34 a share in January 1967 to a high of $157 in September 1967. The suit, which charged that Joel and the others had pumped up the stock by "manipulative and deceptive schemes," was dropped a month later when the plaintiff suspiciously failed to appear for pretrial questioning, claiming he had a cold and had to stay in bed.

Then, in August 1970, the SEC temporarily suspended Marty Joel from doing business after an investigation found that between January 1966 and January 1968—when he was sharing office space with Bernie—Joel had at various times violated the antifraud record-keeping and credit provisions of securities law.

He was banned from associating with any broker-dealer for 75 days, and his firm was suspended from doing business from mid-August 1970 to just after Labor Day. At the time, Joel claimed that the agency's proceedings did not involve his market-making or over-the-counter business, and that his retail business was being phased out. In November 1971, another securities company acquired Martin J. Joel & Company for undisclosed terms and Marty Joel reportedly became a general partner.

After Joel came to work for Bernie as a trader and market maker years later, Bernie lauded him publicly but told nasty stories about him behind his back.

Bernie claimed that the reason he brought Joel on board at Madoff was because he "felt sorry for him, and no one on Wall Street would give him a job." According to a Madoff insider, Bernie claimed he told his longtime friend and colleague, whose family was invested to the hilt in Madoff, "Here's a desk; here's a phone. Do your thing. Don't talk to anyone in the office or in the trading area. You're on your own. If you do anything crooked, I don't want to know about it. You're a separate entity."

Bernie claimed that the reason Joel "was blacklisted" and had problems getting work on Wall Street was because "he taught Ivan Boesky everything he knew—how to work the system legally, and how to manipulate it."

Bernie was the epitome of the pot calling the kettle black.

Some two decades before Bernie Madoff became known as the evil mastermind of the biggest and worst of all financial crimes, Ivan Boesky had held that title. The son of a Jewish immigrant, Boesky had made hundreds of millions of dollars using insider information to take big positions in companies that were about to be taken over. Mergers and acquisitions were then the rage in the early to mid-1980s, and Boesky became the expert in how to cash in—illegally.

It took a long time for the SEC to catch on, just like the agency missed the boat with Bernie. In 1986, however, Boesky was charged with stock manipulation and insider trading, was fined $100 million (half of which he later deducted as a business expense from his income tax), and spent two years in a minimum-security, country club prison in California. This was around the same time Bernie was activating his Ponzi scheme. The *Time* magazine cover of December 1, 1986, had a photo of a tanned and smiling Boesky with the headline: "Wall St. Scam—Making Millions with Your Money." Like Bernie, Boesky became an overnight popular culture figure. The character Gordon Gekko in the film *Wall Street* is said to be based loosely on Boesky.

As time would tell, Bernie shared Boesky's philosophy, which the king of the insider trade had espoused:

"I think greed is healthy," Boesky once declared. "You can be greedy and still feel good about yourself." Family members of Marty Joel—his daughter Patty and her Long Island criminal attorney husband, Howard Samuels—call Bernie's character assassination of him "completely untrue." At the same time, neither had heard about or had knowledge of any association between Joel and Boesky. "Martin Joel was recognized on Wall Street," says Samuels. "He brought companies public. He did underwriting. He was brilliant with the money he made, investing in homes, jewelry, even Wedgwood china."

(In late May 2009, as Bernie was awaiting formal sentencing, he met with Herbert J. Hoelter, considered the crème de la crème of prison consultants, in hopes of lessening his time in the Big House or getting placed in a better Big House. Bernie was in good company. Among Hoelter's past headline-making clients who were sent up the river were Boesky, Martha Stewart, Michael Milken, and Alfred Taubman. Hoelter's Baltimore firm, the National Center on Institutions and Alternatives, had a reputation for so-called sentencing advocacy and arguing for pro-felon use of federal sentencing guidelines by judges.)

While Bernie made it seem as if Joel was a tragic figure for whom he showed his sympathy by allowing him to work at Madoff, there are those who contend otherwise.

"He was on Bernie's trading desk. He was a market maker," says Samuels.

Others say Joel was a force at Madoff because of his many years in the business, and Bernie depended on him to keep things running smoothly, especially to help younger traders when problems arose.

"My father was *instrumental* in the trading room," declares Amy Joel. "He wouldn't be working in any scammo situation. He lived a great life because he made tons of money for himself and Bernie. He traded the most elite stocks. The last time he traded for Madoff was around 2001 when he became ill. He had 24-hour care, but he elected to come into the office some days just to be in an office environment. He would hire a car and with his aide he came to Madoff and walked around and talked to everyone."

The two men—along with another multimillionaire crony, Stanley Shapiro, who made his fortune in the garment business, later had a desk at Madoff, and lost "substantial" millions in Bernie's Ponzi scheme—often spent vacation time together, sharing cabanas at the fancy Breakers Hotel in Palm Beach, schmoozing and smoking cigars, expensive Davidoff stogies that were Bernie's favorite.

Bernie was also with Joel in times of need. For instance, when Joel's first wife died in 1973, Bernie and Ruth were the first ones at the house to help him grieve, and it was Ruth who compassionately told his daughter, Amy, then a college junior, that her mother had passed away.

Joel was so trusted by Bernie and such a part of his inner circle that when Bernie's mother, Sylvia, died sometime in the late 1970s he declined to claim her body and had Joel and Bernie's brother, Peter, handle the matter. "Bernie tracked down my father to go with Peter to claim the body," says Amy Joel. "She died on a cruise in Jamaica, and Bernie was such a wimp he couldn't handle it himself. My father and Peter had to make the arrangements to fly the body home."

Later, after both of the Madoffs had passed away, Bernie confided to Amy Joel that he was saddened because "My parents didn't live long enough to see how successful I became."

■ ■ ■

Marty Joel savored jokingly goading Bernie, because he was aware of his obsessive-compulsive disorder (OCD) issues.

"Bernie had OCD to the umpth degree," observes Amy Joel, who began working at Madoff in 1989, initially for two years in the money-management area—later Ponzi Central—after a long stint at Bear Stearns.

> My dad used to goof with Bernie. It was like a running joke with him. He'd take a piece of thread and throw it on the floor, and Bernie would freak when he spotted it. My father would leave a door a little ajar and Bernie would run out and close it. He'd go, "What's with this?! If you open a door, ya gotta close it," and he'd be screaming. If a window blind was not at a 90-degree angle, the man would go off the wall. He hired three people to clean the office during the day even though the building had a cleaning service at night. That was not good enough for him.

Amy also liked to tease Bernie if she had the opportunity.

> He constantly needed to have a suntan, and if he ever pissed me off I would say, "Hey, Bernie, there's a white spot on your left cheek." And he'd go, "Where? Where?" And he'd ask for my

compact and run into the men's room to look. When he came out I'd say, "*Gotcha!*"

Bernie once seriously lectured Amy Joel about the dangers of entering her apartment wearing the shoes she wore on the streets of New York City, because of the dog and human urine and defecation she might have trod on. He figured she then probably took off her shoes and walked around barefoot in her apartment where she had just walked in her unsanitary shoes. Even worse, he guessed, she probably got into bed with bare feet that were sullied from what she had tracked in. The concept sickened him. "He was like over the top," she recalls. "To stop him I said, 'All right, *all right*, I'll never do it again!' "

At one point during her two decades at Madoff she had worked in accounts payable. "Within three days of a bill coming in," she says, "he made you pay it. If it had 30 days net or 60 days net, he'd say to pay it right away—whether it was a $42 Xerox bill, or a cell phone bill for ten grand, or a bill for rental of line feeds that was $500,000 a month."

The reason? "He didn't want any trouble with creditors."

Every morning, the first thing he obsessively did was check his Dun & Bradstreet rating. Then he'd make his inspection rounds of the office to make certain everything was neat and orderly, that all desk items were in either black or gray, and if by chance he found someone using a desk calculator in another shade, even white, he'd toss it in the trash. He'd be spotted polishing the glass doors to the office, or on his hands and knees on the carpet in front of the elevator bank picking up litter, and making sure the carpet was perfectly straight.

Despite his OCD issues, Amy Joel thought of him as a "stand-up guy," a "very generous" boss who helped his employees when they needed money or time off. "He was so honorable," she believed for years before his thievery came to light and she and her family and her co-workers who had invested in Madoff were left with nothing.

In his early 70s Marty Joel died on May 6, 2003, of lung cancer, at his home in Palm Beach. The services were held at a funeral home in White Plains, New York, and Bernie was there with Ruth to eulogize his close friend and longtime associate. "He had the highest words of praise for him," recalls Joel's son-in-law, Howard Samuels, who was present.

Bernie gave the family the use of his private plane during that difficult time and helped make the funeral arrangements. "He couldn't have been nicer," says daughter Patty Samuels. "Little did I know it was probably our money that he was using, so he could afford to be generous. Right before he died, my father said to me, 'I gave all the money to Bernie, and he's going to take good care of you.' I paid a fortune in taxes—a *fortune*—on the profits, which weren't real."

Adds her husband, Howard:

Marty Joel would come out of his grave and choke the life out of Bernie if he could.

At their father's funeral, Bernie took my wife and Amy aside and said how sorry he was, how close he was to their father, how he was the greatest guy in the whole world. He told them, "Look, the only good thing is you're never going to have to worry about anything financially ever again in your whole lives. Your accounts are with me."

Worry, indeed. After all, Bernie was the trustee of Joel's multimillion-dollar account at Madoff.

By the winter of 2007, Amy Joel saw that Bernie was distracted, that he was often gone from the office for long stretches of time. She believed he was enjoying himself but later came to the conclusion that "he was sucking in the very wealthy, going to where the elite went, where he attracted investors" for his Ponzi operation. Mostly, though, she was increasingly concerned that he wasn't giving careful and proper attention to her late father's sizable investment.

Says Joel:

I had an employer-employee relationship with Bernie. I had an investor relationship with Bernie. We were friends, and he was the trustee of my dad's account, so I confronted him. I said, "Bernie, you're the trustee and certain things are not adding up.

I need you to get more involved." He put his index finger so close to my nose that I had to smack it away, and he said, "I don't really have the fucking head to handle your dad's estate." And I said, "Well, you better get the fucking head, because you agreed to this 15 years ago when he was making multimillions of dollars on your trading desk in the years before he became ill."

Bernie nervously blinked, twitched, turned around, and walked away.

Sometime later I had another discussion with him because I realized things were not going well, and he used the same language with me—"I don't have the fucking head . . ."—and I said, "But now I know that you and only you can change who the trustee is, so please step down and change the trustee."

He never did.

Bernie could not look me in the eye after my father died. People were making excuses for him. His secretary, Eleanor, used to say, "Oh, you remind him so much of your father," all sorts of bullshit like that. My father always had a good impression of Bernie. He made a lot of money for Bernie. He wouldn't deal with snakes. He had severed two or three friend-ships because he knew that the people were underhanded. Maybe my father was blindsided because he and Bernie were such good friends.

The Madoffs were a family I thought I could trust.

Now I want the man hung. I want the wife hung. I want the kids hung.

■ ■ ■

The financial ties between Madoff and the Joel-Samuels family became public in March 2009 when Howard and Patty Samuels' son—22-year-old Andrew Ross Samuels, a student at Brooklyn Law, where Bernie had gone for a year to escape the military—alleged in court papers that a college trust fund established in 1997 for him by his grandfather, Marty, had been obliterated in Bernie's Ponzi scheme.

Ironically, the trust was in part funded by Marty Joel's and the Samuelses' close friends at the time, Bernie and Ruth, who each gave a gift of $10,000.

As the *New York Post* observed, "Bernie Madoff Giveth—and Bernie Madoff Taketh Away."

Bernie's brother, Peter Madoff—the senior managing director of Madoff, director of trading, chief compliance officer, and general counsel with a law degree from Fordham University—was the trustee. For 40 years he had been Bernie's number two honcho. He played a key role in the firm. It was even said that the two brothers flew in separate planes because if there was a crash and Bernie was killed, Peter would be the one to take over.

(It was the second lawsuit filed against Peter Madoff since his brother took the entire rap for the whole Ponzi scheme.)

After Marty Joel died, Peter Madoff invested the $478,000 trust in the Madoff money management operation—the heart and soul of the Ponzi scheme.

Based on the allegations, a justice of the Nassau County, New York, Supreme Court issued an order temporarily freezing 63-year-old Peter Madoff's assets. At the time, an attorney for Peter Madoff; his wife (the former Marion Sue Schwartzberg, also a Laurelton native); and their daughter, Shana, the trading room compliance officer at Madoff, declared it was "absurd" that Peter Madoff had anything to do with his brother's crimes, and further stated that his client had lost millions of dollars in Bernie's scheme.

The asset freeze on the younger Madoff prohibited him from moving money around, or from selling or borrowing against his assets, such as the family mansion in Old Westbury, New York, or the house in Palm Beach near Bernie's place. Some years earlier, the brothers had transferred ownership of many of their properties to their wives. On the Palm Beach property, Marion Madoff got a $25,000 homestead exemption in 2007. Ruth got a similar exemption on the $9.3 million home she and Bernie had in Palm Beach. Florida law protects homes from seizure.

Earlier, shortly after Bernie was arrested, Peter reportedly had agreed with federal prosecutors to a voluntary freeze on his assets.

Howard Samuels called the court freeze "completely justified" and declared, "Peter never acted in the capacity he was supposed to perform, protection of my father-in-law's grandson. He absolutely dropped the ball." For instance, one of the things that Peter Madoff was supposed to do, which he didn't, was notify the young Samuels that he could have terminated the trust when he turned 21 in 2007. Peter Madoff resigned as trustee in May 2008, leaving the young man's money in the Ponzi fund.

In April 2009, the judge in the case allowed a change in the freeze—basically modifying it so as not to interfere with federal prosecutors probing the broader Madoff case, and permitting Peter Madoff to use $10,000 a month of his assets as living expenses. But he was still restricted by the court from transferring his property or assets.

Peter Madoff had complained that the asset freeze kept him from buying "even a cup of coffee."

One Madoff investor who lost the farm says he was dumbstruck when he read about Peter's complaint about not having enough money to live on. "He lives like royalty, with fancy cars and a big house, and he's whining about not having enough pocket money. So many of us don't have a pot to piss in now because of what his brother did to us."

■ ■ ■

Andrew Samuels was not the first to publicly connect Peter Madoff to Bernie's fraudulent activities. Rather, the first lawsuit against Peter Madoff involved a prominent politician.

Two months after Bernie was arrested, attorneys for the family foundation of New Jersey Senator Frank R. Lautenberg and his two adult children, Joshua and Ellen—who were taken for more than $7.3 million in the Ponzi scheme—sued Peter. The suit, filed in federal court in New Jersey, accused Peter, as chief compliance officer of the firm, of either failing to find evidence of the scam or actually concealing it.

"There were many obvious material red flags evidencing the giant Ponzi scheme that were recklessly ignored," according to the complaint. The lawyer for the Lautenbergs, Ronald Riccio, said that Peter Madoff "had a duty to protect the individuals and entities that invested in the firm from fraud and misconduct."

The Lautenbergs' private foundation, which had made investments in 2001 and 2002, saw its money more than double to $15.4 million in the month before Bernie was arrested. But that spectacular growth was just on paper based on the fraudster's bogus investments. It was pure hot air. The recipients of the foundation's money included a New Jersey hospital and a Jewish organization.

Lautenberg, the senior senator from the Garden State and a liberal Democrat, was among a number of politicians to whom Bernie had made campaign contributions—no surprise in Lautenberg's case since he was one of the richest in the U.S. Senate, and one whose foundation saw Madoff as a good place to invest.

The *Record* newspaper of Bergen County, New Jersey, analyzed election filings and found that more than $400,000 in campaign contributions had been given to federal candidates in New Jersey since 2006 by Madoff and family members tied to the firm. Lautenberg received $13,600 for his 2008 reelection campaign.

The senator's spokesman said after the suit was filed, "We will be ridding ourselves of the contribution."

Lautenberg's son, Joshua, had invested $1 million with Madoff in 2003, and by the month before Bernie was arrested, his principal had also grown on paper—to $1.78 million—and daughter Ellen Lautenberg's $600,000 investment in the same year had grown to $1 million, the lawsuit claimed.

But, now, all of it was lost.

Chapter 10

A Madoff Speaks Out and an Empty Promise

In the months leading up to the formal sentencing of Bernie in late June 2009, the close-knit Madoff family remained tight-lipped, refusing to make any public statements, except through attorneys as many of them came under scrutiny for their intimate business connections to the patriarch-felon.

On her visits to see her jailbird hubby at the Metropolitan Correctional Center in lower Manhattan, Ruth Madoff, the once coiffed and beautified matriarch of the now embattled and infamous dynasty, looked drawn and pale and thinner than her usual sprightly 100-pound self, and was mum whenever journalists approached.

On one such visit, however, an aggressive ABC News field producer pursued Ruth on camera and asked whether she had anything to say to her husband's many victims. "I have no response to you," she said, and then it was reported that she had added, "Fuck you" under her breath as she got into a taxi. Her purple language was not out of character. Bernie's longtime secretary, Eleanor Squillari, asserted that Ruth could speak "very harshly to people. If Bernie said something to Ruth that annoyed her, she'd say, 'Go fuck yourself,' or 'I don't give a shit.' That's the way they talked to each other."

To make matters even worse than having been branded Bernie's trash-talking moll, Ruth had been banned from her chic Upper East Side Manhattan hair salon, Pierre Michel, where she'd been a VIP client for a decade, getting her conservative and preppy bob cut and colored—at 69, the gray naturally was starting to show. After the *New York Post* ran a "Page Six" gossip item declaring that "Bernie Madoff is costing his wife her looks," a representative for the salon, which billed itself as a "magnet for celebrities, socialites, fashionistas, and trend-setters" said in a statement: "The Pierre Michel salon's clients are among some of Manhattan's most elite. Unfortunately some of those clients were victims of the Madoffs and therefore Pierre Michel didn't feel comfortable having her in the salon."

While Ruth had not been charged with any crimes, she had now been sentenced to the hardship of finding an upscale Manhattan salon that didn't have Madoff victims as clients—a difficult task indeed—and one that would treat her in the manner to which she was accustomed.

She wasn't the only Madoff woman who was so snubbed. Not long after Bernie was arrested, Peter Madoff's wife, Marion, was said to have been in a tony salon in Manhasset, on Long Island, and was overheard "talking about going on a vacation," according to Madoff victim Sherry Fabrikant. "Two of my friends were there and were disgusted, and they told me, 'We left.'" The salon in question declined to confirm or deny that Marion Madoff was a client.

■ ■ ■

The only Madoff family member who granted the author an interview (in response to a message from the author) was Jennifer Madoff. Not only was Jennifer a victim of Bernie's fraud, but she was also a widow whose young husband, Roger Madoff, Peter and Marion's son, had died on April 16, 2006, from leukemia at the age of 32.

The lengthy death notice that appeared in the *New York Times* the next day had loving eulogies from Madoff family members and friends. There were even some kind remarks from those who would be Bernie's victims, among them his close friend, the Boston philanthropist Carl Shapiro, who later came under investigation, and Susan Blumenfeld, Bernie's interior designer who also had the task of helping Ruth choose her wardrobe, and who along with her developer husband, Edward, lost millions. Roger's cousins, Mark and Andy Madoff, wrote, "Our dear Roger, you fought bravely to the end, never losing any of the wonderful spirit of you. . . . You will be in our hearts forever." His parents called him their "most special, courageous son. . . . May you rest in peace. We love you. XOXO, Mom and Dad."

After Roger died, Jennifer Madoff had self-published a touching, inspirational, and often humorous memoir he had written while he was dying entitled *Leukemia for Chickens: One Wimp's Tale about Living through Cancer.*

Thinking of himself as "the black sheep of the family," young Madoff had reluctantly left a career he loved—writing about and covering business news for Bloomberg News—to work in a new Madoff family venture called Primex Trading at the behest of his father. He described himself as "becoming the last of my generation of Madoffs to succumb to joining the family firm." Peter Madoff envisioned Primex to be a virtual reality type of Big Board. "My father is an entrepreneur and always looking for new ideas," Roger said in his book. "My father had become enamored with this concept and had laid the groundwork for the project."

Because of the Madoff firm's sterling reputation back in 1999 when Primex was born, two giants of Wall Street—Merrill Lynch and Goldman Sachs—had joined in the venture. But Roger had once told a friend in an e-mail, "This job is killing me."

Primex never succeeded.

Jennifer and Roger had married on August 30, 2001, in a big and flashy affair in the atrium of the old Bowery Savings Bank on 42nd Street. They were on their honeymoon in South Africa when 9/11 happened, and their apartment was just a mile north of Ground Zero where the World Trade Center towers had once stood. The two had been introduced some years earlier by her roommates at Cornell University, who had been his friends growing up, and at the time they met he was a student at Duke University.

Roger got leukemia when he was 29, when they had been married only three years.

Still heartbroken by her husband's death, and furious about the ramifications of Bernie's crimes—a promised grant from the Madoff family in her late husband's name to help emerging writers in Queens was never given—Jennifer Madoff was devastated, but defensive of everyone in the Madoff family except, of course, Bernie.

In an interview lasting more than 20 minutes, she never once uttered Bernie's name, clearly viewing her late husband's uncle as a pariah.

Late in February 2008, after Bernie's arrest but before his shocking guilty plea and other revelations about the scheme and the Madoff family, she said to the author:

> Members of my family have, unfortunately, had their lives destroyed, and the family is being torn apart [by the crimes committed by Bernie]. No one can grasp what's going on, and how huge and deep this runs. It's unimaginable to all of us.
>
> Everybody's in shock and feeling completely devastated.
>
> My heart is breaking for my in-laws, Peter and Marion, as I think they've suffered enough in this. I'm so heartbroken for my father-in-law. What it comes down to is he's losing another member of his family—I mean losing a brother [Bernie] after his son is gone. It's devastating.

Jennifer says "it goes without question" that Bernie's crimes had caused a major breach with his brother, Peter. "He's just shocked and devastated by all of it."

Her honesty and concern for both the legacy of her husband and her family were sincere, and the hurt could be heard in her voice. Had at that point the public heard something similar from Ruth, Peter Madoff, or Bernie's sons, the perception of them, even by many victims, might have been different. But there would be no expressions of contrition, no words of sadness for all those who had been hurt or even for their own feelings from Ruth until much later. All were listening to their lawyers' advice, which surely was: don't say a word.

■ ■ ■

In the very early years of the new millennium—when Bernie's Ponzi scheme was going full tilt—cancer was frighteningly ravaging the Madoff clan. Within a time frame of just six months, three closely related family members were diagnosed with blood cancers. As Roger Madoff was going through the hellish and ultimately unsuccessful treatments for his leukemia, his cousin, 38-year-old Andy, Bernie's son, then the head of the trading desk at Madoff and the father of two, was diagnosed in March 2003 with a rare form of lymphoma after a lump was discovered in the crook of his neck. Another cousin, 9-year-old Ariel, the daughter of Madoff executive Charles Wiener, Bernie's sister's son, had also been diagnosed with leukemia, and Peter Madoff had previously had a couple of bouts with cancer that were said to have entailed surgery.

"My family's luck of late made me wary," Roger stated in his book.

A very dark cloud had settled over the family, and a still darker one was yet to come.

With cancer striking family members, the Madoff family started a foundation to fund leukemia and lymphoma research and treatment.

"Using resources from the family's trading and investment business," Roger Madoff disclosed in his book, "the fund ballooned in size to well over eight figures. To me, the sum was enormous. Not being closely involved in the trading operations, I hadn't realized the extent of the wealth that existed there.... In less than a year, the Madoff family became the largest benefactor for leukemia and lymphoma research in the U.S., and probably the world. We didn't make public pronouncements about our charity. Different members of the family had different reasons for keeping quiet. For me, the fact that three family members were suffering acutely from blood cancers seemed reason enough not to crow about research funding."

Roger never explained the reasons for remaining mum. Was it possible that Bernie didn't want it revealed because of the impact it might have had on his firm? Or was it simply that people prefer to keep cancer a secret when it strikes? Even today it's sometimes still described in obituaries as "a long illness."

One also has to wonder whether any or all of that eight-figure endowment came from money stolen from the accounts of Bernie's money-management investors. And was the Madoff family's donation kept secret in order to not scare away investors in Bernie's very exclusive fund with the specter of cancer looming over the family?

A few weeks after Roger Madoff died, Ruth was chairperson for the Gift of Life Bone Marrow Foundation's sixth annual Partners for Life gala at New York's Grand Hyatt Hotel, which was hosted by the Tony Award–winning actor Ron Rifkin. A photograph in the organization's magazine showed Bernie and Ruth, benevolently smiling.

Jennifer Madoff, a strong and self-confident young woman, emphasized in her interview with the author that the public and the media, and even the thousands of Ponzi victims, don't personally know the Madoff family members, and she considers that a shame. Specifically she mentions "my father-in-law and his kindness, and his generosity, and his wonderful loving nature. If they don't know everyone personally, they just associate it with how awful this all is."

For instance, she's very defensive of her sister-in-law—Roger's sister, Shana Madoff Skoller Swanson—who tried to save her brother's life by being the donor for a stem cell transplant. "We're very close," asserts Jennifer. "I'm the godmother of her daughter [Rebecca]. She and Roger were very close, so I feel very protective of her." Jennifer says she was particularly upset "and kind of repulsed" by the *New York* magazine cover story on Bernie that went into details about Shana's private life and her second marriage—to Eric Swanson, a former lawyer at the Securities and Exchange Commission. "Unfortunately, their loving, wonderful relationship is being dragged through this for no reason whatsoever."

However, her late husband in his memoir—published posthumously by Jennifer herself—also revealed some very embarrassing details about his sister's private life, details more appropriate for a tell-all, but he had his reasons.

He wrote:

> Her personal life had become more of a concern to me once I learned that I had relapsed, since the next phase of my treatment would require her to donate stem cells, shown in previous tests to be a "perfect" replacement for my damaged bone marrow.
>
> My sister was thirty-two at the time . . . [and] worked at our family's trading firm as its Head of Compliance making sure everyone played by the rules. Besides being a single mom, she had an active social life. . . . She was rail thin and attractive and had little trouble meeting potential mates. Her longer relationships always seemed to be with previous boyfriends. No matter how difficult the breakup, Shana's beaus never disappeared for long.
>
> In that summer of 2003, Shana was spending most weekends at the Hamptons beach house of her current boyfriend, Randy. Occasionally, Shana wouldn't stay at Randy's for the entire weekend, usually because a row had erupted between them. Although Randy never threatened Shana physically, if the two had a heated verbal spat, Shana wouldn't flinch at packing her bags and driving home to Manhattan at any hour of the night.
>
> Normally I found Shana's dramas amusing. But that summer Jen and I were more frightened than amused by them: frightened because we now saw Shana as my lifeline. I tried to convey my unease to her. . . . Jen seconded my feelings in a separate talk.

Roger quoted Shana as telling his wife, "I know you think I'm reckless. But I would never do anything to put Roger in jeopardy."

He then revealed that after Shana had taken two routine blood tests to make sure she was a "perfect match" for the stem cell procedure, a major problem was found. She came into her brother's hospital room and, laughing nervously, declared, "Well, I'm pregnant! I guess it happened last weekend. They said it just barely showed up on the test."

Peter and Marion Madoff were in the hospital room and were shocked by her announcement, while Roger "was floored, speechless."

Shana then told her brother that it was probable that the much-needed stem cell harvest would damage the fetus.

He disclosed that Shana attempted to abort the pregnancy by taking a morning-after pill; the first time it failed, but the second time she took the pill it worked.

"The immediate crises," he said, "passed, but indefinable feelings of hurt lingered on both sides."

At the Gift of Life gala of which Ruth was chairperson, Shana spoke "proudly" about donating blood stem cells to her brother, "and talked lovingly of his courageous battle and kind spirit." She told the wealthy gathering, "Roger lost his fight, but the memory of the passion and promise with which he lived will always be with us."

Naturally, there was nothing said about the scandalous situation that her brother had revealed in his memoir.

Among those listening in the audience were a number of future Madoff victims such as Fred Wilpon, the hugely wealthy real estate investor and owner of the New York Mets baseball team, who had turned over hundreds of millions of dollars to his longtime friend Bernie to invest over the years.

Prior to Bernie's confession and incarceration, Jennifer Madoff notes that "everybody in the family was close, everybody worked together, so many of the cousins worked together. They had a nice, close relationship. It was a big, happy family. Now everyone is crestfallen—that's the best way to describe it. Everyone is just reeling. In the wake of this, they're all trying to understand it themselves—it's devastating, like an earthquake. You don't know that it's coming and it just turns your world upside down. As the news comes out, everybody in the family feels crushed."

She adds sadly, "I hate the idea that my late husband's name and his legacy would be associated with this *horror*."

■ ■ ■

The Madoff family, in particular Roger's parents and Bernie and Ruth, had pledged to fund the Roger Madoff Literary Fellowship sponsored by the Queens Council on the Arts. Compared to the billions lost by investors, and the promised Madoff funding for education and research that was lost, the $10,000 fellowship was minuscule, but it had enormous meaning for those involved.

The council's director, Hoong-Yee Lee Krakauer, says:

It was intended to really bring focus to the literary community of Queens, which is populated by some amazing writers from different countries. Peter and Bernie knew this.

They're Queens guys. They know what Queens is, so for us to be able to offer a fellowship that was large enough to really confer validation upon an emerging writer, and to attract other funders to support translation services for an anthology was very exciting on many fronts.

The Madoff money just made it more exciting because it would have really put this fellowship on the level of the other fellowships in the literary world—highly endowed and highly publicized—and give emerging writers that are sort of in the backwater a chance to write.

Everything was in place on December 4, 2008, when the deadlines for entries had closed. Panelists had been chosen for judging; a Queens public access cable TV program about the fellowship had been taped with Jennifer Madoff and was ready for airing, and publicity was being generated.

Then, on December 10, the eve of Bernie's arrest, the night of the Madoff Christmas party, Krakauer, who was overseeing the program in conjunction with Jennifer, received a telephone call from one of the panelists who was in the literary-film business and a good friend of the Madoffs. She says the caller told her, " 'Tomorrow in the news Bernie Madoff is going to make an announcement that his entire business is bankrupt.' Ponzi scheme wasn't mentioned, but that [Madoff] was a house of cards, or something to that effect. I said, 'You're joking. There's no way,' because they said, 'Whatever you're doing with the Roger Madoff fellowship—it should come off your web site. You should notify everybody. It's not going to happen.' I said, 'That's just *crazy*.' "

It wasn't, of course.

"According to Jennifer," says Krakauer, "the check was being written and they were going to send it out before the year's end, but then the whole thing fell apart [with Bernie's arrest]. So we never got the check, and so maybe that was a good thing because I think it would have bounced."

Krakauer, an alumnus of Bernie and Ruth's Far Rockaway High School, had been "social friends" with Peter and Marion Madoff for a quarter-century, having met in the early 1980s. When she married her husband, Seth, the Madoffs were among the guests. Over the years they'd get together at seders and Thanksgiving gatherings. "Peter and Marion were a lot of fun—the two of them, with a great sense of humor. Shana and Roger were like big brother-sister to my kids, and then my daughter and my kids were kind of like big brother-sister to Shana's daughter, Rebecca. Our kids intermingled. We shared that."

Krakauer viewed Peter as "an alpha male" who was domineering and "*had* to cut the turkey" at holiday get-togethers. She also noted the kind of obsessive-compulsive problem in Peter that possessed Bernie, whom she did not know.

She says:

We used to kid around with Peter because we knew his pet peeves. If the table was set for 12, we'd make sure there were only 11 settings, so he'd get crazy when he counted them. It was those kinds of things that we knew he'd go nuts over. People in our circle would make things for our dinners. One friend used to make his own ice cream, and someone else would make pies or cakes, and they took pleasure in doing that. But Peter would criticize and nitpick—"It's *too* salty," or "It's *too* sweet." It was always something, so we used to tease him about that—friendly nudging.

Marion Madoff, a large-size woman with a sweet smile, according to photographs, was a jock of sorts who played golf and loved football. The Madoffs and the Krakauers went to a few Super Bowl parties together. "Marion was right in there with the guys, so I thought they were not a perfectly matched couple in the same sense as what I knew of Bernie and Ruth, whom I didn't know. Marion had a *personality*. That's all I can say. I could see Peter and Marion bickering. If you have two strong people in a marriage like they were, you're gonna have a lively marriage."

In all the years the Peter Madoffs and the Krakauers were friends, Bernie and Ruth never joined in the circle.

"Maybe it was a blessing," observes Krakauer after the Ponzi scandal broke. She says that in their social circle with Peter and Marion was another couple "who lost a significant amount of money" in Peter's brother's scheme.

There was also a big difference in terms of lifestyle between the two couples. While the Krakauers lived in middle-class Rockaway, Peter and Marion Madoff had spectacular homes at 975 Park Avenue and in a ritzy section of Long Island with the odd name of Muttontown. Years earlier, when Bernie and Peter were installing sprinkler systems, both had discovered Muttontown on the Gold Coast of Queens on Oyster Bay, and thought it would be the most wonderful place in the world to live—a regal out-of-the-way town with stately mansions. Eventually, Peter, working side by side with Bernie, would own one of those palaces

But Krakauer stresses that Peter and Marion "were not ostentatious people. They never threw things in your face. We were never made aware of major shifts of wealth. We knew they were flying down to Florida in their plane, but he never said, 'I'm flying down in a bigger plane to a bigger house in Palm Beach.' They had a lot of money and lot of affluence, but they never gloated about it. Maybe every single time we saw them they had a new car—and they had great cars, different Mercedes-Benzes all the time. When they bought the house in Muttontown, Marion was telling me, 'Oh, it's great. But it's not *me*. I have to do this, I have to do that.' I thought, 'Oh, my God, you have to do all this stuff to all these rooms. That's a *lot* of money.'" They later sold the place for and an even more spectacular home in Old Westbury.

Yet it wasn't all peaches and cream. Krakauer saw Peter Madoff's tough business side when she and the family began talking about the Roger Madoff fellowship. She recalls:

It became clear to me that he didn't know anything about nonprofit arts. Peter grilled me like we were talking about a business plan. He was more interested in the numbers and the business in that particular project than the actual cultural impact. If he was a cultural maven—and I have a lot of those guys on the board who say, "Whatever it is, whatever you want"—but Peter was not like that. He was, "Well, what's the return on the investment?" And I'd have to say, "Peter, it's *nonprofit!*" But that's what he always reverted to—the business.

After the Madoff scandal became public and the $10,000 check for Peter's son's fellowship was never sent as promised, the Madoffs had no contact whatsoever with Krakauer or the arts council. "I've been in touch with Jennifer, but even she has said to me that it's been very difficult for her with Peter and Marion. I wasn't surprised, because that was a project I really worked on very closely with Jennifer, and Jennifer is also going through a very difficult time, and Peter and Marion are going through hell, and the elephant in the room is Bernie.

Bernie never knew how to send an e-mail, and Peter is brilliant. If they are so close, the obvious question is: How involved was Peter? If that's so, and the answer is yes, he was involved, then he actually took down everybody we've had dinner with for 25 years. And no, if he wasn't involved, then who was?

Either way it's such an uncomfortable situation. Even my friends who did call and try to have a conversation with Peter and Marion say they can't because you look at somebody whose brother just took all this money from you—how can you have a conversation?

With me, I didn't lose money personally, but I lost momentum. I had disappointment, dreams, things like that which I think are just as valid, so I have no incentive to pick up the phone and call Peter and Marion.

I can't imagine what I would say, except *Why?* I just want to know how the family was involved. I just want to know who was I having dinner with for 25 years.

A lot of people want to know: Who was this guy? Who is this family?

Chapter 11

Mr. Outside versus Mr. Inside versus the SEC

B ernie, the elder, and Peter, the younger, had a brotherly love–hate relationship.

Their sibling rivalry had started when Bernie realized his baby brother, seven years his junior, was so much smarter than he was. He was envious when Peter got admitted to prestigious Brooklyn Tech High School whereas Bernie never could have made the grade there.

Peter, however, wasn't anywhere near the top of his class, either. His transcript, according to a knowledgeable source, showed that he was 484th out of a June 27, 1963, graduating class of 941. His final average was 81.7, and he was a B student in the subject in which he was seen as superior, math.

Nevertheless, he had gone on to a better college than Bernie, Queens College, where he met his future wife, Marion. While Bernie was hawking penny and over-the-counter stocks listed on what were called the Pink Sheets, and making a nice buck at it, along with building his private investment advisory business, Peter was earning a law degree at Fordham Law School (graduating in 1967)—the degree Bernie never got because he left law school after one year. Moreover, women thought Peter was better looking than Bernie, which always bruised the older brother's macho ego.

From day one, Bernie lorded it over Peter, who had begun working with him around 1965 at the 39 Broadway offices of Bernard L. Madoff Investment Securities, and Bernie would continue to be the dominant one through the years.

Bill Nasi recalls how Bernie started Peter at the very bottom in the business. "Basically," he says, "Bernie had him licking stamps and doing the mail room."

It was the start of a more than four-decades-long partnership, or at least that's how many personally, or socially, connected with the brothers perceived the arrangement. On the surface, as the years passed it appeared to be a 50–50 collaboration—one, though, that was ultimately doomed.

In fact, it clearly wasn't an even deal.

■ ■ ■

The Madoff firm had moved from 39 Broadway to 110 Wall Street in the 1970s, when Bernie's firm first started trading New York Stock Exchange (NYSE)–listed stocks. The trading floor was a giant rectangular wooden platform with all the workstations surrounding it. "Bernie was a workaholic," says Bill Nasi, who helped with the move. "Bernie loved to keep the place spotlessly clean, and he was on his knees hammering nails into the platform to make sure it was upright."

In the late 1980s, Bernie moved uptown to the new and futuristic 34-story skyscraper on Third Avenue between 53rd and 54th Streets designed by John Burgee and Philip Johnson known as the Lipstick Building—so named because it looked like an enormous tube of lipstick. A part owner in the flashy building was Bernie's chum, investor, and eventual victim, Fred Wilpon. By moving to midtown and out of the financial district, Bernie felt he could operate his trading and money management operations in greater secrecy; Wall Street had always been a hotbed of financial gossip-mongering and spying on the competition. Bernie liked to keep his investment strategies and business operations close to his vest.

One morning Bill Nasi had gotten into the Lipstick Building offices of Madoff very early. Thinking he was the first to arrive at work, he entered the reception area only to be startled by Bernie's voice, usually low, but at the moment loud and frightening. Nasi recalls:

> He was screaming at Peter. *Screaming.* He was saying, "I want you to go outside and look to see whose name is on the door! You own 1 percent of the business, so until *your* name is on the door you keep your fucking mouth shut! I run things here!" I assume they thought they were alone in the office. I was so embarrassed I backed off and went down to the lobby. I learned one thing that morning. Because Peter's name wasn't on the door, Peter couldn't make any decisions. It was terrible to hear that.

Bernie's secretary, Eleanor Squillari, overheard a similar outburst aimed at Peter, known as the "Energizer Bunny" because he never seemed relaxed, though he didn't have his brother's facial ticks and squints. She recalled to *Vanity Fair* how the two had once checked in with her on separate phone lines from an airport to see if there were any messages. When she told Bernie that Peter was calling in on another line, she overheard him blast his brother.

"Hang up the fucking phone. She's *my* secretary!"

Bernie was the ultimate control freak, even with his closest partner, Ruth.

A Madoff intimate was in the process of having her fancy Sutton Place apartment renovated and was telling Ruth about her plans. As they were discussing architects Ruth made it a point to say, "I hope you can make your apartment livable." Surprised, the friend responded, "Of course, Ruth. Why wouldn't I make it livable and comfortable?" Ruth's shrill answer floored her. "Because I can't sit on most of the furniture in our place. They're rare antiques, and Bernie doesn't want me to sit on them."

Bernie governed Peter in the same way he exercised control over Ruth, despite the fact that it was the younger brother who was the technology and computer expert and multitasker.

Whenever it came time to claim credit for pioneering the use of electronic trading and bringing high-tech capabilities to the Madoff business, it was Bernie who took the bows while Peter waited in the wings applauding like a stand-in.

As one observer notes of the relationship between the brothers:

> It was more of a Mr. Inside–Mr. Outside type of situation. In the garment industry they almost always have partners. Mr. Inside is the person who knows the techniques and the fiscal ins and outs of running an operation, and that was Peter. Mr. Outside's the schmoozer, the person who gets the customers, the person who deals with public relations. Bernie was an excellent Mr. Outside.

And that assessment appeared to be on the mark.

Traders Magazine, which had covered Bernard L. Madoff Investment Securities (BLMIS) over the years, observed that by the 1990s,

> Bernie had become something of a senior statesman in the industry, serving on the NASD [National Association of Securities Dealers] board, non-executive chairman of Nasdaq, and as head of the Securities Industry Association's influential trading committee. For a while he was spending one-third of his time in Washington as an unofficial lobbyist for the dealer community.

He was Mr. Outside to the nth degree.

With Bernie on the cover in a lengthy March 2009 profile called "Before the Fall," the magazine noted that Peter "was the firm's original computer whiz and eventually assumed responsibility for the trading operations. It was Peter, in fact, who saw the potential in trading securities listed on the New York Stock Exchange. And it was that decision that catapulted the firm into the big leagues of wholesaling."

He was Mr. Inside to the nth degree.

A former Wall Street big recalled how it was Mr. Outside who "always made himself available in the early days of Nasdaq when it was hard to get volunteers. . . . After a while, he became a leading voice and was influential and valuable to Nasdaq." Another told *Traders Magazine*, "Bernie's strategy was to get actively involved in all aspects of the industry," and noted that he had "a much bigger presence than the size of his firm would naturally warrant. By being visible, he'd boost his business. . . . It was a very smart move."

When, in the late 1970s, Madoff bought seats on the Cincinnati Stock Exchange—a competitor of sorts to the NYSE in terms of trading platforms and operational styles—Mr. Inside, Peter, was elected to the board, and also joined the Cincy's trading and technology committees, mainly because of his expertise in those areas, not because he was seeking to overshadow his ruling brother; Bernie would never allow it.

By the early 1980s, Bernie "could hang out his shingle as a full-fledged alternative to the New York Stock Exchange," stated *Traders Magazine*. Bernie, always the spokesman, was quoted as declaring, "We set the standard at the Cincinnati," and he began securing steady order flow from the likes of Charles Schwab & Company.

Madoff was growing bigger every year, with Bernie working the system from the outside and Peter keeping things under control on the inside. Madoff soon had the ability, with Peter's expertise, to execute orders quickly—even faster than the NYSE.

Moreover, brokers were actually being paid by Madoff for their business. Complaints were registered with the SEC by the NYSE and other exchanges that Madoff wasn't playing by the long-established rules.

Bernie's response was to ignore the rules.

■ ■ ■

Business boomed, with Madoff nearing 10 percent of the volume of the NYSE in the 1990s. Madoff had become Wall Street's 70th largest firm during the Clinton years, doing as much as 25,000 trades daily. In that same time frame, Bernie was named to the chairmanship of

Nasdaq's board of directors, and Peter served on the board for several years. But he still ran the firm's trading show and oversaw compliance. He was Bernie's number two in the chain of command, other than those few individuals Bernie may have had working in his clandestine investment advisory operation—the Ponzi scheme, of which Peter later would claim all innocence.

The Madoff joint was jumping.

With Bernie blowing the Madoff horn, the firm was generating positive publicity because Bernie always made it a point to talk to journalists when they called, or invited them over to tour the trading floor.

Laurel Kenner, who had been Roger Madoff's stock market editor at Bloomberg before she left the news service in 2000, recalls how Bloomberg's New York bureau chief at the time, aware that Roger was a member of the "dynamic Madoff family," would visit Madoff headquarters "to meet and greet and hang out and see what was going on." Adds Kenner, "Everybody was encouraged to go out and meet the people we were writing about for story ideas. When we did market preview stories in the morning, we would call Madoff for a London quote because they had the London office."

The business media and Madoff had a beautiful relationship.

After Bernie's Ponzi operation was revealed, Kenner opined that Bloomberg had missed the boat, the biggest financial fraud in history. "It's embarrassing," she says. (After the scandal broke, however, Bloomberg was on the story, breaking a number of exclusives.) And Kenner observes, "I'm so glad Roger isn't here to see this, and second of all, how in the world could Bernie Madoff have pulled off a fraud of such magnitude? Where's the family in all this?"

With Bernie pumping things up, BLMIS was consistently in the business news in a highly positive way for years.

A trade publication, *Wall Street & Technology*, profiled "The Madoff Dynasty" in its August 2000 issue as part of a story called "Family Influence" that examined three families involved in financial technology, and their impact on the industry. The Madoffs were chosen because they were considered to be among "the most influential." The highly complimentary article noted that Bernie's brother, sons, nieces, and nephews orbited around him, but that when the firm was started "there was only his wife, Ruth, who helped with some bookkeeping—and dreams of Wall Street success."

The article pointed out that the day-to-day Madoff business "found its way to the dinner table at home."

Mark Madoff, who joined the firm in 1986 after graduating from the University of Michigan, was quoted in the article as saying, "All of his [Bernie's] family members grew up with this being our lives. When it is a family-operated business you don't go home at night and shut everything off, so you take things home with you, which is how all of us grew up. . . . What makes it fun for all of us is to walk into the office in the morning and see the rest of your family sitting there. That's a good feeling to have. To Bernie and Peter, that's what it's all about."

Affirming Mark's statement, Kenner recalls a wide-eyed Roger telling her that his cousins "all could remember 14 different stocks, and keep all the prices in their heads."

But less than a decade after the Madoff profile appeared, Mark had to change his tune, since it was Mark and his brother Andy who turned in their father to authorities. Andy Madoff melodramatically told a friend that what their father did was "a father-son betrayal of biblical proportions." While the sons consistently maintained through intermediaries that they were hoodwinked just like all of Bernie's other victims, their dealings with their crooked father came under investigation.

"I'm unemployed, I don't have any money, and I'm just trying to stay out of jail—my name is mud," Andy whined to a friend, according to *Vanity Fair*.

The brothers cut off all communication with their mother, likely because of legal advice, and refrained from visiting their father in the slammer.

But before the fall of Bernie, it all looked so perfect to outsiders like the business reporters, and even to family insiders like the innocent Roger Madoff. But a longtime family friend, veteran Madoff employee, and eyewitness asserts, "There were massive fights between Bernie and Peter, and between Mark and Andy—but no long-term feuds."

With Bernie behind bars, and with a number of the Madoff family business principals being scrutinized by authorities after the patriarch's arrest, the reporter who wrote the "Madoff Dynasty" story almost a decade earlier, Anthony Guerra, observes, "It's very difficult to know somebody from the level of the stories that we do in journalism when you're looking at their business life. That's a surface-level snapshot. You would have probably had to dig so, so, so deep, and you're talking about a situation where family members may not have known."

He adds, "It's a sad story to me that you can have so much, and it not be enough. That's the larger human drama in the Madoff story."

■ ■ ■

Red flags, however, soon started to be furiously waved.

In May 2001, *Barron's*, under a headline "Don't Ask, Don't Tell: Bernie Madoff Is So Secretive, He Even Asks Investors to Keep Mum," reported, "Some folks on Wall Street think there's more to how Madoff generates his enviable stream of investment returns than meets the eye. . . . Even adoring investors can't explain his enviable steady gains." The report by Erin Arvedlund noted that "few on the Street" were aware that Bernie was managing billions of dollars for rich clients, enough to rank Madoff among the three largest hedge funds in the world.

Bernie called the Wall Street speculation "ridiculous." And when asked by *Barron's* to explain how his money-management operation "never had a down year," he responded, "It's a proprietary strategy. I can't go into it in great detail."

Bernie said it was called a "split-strike conversion," which was gobbledygook to most.

His real strategy had been conceived some eight decades earlier by the man whom Bernie would surpass as the greatest swindler of his time, Charles Ponzi, from whom the term *Ponzi scheme* was derived—whereby early investors are paid with ill-gotten funds from later investors.

As it turned out, the Jewish guy from Queens had out-Ponzied the Ponzi guy from Italy who came to America to commit his crimes.

Like Bernie, Ponzi had a respectable-sounding firm, Securities Exchange Company, to hustle his fraud. And like Bernie, Ponzi was a dapper schmoozer, a *macher*, a Mr. Outside.

Ponzi's scheme began shortly after the end of the Great War and at the start of the Roaring Twenties.

As with the reporter from *Barron's*, a business writer raised the first red flag that questioned Ponzi's high returns. With incredible chutzpah, Ponzi sued and won a $500,000 libel suit. But his scheme soon ran out of steam. With revelations that he was robbing Peter to pay Paul, there was a run on his company with investors seeking their money—millions of dollars back then, not anywhere close to Bernie's billions.

In the end Ponzi was charged with 88 counts of mail fraud. He pleaded guilty to one and spent three and a half years of a five-year sentence in a federal prison. He was later charged with larceny by the state of Massachusetts. It took three trials before he was found guilty and sentenced to a maximum of nine years in prison. He was eventually deported to his native Italy, where he pulled off more scams. He died in a charity hospital in 1949.

And it was expected that the biggest Ponzi artist of all, Bernie Madoff, would die in prison.

■ ■ ■

Around the time *Barron's* ran its probing story about Bernie (which received scant public attention, especially from investors in Madoff, who were happy enough with the returns they were getting), a genuine financial wizard, mild-mannered and studious Harry Markopolos, was assigned by his employers at Rampart Investment Management, a Boston options trading firm, to determine if there was any way they could come close to matching Madoff's steady returns—incredible double-digit returns—in both up and down markets.

Markopolos attempted to reverse engineer Madoff numbers using data from Madoff's trades in options and stocks, but all efforts at simulation failed. A math whiz, Markopolos was stymied. As he later observed in a newspaper interview, "You can't dominate all markets. You have to have some losses." He finally came to the conclusion that what he was trying to match was, in fact, a genuine, full-blown, red-blooded, all-American Ponzi scheme.

Suspecting that a major crime was taking place at BLMIS, Markopolos contacted the New York office of the SEC, expressed his concern, and began supplying the agency with memos and data. There had been little, if any, response by the time he left his job at Rampart in 2004 to start a financial fraud investigation business. Initially, he had hoped to make some money himself from the evidence he had gathered—a reward the SEC and other government agencies pay to whistle-blowers if a prosecution is successful. But with no action on the SEC's part and no financial reward forthcoming, he decided to pursue the case he had gathered with even more gusto; his goal now was simple: He wanted legendary Wall Street titan Bernie Madoff's ass in a sling.

In 2005, the tenacious Markopolos sent the SEC a scrupulously researched memo with the straightforward title: "The World's Largest Hedge Fund Is a Fraud."

Still no immediate action was taken.

Markopolos later revealed that in taking on Bernie, he feared for his life and the lives of his family members because Bernie "was one of the most powerful men on Wall Street and in a position to easily end our careers, or worse." He said he initially acted anonymously with regulators because of this fear.

Was Markopolos afraid of a Madoff-dispatched hit man?

Did he fear Bernie was the Tony Soprano of the Madoff family—the Godfather?

Indeed he did. He had started checking his car for bombs.

It was not out of the realm of possibility, since the Mob had gotten into Bernie's kind of business. While Bernie was operating his Ponzi scheme, a real-life soldier in the Luchese crime family had set up a bogus hedge fund in the early 2000s with the confidence-inducing name America's Hedge Fund, conned investors from the Midwest, and, like Bernie, sent them bogus statements showing generous returns. The crew made millions before they were busted.

Markopolos asserted that Bernie's fund "posed great danger" to anyone who investigated it. While there was an industry self-regulatory agency called the Financial Industry Regulatory Authority (FINRA), Markopolos said he never took his allegations there because the Madoff brothers—Bernie and Peter—had power and influence within the organization.

Because no action was taken by the SEC, Markopolos declared, "I became fearful for the safety of my family until the SEC finally acknowledged, after Madoff had been arrested, that it had received credible evidence of Madoff's Ponzi scheme. . . . "

Just as Markopolos feared Bernie, Bernie feared the SEC, and as the world came to know, he had good reason.

Whenever SEC representatives announced even a routine inspection visit to Madoff headquarters every three or four months, the boss went ballistic. "Bernie was like a chicken with his head cut off," recalls eyewitness Bill Nasi. "He freaked out in the sense that his voice became high-pitched and he was running around the office and was very agitated. My supervisor told me, 'Keep out of Bernie's way today, because he's having conniptions—the SEC is coming in today, and when that happens he's super-agitated like the Energizer Bunny on high speed.' "

Bernie instructed everyone to dress up, be on their best behavior, and just keep working with their heads down.

"A small army [of SEC people] would come in," says Nasi. "I'd see them scrutinize everything, and everyone had to look hard at work. It's as if someone had thrown a switch on Bernie. He was having a shit fit."

Curiously, Bernie never asked anyone for receipts, except when documents had to be delivered to the SEC offices in lower Manhattan, according to Nasi.

> Then he was on pins and needles. I had to bring the receipt back. If I was late he would be beat me up, page me—"Where's Bill Nasi? Get Bill Nasi in here!" I'd go back to his office and he'd be in a frenzy. He'd ask me was I sure I delivered it to the SEC and not some other office. I told him I had to sign in and go up on a special elevator. "You got it? You got the receipt? Gimme it!" He was just like that.

The other odd quirk Madoff employees like Nasi noted was that Bernie would never give up his Social Security number to anyone. In a world where identity theft is prevalent, that's not a surprise. But in Bernie's case, he went to extremes. "When a vendor wanted to open an account with Bernie, they'd ask for his Social [Security number]," says Nasi. "But Bernie would rather send them a check for $250,000 and tell them that 'at the end of the year, if you haven't used up all the money you can always return it.' But he wouldn't turn over the number. Those vendors, like the ones who serviced the backup computer systems, had to break their own protocols about Social Security numbers or face losing the business." (Ironically, Bernie's SSN has been released in publicly filed court records as 069-30-9552.)

Meanwhile, it appeared authorities were finally going to take a hard look at what was going on inside the walls of Madoff.

Finally, in January 2006, based on Markopolos's allegations, the SEC opened an investigation, and then quickly blew another opportunity to nail Bernie and expose his crimes. The agency learned that he had given it questionable information about how he managed the money of his customers. The SEC asked for documents, and even interviewed Bernie. The investigators appeared to be getting close to the case laid out by Markopolos. But in the end the SEC gave Bernie an easy out—it asked him to register as an investment adviser, and he quickly did so.

Case closed.

The SEC's final report on the matter said the investigation was terminated because the discovered Madoff violations "were not so serious as to warrant an enforcement action," the *Wall Street Journal* reported.

It was shades of the SEC's decision to end its probe of unregistered Madoff feeder fund principals Frank Avellino and Michael Bienes almost two decades earlier when they quickly agreed to return investors' money, thus keeping agency probers from looking more closely at Bernie's operation.

In early February 2009, with Bernie under penthouse arrest after admitting his fraud, the SEC came under scathing attack in a fiery hearing held by the House Financial Services subcommittee.

The key witness was the man who had started nosing around nine years earlier—52-year-old Harry Markopolos, now vindicated and hailed as a hero. He hammered the agency as incompetent, declaring that it "roars like a lion and bites like a flea. . . . I'm saying that if you flew the entire SEC staff to Boston, [and] sat them in Fenway Park for an afternoon, they could not find first base. . . . The SEC was never capable of catching Mr. Madoff. He could have gone to $100 billion. . . . It took me five minutes to figure out he was a fraud."

SEC officials such as Linda Chatman Thomsen, the agency's enforcement director, were placed on the hot seat and attacked by legislators for their investigative and regulatory failure. Typical were the sarcastic and caustic words of furious New York Congressman Gary L. Ackerman, a Democrat, who declared: "We thought the enemy was Mr. Madoff. I think it is you."

The *New York Post*'s headline blared: "How SEC Bozos Blew It."

A week later the embattled 54-year-old Thomsen, who had headed enforcement since 2005, resigned after being blasted by critics for "turning a blind eye" to tips that could have caught Bernie earlier.

Markopolos also claimed that he had tipped off the *Wall Street Journal* about Madoff's scam in December 2005, and evidenced e-mail correspondence with a *Journal* reporter who wanted to investigate. But Markopolos said the story was never done because the reporter couldn't get approval from upstairs to pursue the lead. The journalism trade publication *Editor & Publisher* contacted Paul Steiger, who was the *Journal*'s managing editor at the time, but he claimed he never heard of the paper getting such a tip. He said that any "assertion that we were afraid of Madoff is just preposterous; it is silly."

As the Madoff investigation dragged on through 2009, agency officials promised reforms in order to restore shattered investor confidence. It even went so far as to hire a government-funded research organization, the Center for Enterprise Modernization, to examine and come up with better ways for the SEC to deal with Markopolos-like tips about bad guys in the financial sector.

A new sheriff was put in place to police Wall Street—it was hoped. Her name was Mary Schapiro, chairman of the SEC. But she was quickly criticized.

In a lead editorial, the *Wall Street Journal* in early February 2009 declared:

> Judging by her first public address . . . Mary Schapiro had developed a novel response to Bernard Madoff's alleged fraud [alleged because he had still not pleaded guilty]. In Friday's speech to the Practicing Law Institute, the new SEC boss never uttered the word "Madoff." Odder still . . . [she] had decided that what her enforcement staff really needs is less supervision from the top.

However, the walls were closing on Bernie Madoff. The fall of the Madoff dynasty was at hand.

Chapter 12

Life inside the Madoff Piggy Bank, Flashing the Plastic, and Losing the Farm

N
ot long before Bernie was arrested he and Ruth had visited their multimillion-dollar abode in Palm Beach, the wealthy, somewhat Jewish enclave where investors in Madoff would lose hundreds of millions of dollars. One of Bernie and Ruth's favorite men's shops that also sold some women's wear was the chic Trillion boutique under the palms on ritzy Worth Avenue, an amalgam of trendy Rodeo Drive in Beverly Hills, Paris's glamorous Avenue Montaigne, London's tony Oxford Street, and Milan's stylish Via della Spiga.

The Madoffs had shopped at Trillion for some three decades.

Bernie, whose mother wouldn't buy him Keds sneakers when he was a kid, which made him feel like a Laurelton outcast, spent money like a kid in a candy store at Trillion.

The store offered a very special $7,400 unconstructed, handmade vicuna and cashmere, cream-and-brown herringbone jacket that took a very special buyer to see it for what it was—and afford to pay for it. Bernie was that kind of guy, says Trillion's owner, David Neff, who personally served the Madoffs, and bonded with Bernie.

> That jacket was unique and it was really expensive, and not everybody could appreciate it for a multitude of reasons. It takes a certain attitude; it's not for everybody. But when Bernie saw it he just lit up, and said, "Yeah, yeah, yeah—I like that." There are two reasons he liked it. First of all it really is very special, but secondly he has every kind of sport coat that he could want—so this was a step up, and he recognized it. Not many people did.

Bernie also favored Trillion's navy crewneck wool sweater that he bought at $1,200 a pop, and it wasn't even cashmere. The $2,000-a-pair conservative charcoal flannel pants went well with the sweater. Bernie bought those, too. Observes Neff, "The guy that's wearing those says, 'Holy smokes, am I a lucky boy.'" Bernie also liked the cotton and cashmere corduroy trousers—the ones that "don't wrinkle, are a pleasure to wear," came in 18 "unique" colors, and cost him (or probably his bilked investors) $1,200 a pair.

Speaking of Bernie, Neff observes:

> There are people that trust their own taste and are hedonistic enough to appreciate these very expensive items. Just those three items, two pairs of pants and a sweater, cost $4,400. If somebody didn't care about money, it didn't matter. But Bernie didn't throw it around and he didn't just come in and make big stacks—he was discerning, conservative. His closet wasn't jam-packed with all the purchases he made every other Sunday—but just with the good stuff.

Bernie certainly was discerning in apparel and in people. He cleverly chose the investors who became victims in his Ponzi scheme very carefully. For the most part they had to invest multiples of seven figures, and they had to be the kind who didn't ask too many questions. Most of them who actually knew Bernie felt he was conservative—to them he was low-key and he didn't flaunt all the goodies he had. He saved his brashness, of which there was plenty, for those in his inner circle.

■ ■ ■

As David Neff rightfully perceived, Bernie was proud of the contents of the enormous custom-built walk-in closet in the dramatic mahogany-paneled master bedroom of the Madoffs' East 64th Street co-op apartment—Penthouse 12A (and for a time Bernie's Big House before he pleaded guilty and was put into a real prison cell). Even though Bernie amazingly banned Ruth from sitting on the antique furniture, the penthouse was in her name—a legal dodge, they both hoped, against possible seizure.

Bernie treasured the duplex apartment with its dramatic curved staircase like something out of a 1940s Hollywood movie set; it showed the world that the poor boy from Queens had made it big, and it gave him bragging rights because his place was the last to be done in Manhattan by the interior designer Angelo Donghia before he died from AIDS-related illnesses. Donghia was known for his chic, sophisticated interiors for clients who included, besides the Ponzi artist, such luminaries as Donald and Ivana Trump, Liza Minnelli, Halston, Ralph Lauren, and Mary Tyler Moore.

Ruth once told Bernie's Far Rockaway High School chum and eventual Ponzi victim Cynthia Greenberger Lieberbaum that she had found him overwhelmed with emotion and weeping in his chicly decorated living room as he contemplated his meteoric rise to the top, the riches that he had accumulated, and the luxury that enveloped him, according to Cynthia's brother, John (Greenberger) Maccabee.

Bernie's closet, says Maccabee, was on the Madoff penthouse grand tour, and he had the displeasure, as he later viewed it, of being guided through the realm by the lord of the manor.

The closet was brimming with the clothing treasures imagined by Trillion's owner, only more extreme.

Each drawer of a slender dresser displayed just one shirt, but there were 16 drawers, each with a shirt in the same shade of blue, matching Bernie's eye color, and each shirt had a similar cut. In another part of the closet hung his suits, also all identically cut—expensive and British, all of them the same charcoal gray and double-breasted. The pants each hung on separate hangers, as did the jackets, each with a bit of space between them. His shoes, handmade, at least a dozen pairs in all, were shined and lined up military-style in two rows.

It was all laid out as if for a GQ photo shoot.

Everything was hung with the greatest of care and put in place in such a way as to unconsciously underscore Bernie's rampant obsessive-compulsive issues.

"His closet was *so* anal," says Maccabee. "A lot of people will toss off 'Oh, Bernie was crazy.' Well, he *was*. He was fastidious about cars, his boats, his houses, so when he took me on a tour of his closet my mouth sort of dropped open. But it was in keeping with what I knew about him. It always felt like it was insecurity to me. It's common after I moved to L.A. for people to do that—to take you on a tour of their house and to show their closet, and the next thing I knew I was staring at little suits and little dresses. But the first person I knew to actually do that was Bernie—Bernie and Ruth. He was definitely showing off."

Bernie had a closet full of similar suits at Madoff headquarters in case he needed to make a change for a special client or meeting.

The money didn't matter. It was always there for his taking.

Moreover, he actually had his suits cut in London not only for his body shape, which was teddy-bear chubby, but also for the very slender cell phone he always carried, the RAZR, which Motorola had started marketing in 2004 as an expensive, exclusive fashion phone for the hip and trendy. Bernie had first discovered the phone in Europe two or three years before it was sold in the United States, and he had paid $3,000 for the bragging rights to carry one.

In the July before his arrest he had gone phone shopping with his firm's head of purchasing, Amy Joel. The phone store salesman showed Bernie all the latest gadgets, but he rejected them. Joel says, "He took out his RAZR and told the clerk, 'See this phone? I have all my suits built around this phone. It flips me out when I see men with their gawky phones in their pockets. It just doesn't look right. With this, you can't even tell it's in my pocket. I want three of them.' I could see the salesman going *ka-ching, ka-ching, ka-ching* in his head," adds Joel. "When we walked out I said, 'What's wrong with you? I'm here to negotiate and you're bragging about how much money you have and you buy three of these things,' and he turned to me and out of the blue said, 'You're a fucking psycho!' "

■ ■ ■

Bernie also matched his custom-tailored suits (and phone) with another passion, buying and possessing some of the finest and most expensive wristwatches in the world. For more than a decade, he had been a customer of the very exclusive Somlo Antiques shop in prestigious Burlington Arcade in London, where the international division of Madoff was located.

George Somlo, the managing director, sold watches going back to the sixteenth century, and was an expert in horology, the science of measuring time. Besides his shop, Somlo participated in shows that catered to the wealthy—the Palm Beach Jewelry, Art, and Antique Show and the International Fine Art & Antique Dealers Show in New York. Although Somlo and Bernie bonded at both places, Bernie usually shopped with Somlo in London when he was there doing business.

"He did have very good taste in watches," says Somlo. "He was very particular in what he liked."

Bernie favored the slim Patek Philippes and Rolexes—"particularly the very discreet, not flashy, Rolex chronographs from the Forties and Fifties"—like the two he wore simultaneously on one wrist so he could easily tell the time between his New York headquarters and his London branch. "The watches he bought were very much collectibles," notes Somlo. "Items that he bought from me long ago became considerably more valuable—if he had spent $10,000 for a watch, it became worth $50,000 or $60,000." But, as Somlo pointed out, the value of Bernie's watch collection was minuscule compared to the billions he swindled. "In the whole big picture, it doesn't really amount to much"—not even the most expensive watch he had bought that cost Bernie $80,000, which he charged on his credit card. About the watches Bernie bought, Somlo noted, "If you saw one on his wrist, you would think they were nothing, unless you understood watches. They were very discreet."

Somlo found dealing with Bernie, and meeting with Ruth, always a pleasurable experience.

"I would have trusted him with anything," he asserts. "He was always so presentable. He was always very honorable. He didn't offer me ludicrous prices—he was completely the opposite" of the stereotypical Ugly American.

Somlo recalls,

> I found him to be the American version of the English gentleman. I posted him a fair price, which is what we do with clients we've known for many years, and he'd say, "Fine, I'll take it" or "No, I don't want it." There were lots of things he declined because he had similar ones.
>
> He wasn't buying just for the sake of buying. He bought what he liked. Watches were a passion for him. He loved them. I held things for him, which I thought he would like. He was a good client. We had a rapport. He knew me as George and over the years I knew him as Bernie.

Oddly, Bernie placed a ceiling on how much he would spend on his passion, the tops being that $80,000 watch—a 1940 Patek Philippe chronograph that he purchased in late 2007 as a Hanukkah present for himself. From dealing with Bernie for years, Somlo knew that he wasn't a watch *expert*, but rather made his purchases based on how a watch *looked* and the kind of watches Somlo recommended. Notes Somlo:

> Considering the amount of money he had, or didn't have, he had this price of around $80,000. He wouldn't buy anything for $100,000 or $120,000. There was never any point in my offering him anything over that price, because he was adamant

that he wouldn't pay that much. The Patek Philippes were easily $80,000. He had this sort of cutoff point, and he probably wouldn't have felt comfortable wearing a watch for $250,000 on his wrist. The ones he bought early on were $20,000, $25,000—wearable things.

In conversation with Bernie, Somlo learned that he had been collecting expensive vintage watches for years, long before he had become a customer of his. The two watch lovers became close enough that Bernie and Ruth invited Somlo and his wife to their New York penthouse about 18 months before Bernie was busted, and Bernie sent customers to the horologist, but never asked him to invest—luckily for Somlo.

"They were an adorable couple," says the dealer, "so my wife and I were *astonished*, were just *floored* when he was arrested and when all this terrible news came out about him. He's the last person in the world we would have expected anything like this to happen [to]. I knew someone else who lost a fair amount of money with him who was also collecting watches, a business colleague of Bernie's from California. I also met somebody here in London who was part of the Fairfield Greenwich Group. His daughter went to the same school in America as my son, and he told me, 'I'm completely bust.' All I heard when I was in Palm Beach were horror stories.

"I was surprised to hear that Bernie didn't kill himself."

■ ■ ■

When he was in Palm Beach, Bernie enjoyed hanging out with David Neff at Trillion, and usually Ruth was at his side, although she had no role in helping him choose his clothing.

Observes Neff:

Of the two, Bernie was the more *tasty*. I was never impressed with Ruth's taste level. Most men will say to me, "I've got to get my wife" if it's a choice between three things. Bernie never said that. They were really tight, but between the two of them it was never "Oh, Bernie, I hate that on you," because Bernie wouldn't put something on that anyone would hate on him. He was worldly. He had a certain confidence in his own taste and the knowledge of what he was looking at.

Since I've been in business, I met a lot of cool people here in Palm Beach, and I would have to put Bernie Madoff in the top five, and Jimmy Buffett and people like that are in my top five, people that are just cool, low-key people that are never in a hurry, have plenty of time to ask questions personally.

Although he blinked and twitched a lot, Bernie never looked like he was under pressure.

The two had a camaraderie, just like Bernie had developed with George Somlo.

Bernie talked about his several boats, each called the *Bull*—the one in Florida was a gorgeous classic wooden Rybovich fishing vessel, the best there is—and boasted about how he used the same decorator for his boats who also did the interior design on his home in France, and the interior of the plane he co-owned. Once again, everything was always done in black and gray. Even though he co-owned a jet, he mused about the fastest plane he chartered when he went to Europe, and about his preferred craft to get him around quickly when he was on the Continent.

To avoid the heavy traffic on the road between Cannes and St. Tropez, the *macher* from 228th Street in Laurelton decided that it would be best to travel on his yacht rather than by car. "So Bernie and Ruth would get on the boat and they'd go to St. Tropez for the weekend," says Neff, "and I thought, oh, that is *so* cool; that makes so much sense." Bernie's only complaint was that he had to hire a captain whose salary he had to pay through the winter even though Bernie and Ruth were usually there for only a month.

Neff saw Bernie as one of his true power customers. "People I know who would come into the store would bow to Bernie," he says. Among those customers was a major Madoff investor, philanthropist and victim Jeffry Picower (and his wife Barbara). Picower would later come under investigation for allegedly telling Bernie how much in returns he wanted for his investment.

Bernie liked the way Neff treated him, and once offered him a tour of his offices in the Lipstick Building. "I had telephoned him about this fabric that I was getting for worsted spun-cashmere suits. He said he couldn't picture it, so I came to New York wearing the suit and he said he'd take one. He was very cordial, and showed me around, and told me what he did there—but I didn't know anything about that office on the 17th floor."

To Neff, Bernie maintained that he only played golf with Ruth at what would turn out to be the Ponzi-ravaged Palm Beach Country Club, where the initiation fee was more than $300,000 and there was a long waiting list, and where as many as a third of the members had put their money in Madoff. And he bragged that he refused to attend any of the ritzy parties and charity balls to which he was constantly being invited as an A-lister in Palm Beach by his very grateful private clients—such as Carl Shapiro, the elderly entrepreneur who once owned Kay Windsor clothing, and who had begun putting his money with Bernie when he was just starting out.

After knowing Bernie for so many years as a customer and sort of like a friend, although they never socialized outside of the store except for that one visit to New York that was strictly business, Neff said he "enjoyed telling people that Bernie Madoff was my go-to guy when I'd read some wild story about some malfeasance on Wall Street. I'd say to Bernie, 'What about Joe Schmo? I can't believe what I read this week.' And Bernie would say, 'I know. Can you believe that guy? How did he think he was going to get away with that?' "

Later, after Bernie's scheme became public, Neff discovered that a number of his store's customers were taken for a ride "big time," as he put it. "There are so many horrible, horrible stories. I've talked to too many guys who have said to me, 'You know, I can't start over again because I'm too old.' "

Ruth didn't fare as well as Bernie in Neff's eyes.

"I thought she was a funny little creature," he says, "kind of quirky, pleasant enough, but nowhere near as friendly as Bernie. She was kind of a zero."

The very last time the Madoffs shopped at Trillion before Bernie was taken down, Ruth bought a $4,000 double-face cashmere (meaning cashmere on the outside *and* on the inside) little blue jacket, similar to a cardigan but actually a blazer. It had to be recut to her small size 4 because she always bought mediums.

"She liked to buy things big in size," says Neff.

Then came the incident that dropped Neff's jaw, the final straw in his Bernie and Ruth saga.

The first thing on Monday, December 15, 2008, after Bernie's arrest, Ruth Madoff placed a call to Trillion.

Recounts Neff:

She wanted to make sure that we would send her blazer up, because she didn't think she'd be down here for quite some time. It just amazed me that this jacket was on her mind on that horrific Monday. It's like, "Where is your head?" We shipped the jacket, and I never heard from Ruth or Bernie again.

There was, however, a postscript.

On that last visit to Trillion, Bernie had fallen in love with another pair of $2,000 slacks. Unfortunately, Neff had to tell one of his favorite five customers that his size wasn't in stock and that the garment had to be special ordered from Italy. By the time the pants arrived, Bernie had confessed to his Ponzi scheme and was under 24-hour house arrest. Neff immediately put Bernie's American Express Platinum card through the charge machine, not wanting to be stuck with his order. But the card had already been canceled. The slacks wound up back on the rack waiting for another customer with Bernie's fine taste to come along.

■ ■ ■

Before the plastic was canceled, the Madoffs had used it, or their corporate card, to charge a king's ransom of goodies. Bernie, Ruth, and other members of the family, as well as a few close associates at Madoff, had turned Bernard L. Madoff Investment Securities into their very own personal piggy bank of conspicuous consumption.

In early May 2009, the firm's corporate American Express statements for January 2008 and later were among numerous exhibits filed in U.S. Bankruptcy Court in New York by the trustee, Irving Picard. Picard had the job of pulling in Madoff assets to distribute to Bernie's thousands of victims. (By late spring 2009, he had recovered just over $1 billion, and was seeking close to another billion dollars—far less than the estimated $65 billion lost in Bernie's Ponzi scheme. Adding insult to injury, Picard was being faced with lawsuits from Madoff victims who didn't like the way he was deciding who got how much.)

In filing the credit card statements and other records, lawyers for Picard said that for many years Bernie's firm "was Bernie Madoff and Bernie Madoff was BLMIS, each the alter ego of the other. . . . The entanglement permitted Madoff, at his whim and desire, to engage in innumerable financial transactions wherein he essentially used BLMIS as his personal 'piggy bank,' having BLMIS pay for his lavish lifestyle and that of his family. Madoff used BLMIS to siphon funds which were, in reality, other people's money, for his personal use and the benefit of his inner circle. Plain and simple, he stole it." Those credit card statements are a mind-boggling snapshot of the Madoffs' lifestyle—very *fancy-schmancy*, as Bernie would say.

Besides Bernie and Ruth, the cardholders included Peter and Marion Madoff; Mark and Andy Madoff, and Andy's soon to be ex-wife, Deborah West Madoff; Peter's daughter, Shana; and Bernie's nephew, Charles Wiener. Among Bernie's loyal top lieutenants at Madoff who used the card were Frank DiPascali, Annette Bongiorno, and JoAnn Crupi. Even the captain of Madoff's yacht, Richard Carroll, made charges.

Probably fearing a paper trail and detesting receipts unless they were from the SEC for delivered documents, Bernie showed no personal charges on the late 2007–2008 corporate card. More than likely, he probably paid for goods and services over the years with a personal credit card or with cash—there was plenty if it always available to him, though it belonged to others.

Ruth was another story. She charged thousands of dollars on the card. Ruth was the ultimate shop-til-you-drop obsessive.

"There's a scene in the mob movie *Goodfellas* where the mobster's wife asks him for some spending money to go shopping," notes a close longtime Madoff family circle observer. "He asks her how much and she holds her thumb and forefinger about an inch apart. *That* was Ruth."

Even after Bernie was behind bars, Ruth was out spending like there was no tomorrow, and she may have realized there was no future left as the scandal escalated and she came under scrutiny. Though Ruth wasn't in court standing by her man when Bernie pleaded guilty and was hauled off to jail to await formal sentencing, his mate of half a century was out shopping a week or so later, according to a longtime Madoff family friend who lost a bundle to Bernie.

Continues the friend:

Unless Ruth was scared for her own protection, she didn't go to court with him.

I expected her to be at his side. I said to myself, "Wow, *this* is interesting. *This* is intriguing." Bernie didn't know whether he was coming back to his $7 million penthouse or if he was getting put in the slammer. Wouldn't you think that she would be by his side?

Perhaps more interesting, Ruth had invoked marital privilege, meaning she would never have to testify against her husband if she didn't want to. The question remained, however, whether she would be formally brought into the case or would be considered simply an enabler—the little-woman-at-home bystander who never questioned how they got all those homes and boats and jewels and cars and all that other stuff they had.

The friend adds:

So while he's in the Metropolitan Correctional Center I see her coming out of this fancy, very expensive home furnishings store on Lexington Avenue in the 60s [where a dinner plate by Raynaud from France costs $118] and she's carrying three large shopping bags. I mean Ruth has everything in the world, and here she is carrying three more shopping bags of stuff—I mean the woman is crazy.

She didn't see me. I said to myself, "Oh, my god, if I come face-to-face with her I'm going to punch her lights out, spit in her face, and get arrested," so I crossed the street.

A few days later my cousin went into the store and asked whether Ruth Madoff was one of the better customers, and they go, "Oh, yeah. She just bought three shopping bags full of china for thousands upon thousands of dollars and she was headed to her Palm Beach estate. We're going to be starving now because he's in jail."

In the wake of that shopping sighting, Ruth was spotted enjoying Palm Beach with some friends—with a precious $7,500 Birken bag on her arm.

The evidence of Ruth's piggishness was in black and white.

Her charges on the Madoff corporate American Express Platinum card just for December 2007 through January 2008 totaled $29,887.94. The total Amex bill for that month for the Madoff clan was $100,121.99, paid in full.

In a one-day shopping spree in Paris she splurged at Armani ($2,000), Jil Sander ($1,237), and a shop called Marni ($555), and back at home her wardrobe bloomed with new things totaling almost $1,800 from Polo and the Diane Firsten boutique in Palm Beach. She charged $5,015 at the Montauk Yacht Club. She used the card for everything from mundane groceries at a Publix supermarket in Palm Beach to a fancy Manhattan shop specializing in "the world's best caviar." There were movie tickets, wine, lots of prescriptions, purchases at Tiffany and Gracious Home, and hundreds of dollars over several weeks in dry cleaning. She even charged charitable contributions—$1,000 to Project Sunshine, $10,000 to the 92nd Street YM-YWHA, among others.

As a commenter on the *New York Times* DealBook blog observed, "This woman used the credit card to make charitable contributions. But it wasn't HER personal card . . . she was using stolen money to contribute to charities. And from whom was the money stolen? Other charities—at least in part. . . . "

Because of her initial failure to show any sympathy or remorse for the Ponzi scheme victims and suspicions that she knew all along what her mate was up to, Ruth had become a pariah in the eyes of the American public, the wealthy circle she had run in, and especially the many investors who had once liked and trusted her.

Aside from being banned from coming to the beauty salon where every month or so for a decade she'd get foil highlights—Soft Baby Blonde, revealed the *New York Times*—done by a colorist whose hair work had been mentioned in fashion magazines, the Pierre Michel salon, also refused her request to do her hair in the privacy of her penthouse.

That wasn't the only place from which she was 86ed.

A florist in Amagansett in the chichi Hamptons, where the Madoffs had a spectacular beach home, refused to do business with her after the scandal broke. Every summer for years the florist had supplied flowers for the Madoffs' annual company beach bash.

Ruth had been a regular at a trendy Upper East Side gym—she liked to keep in shape for Bernie, knowing he had a roving eye and past dalliances—but she stopped going, possibly suddenly unable to afford the $1,200-a-month membership, or actually having been told not to show her face there, or even because Bernie was now locked away and she didn't have to worry about looking good for him. (A joke emanating from the Metropolitan Correctional Center was that obsessively clean and neat Bernie had been renamed "Susan" by other inmates.)

Bernie and Ruth frequently had dined together at fancy Upper East Side Italian restaurants where they walked in hand in hand from their penthouse. But after Bernie was taken down, the owners had a hands-off policy toward the inmate's mate. Marco Proietti, general manager of Bella Blu, didn't think he'd serve her because "People definitely think she knew what was going on . . . one of our customers lost $10 million." Sette Mezzo was another chic Italian eatery where the Madoffs often dined. The general manager said he'd consider Ruth as a customer again—but only if she ponied up the $160 for the bill he was left holding after the Madoffs had dined there shortly before Bernie's arrest.

"She's perceived as the succubus to Bernie's incubus. She was inside a circle of people whose wealth has been sucked out of the system," observed Richard A. Shweder, a professor of cultural anthropology at the

University of Chicago, in a story in mid-June 2009 that the *New York Times* Sunday Styles headlined "The Loneliest Woman in New York."

Not only was Ruth becoming lonely, but she was also experiencing a major lifestyle overhaul.

Ruth was a limo, town car, or worst-case scenario, taxi kind of girl, but the extent of how far she had fallen in the lifestyles of the rich and infamous food chain was graphically documented in the *New York Post* four days before Bernie's sentencing. There she was—in a color photo that practically filled page 3—the despised Madoff wife riding on the New York subway system's grungy F train, transport for the city that never sleeps commoners. Her green eyes covered by trendy aviator-style sunglasses, wearing a sporty outfit that included jeans and loafers, the wife of the most hated man in America was sitting under an advertising sign that trumpeted "99¢ Does More." As the *Post* noted in its caption, the ad reflected "about how much her hubby left some victims."

Spotting the photographer snapping her picture, Ruth snarled, "Are you having fun embarrassing me—and ruining my life?"

The *Post* headline blared: "The Ruth Hurts."

■ ■ ■

Like their mother, the Madoff boys were big spenders, as verified by their charges on the Madoff corporate American Express card.

For a holiday vacation in Wyoming, Mark and Andy Madoff combined racked up more than $35,000 in expenses and other goodies. Despite their royal standard of living, Bernie and his scions weren't known as big tippers—Andy had one restaurant tab for $1,126.41, but left the waiter a chintzy $60.

In a July 2008 Amex bill, Mark charged a whopping $77,388.21 with a Connecticut aviation company for an apparent airplane charter while vacationing in Nantucket. That same month, his brother had charges for the month of almost $19,000, including $4,464 for a flight to Nice in the south of France, and $2,395.41 for casual wear at Ralph Lauren Polo in New York. The total for the Madoffs' July bill was $137,171.01. Every bill was paid immediately.

But their spending wasn't limited to airplanes, vacations, and clothes.

In the months leading up to the patriarch's arrest, the younger generation of the Madoff dynasty were on a home-buying spree—at a time when the nation's real estate market was in the toilet and thousands were being foreclosed on and made homeless. Bernie's boys were spending big bucks for roofs over their heads: Mark Madoff, with a loan from his father, paid $6.5 million for a Nantucket home on more than three acres after selling another Nantucket house for more than $2 million. Two months before his father's arrest, Mark's brother, Andy, also with his father's financing, paid $4.3 million for a condo on the Upper East Side of Manhattan, in close proximity to the building where his cousin, Shana, had planned to live; but then Uncle Bernie was busted.

As the blogger known as "Mrs. Panstreppon," who wrote much about the Madoff affair, observed: "Were the Madoffs trying to stash as much cash as they could in the months before their empire collapsed? Sure looks like it."

■ ■ ■

Bernie's close associates at BLMIS were also racking up charges.

On the August 2008 Amex bill, Madoff associate 52-year-old Frank DiPascali racked up $10,066.81, mostly for eating out. One charge was for $2,355 at a Shell station, apparently to fuel his boat, the multimillion-dollar 61-foot Viking sportfishing craft *Dorothy-Jo*, named after his daughter and wife. In 2007 aboard the boat he won the South Jersey Mid-Atlantic Tuna Tournament, raking in the prize of $55,070. The captain of the *Dorothy-Jo* was listed as an employee of BLMIS. Besides the boat and a salary estimated at seven figures, DiPascali owned a seven-acre estate in Bridgewater, New Jersey—not bad for a high school graduate from Queens who started with Bernie at the bottom and came to work every day in jeans.

Fortune reported in late April 2009 that 33-year Madoff veteran DiPascali—"the chief lieutenant" in Bernie's money-management operation on the 17th floor of the Lipstick Building—was trying to work out a deal for himself with federal prosecutors, although he hadn't been charged with any crimes at the time. The magazine stated, "In exchange for a reduced sentence, he would divulge encyclopedic knowledge of Madoff's scheme. And unlike his boss, DiPascali is willing to name names."

Like DiPascali, JoAnn Crupi, a Jersey girl, was a Madoff employee for a quarter century, and worked in the 17th-floor asset-management area where the Ponzi scheme originated. Court filings indicated that she received $2.7 million from company funds to buy a waterfront home. Before Bernie pleaded guilty in March 2009, Crupi and two other Madoff employees, including DiPascali's brother-in-law, made deals with the prosecutors to talk about DiPascali's role in the company in exchange for an agreement that what they had to say, as long as it was truthful, would not be used against them.

The family's and friends' credit card charges were just the tip of the iceberg of how and where the Madoff money went. Real estate, yachts, private planes, country club memberships, loans, housekeepers, boat captains—"In Bernard Madoff's world nearly everyone seemed to be on the payroll," the *New York Times* observed.

For example, Marion Madoff, Bernie's sister-in-law, was said to have been paid a salary of $163,500, though it was known that she didn't work at the firm. According to a former Madoff executive, Marion's only contact with the company was to have her BlackBerry fixed or replaced, and to partake in the orchids the firm bought.

■ ■ ■

Big so-called loans that never had to be repaid were another perk of being a Madoff.

In December 2007, for instance, a year before Bernie was arrested, Peter Madoff received $9 million in Madoff largesse. The unsecured promissory note had a maturity date of December 2012, with an interest rate of 4.13 percent per annum, and came out of the Madoff account at the JPMorgan Chase bank, where Bernie had been keeping the funds of his money-management clients—the Ponzi victims—rather than actually investing it.

There was speculation that the loan to Peter was used all or in part as a wedding gift for his daughter, Shana, and her groom, Eric Swanson, the former SEC attorney.

Five months after Peter got the loan, the newlyweds paid $2.8 million for a home in the celebrity-studded town of East Hampton, on Long Island. The Swansons also had planned to plunk down a whopping $4.195 million for an apartment in the Diamond House condominium building on the Upper East Side. Their bid was accepted, but then Shana's uncle was arrested and that same day she and her groom withdrew their offer; they claimed one of the rooms was too small.

The Madoff-Swanson nuptials had raised a lot of questions. In May 2009, as Bernie awaited formal sentencing, the inspector general of the SEC, David Kotz, gave the U.S. Congress an update on his internal investigation begun after Bernie was arrested.

While no names were given in the Kotz report, which a New York congressman quickly complained didn't tell enough, CBS News reported in early June 2009 that "Kotz is looking into a former SEC official who allegedly had a personal relationship with a Madoff family member"—a veiled reference to Shana Madoff's husband. The *Wall Street Journal* had previously reported that the SEC was looking into Eric Swanson's relationship with Shana. Swanson had met her "through her trade association work in the industry," according to a spokesman for Swanson. He had left the SEC a year before he married into the Madoff dynasty.

For a decade, he had worked as a senior inspections and examination officer, and his duties included trading oversight at stock exchanges and electronic-trading platforms. At least twice, in 1999 and 2004, he was involved in Madoff firm examinations, according to press reports. It was the Office of Compliance Inspections and Examinations that had probed Madoff, turning up zero evidence of any crime. A spokesman for Swanson said that his client "did not participate in any inquiry" of Madoff "while involved" with Bernie's niece.

Still, at least on the surface, the Swanson-Madoff relationship appeared fishy, and sparked much speculation.

The snarky media web site Gawker, noting that Shana was a fashionista, headlined one story, "Ponzi Schemer's Label-Whoring Niece Married SEC Lawyer."

■ ■ ■

On April Fools' Day 2009, the government started taking away some of the treasured luxuries Bernie and Ruth had accumulated with his investors' money, as Irving Picard had charged. It was the beginning of the federal court–ordered seizure of the $823 million in assets Bernie was known to have just before his arrest, much of it in Ruth's name.

Around dinnertime, U.S. marshals along with members of Palm Beach's finest descended on the Madoffs' $9.4 million, 8,753-square-foot, five-bedroom mansion at 410 North Lake Way, changed the locks, set an alarm, and conducted an inventory of the contents. Property records showed that the house had been purchased under Ruth's name in 1994 for $3.8 million.

The house had a bullish decorative theme that was discovered when marshals spent several hours photographing items in the house for possible eventual removal. "There were bulls everywhere," said Deputy U.S. Marshall Barry Golden. "There were large statues of bulls, small statues of bulls, bull bookends, even bulls on clothing. There's a lot of bull in the house. I've never seen so much bull in my life."

He stated that once the judge signed the seizure order, "It stopped being Bernie Madoff's home."

A "No Trespassing" sign was posted out front.

Further south on Florida's Gold Coast, in Fort Lauderdale, the marshals made another big catch. Just after dawn they swarmed into the Roscioli Yachting Center on the Marina Mile and permanently anchored one of Bernie's prized possessions, his 55-foot, custom-built classic 1969 Rybovich motor yacht that he had named *Bull*. Not long before he was arrested, the $2.2 million boat had been given a complete renovation at a cost of $130,000—from the paint to the keel.

A former close friend who was burned by Bernie in the Ponzi scheme asserts, "Bernie loved that boat more than he loved Ruth.

Believe me when I say that Bernie and the *Bull* were married to one another. He talked about her all the time—*Bull*, not Ruth."

As Robert Roscioli, the marina's owner, said, "The boat is immaculate. It's an antique that has been well taken care of and maintained."

Much like the boat owner's mate.

Golden, the marshall, observed, "A lot of money was put into maintaining that boat. [It] was extremely well kept, extremely clean. The engine compartment was spotless. It looked like somebody took a bottle of 409 and scrubbed it every day."

Shades of Bernie's OCD.

The same day the house and yacht were seized, the marshals also nabbed another of Bernie's fishing boats, a 24-foot Pathfinder—*Little Bull*—that was docked in Palm City, Florida.

A week later, across the pond, French authorities seized the other *Bull* that Bernie treasured—an ultraluxurious $7 million ocean-going yacht, the one he bragged about to David Neff, his clothier in Palm Beach. She was docked at a marina in the chic Mediterranean hideaway of Cap d'Antibes where the Madoffs also owned—in Ruth's name—a million-dollar Riviera getaway located at Villa 2, Chateau des Pins.

The seizure of the yacht—owned by a Madoff company registered in the Cayman Islands—had been demanded by Meeschaert, a French investment manager that was attempting to retrieve losses to clients who had bought shares in a Swiss bank's feeder fund that had invested in Madoff.

"We decided to act quickly to prevent the yacht leaving French waters," said Chairman Cedric Meeschaert.

A heavy chain was thrown around the boat's propeller, and bailiffs posted a warning on the boat, cautioning that "major judicial problems" would result if anyone attempted to sneak off with the vessel.

With Bernie's yachts in tow, a battle ensued between authorities in France and in the United States over the Madoffs' chic French retreat. Both governments wanted to seize the chateau that was purchased under Ruth's name in 2000. Valued at $1 million, it was said to have furnishings worth an estimated $900,000, according to court records.

While the assets seized in Florida and France came off without a hitch, or a fight from the Madoff side, Ruth was reported "ready to rumble" if attempts were made to take her New York penthouse and Hamptons abode, along with more than $60 million in what she claimed were her own private funds—a $17 million bank account and $45 million in municipal bonds. Moreover, she intended to fight for the money from the sale of the Florida boats and home when that happened.

The Madoff attorney, Ira Sorkin, asserted in court papers that the tens of millions in cash and bonds, and the two remaining homes, weren't linked to Bernie's fraud.

But a lawyer representing victims was furious when he heard that claim.

"She wouldn't have it but for her husband's acts and activities," he declared.

Ruth would eventually lose most of it.

■ ■ ■

A skirmish over assets also pitted British authorities against those in the United States. The first round was fired in early June 2009 when Grant Thornton, who was responsible for liquidating Madoff Securities International Limited (MSI) in London, faced off with Irving Picard and victims of Bernie's fraud.

In particular, the American side was seeing red because the Brits had made a sneak attack and seized one of Peter Madoff's toys in Florida, a vintage Aston Martin DB2/4—the James Bond car—valued at $235,000. Wire transfers from the London office to the New York office were used to purchase the classic in the nine months preceding Bernie's arrest. Grant Thornton wanted court approval to take U.S. assets without any hindrance.

If there ever was a Madoff piggy bank, it appeared to be MSI, which was founded in 1983. It was owned outright by the Madoffs—88 percent by Bernie and the remainder by family members. MSI didn't handle private investor money as did BLMIS, and it once did have a legitimate trading business. But it reportedly stopped such activity in the early 2000s and became a "proprietary trading house" that only invested Madoff money. At the same time it was seen by investigators as an entity to pay for the family's extravagant lifestyle, such as Peter's 007 car.

In the month before Bernie's arrest, MSI transferred a reported $164 million to the New York headquarters. British investigators—the government's Serious Fraud Office—were probing the possibility that the London unit was involved in alleged money laundering.

Headquartered on two floors of a Georgian-style townhouse in what was known as "hedge fund alley"—Berkeley Street—in the posh Mayfair district of London, it had more than two dozen employees before the roof fell in. This shocked the UK workers, because in 2008 Bernie was planning for the future; a decade-long lease was renegotiated, and almost $1 million was spent on a new information technology (IT) system and custom office furniture.

Life at MSI had Bernie's signature touch all over it.

The $90,000-a-year manager of the London office, pretty 38-year-old Julia Fenwick, said that Bernie demanded that the facility be the mirror image of the New York office—"everything black and gray."

Fenwick, who had a close friendship with Shana Madoff, was quite aware of Bernie's obsessive-compulsive nature. She told a British reporter:

> We'd spend days before his arrival leveling blinds, making sure the computer screens were an identical height, lining every picture up straight. No paper was allowed on the desks. We'd use black marker pens to touch up the doors. Anything that looked as if it had a mark or a scratch on it, we'd have to retouch. Things like that would drive him nuts.

Fenwick had flown on Bernie's private jet, and like his offices it was painted black and gray. Passengers weren't permitted any carry-on luggage with metal edges or feet so as not to scratch surfaces or tear seats. She recalls Peter Madoff "freaking out and yelling, 'You can't put that there. You might mark something. Bernie would kill me.'"

Bernie and Ruth came to the London operation two to three times a year.

They often traveled with their interior decorator, Susan Blumenfeld, who did his offices, his plane, and even "approved" Ruth's outfits, Fenwick claimed in an interview with the *Daily Mail* in London.

Though Bernie and Ruth dined at fancy Manhattan restaurants, Fenwick noted that in London the Madoffs enjoyed noshing at greasy-spoon eateries, and Bernie wasn't eating kosher, either—she says he savored pork sausages.

For breakfast Bernie always ordered the same sandwich—cream cheese, smoked salmon, and cucumber on brown bread—and both he and Ruth enjoyed the music of Neil Diamond. His expensively cut suits were purchased from exclusive Kilgour in Savile Row near the Madoff offices, and he'd have the tailors come to his office for fittings. Bernie never bothered to buy property in London, but stayed at the Lanesborough, considered one of the world's most expensive and lux-urious hotels, where guests had private butlers assigned to them; the hotel's Royal Suite cost more than $14,000 a night. Bernie always kept a wardrobe of clothing at the hotel, and it would be cleaned and pressed and waiting for him on his arrival.

While Fenwick had a friendly relationship with the Madoffs, Bernie wasn't all that nice to other employees, often using the *F* word. Fenwick recalled him shouting when he got angry, "It's my bat and my ball!"

She says, "He was a bit of a cheeky chappie in some respects" and "a terrible flirt. All the girls in the London office thought so."

One of the office manager's odder experiences with the Madoffs, though, involved Ruth, who demanded that Fenwick handle her pur-chases of a $35 face cream that claimed to reverse the signs of aging.

Miles Goslett, the *Mail* reporter who interviewed Fenwick—who sought and was given money for her story because she received no compensation when Bernie was arrested and the office closed—quoted her as saying, "I had to buy tubs and tubes of Boots No7 Protect & Perfect Beauty Serum. I was buying five or six tubes at a time. We sent them over to Ruth in America. She'd heard about the cream because it had been discussed on television over there, but of course she could not get hold of it in New York, so I bought it for her. It was a key part of her beauty regime."

Fenwick's close friendship with Shana Madoff was the key to earning Bernie's trust. Because of Shana, Fenwick was invited to the 2002
Madoff annual beach party in Montauk, where she noted a rather
bizarre scene. After Mark and Andy Madoff put out the beach chairs,
everyone had to be seated in a specific circular arrangement dictated
by Bernie. In the center were the top traders, and on the far outside
was the mailman.

Shana also invited Fenwick to her wedding ceremony—the marriage to former SEC lawyer Eric Swanson.

When one of the other guests asked Fenwick why she was there,
she jokingly responded, "Oh, I sold my soul to Bernie." Her boss, who
was standing nearby, overheard the remark and told her he intended to
punish her—by making her "sit next to him for the whole evening."

Chapter 13

A Family (and Sometimes an Office) Affair

If Bernie's world in merry old England seemed strange, life at the Manhattan headquarters was even more bizarre. To begin with, the boss had a big say in how the facility was designed, a scheme that appeared to stem from his obsessive-compulsive issues.

Although he had moved his firm to the Lipstick Building in the go-go 1980s because it was so high-tech, the roundness of the structure made him incomprehensibly nervous and uncomfortable. So what did he do? He had the interior and everything in the offices squared off. For whatever reason, he couldn't live with round or elliptical. When the firm moved in, Bernie initially leased only one floor, the 18th, but as business boomed (and more suckers were conned into his investment scheme) he expanded—to the 19th floor and then to a portion of the 17th floor, his Ponzi hideaway.

Madoff's office on 17 wasn't alone. Also on that same floor, but not a part of Madoff, was the headquarters of another major trading firm, Muriel Siebert & Company. Known to Bernie and others in the business as Mickie, she was considered "the first woman of finance" and the first female to own a seat on the New York Stock Exchange. A pal of Bernie's for years, her offices were only paces away from the site of history's biggest fraud, but like so many others, Siebert had no suspicions about his criminal activities.

Besides being a crook, Bernie was a bit of a perv.

Uncle Bernie, as niece Shana Madoff Skoller Swanson affectionately called him, had a thing about coming out of the restroom half unzipped, apparently hoping that his dirty old man act would be a turn-on to his married secretary, Eleanor Squillari, described by co-workers as "once a babe." Bernie, tucking it in, would say to her, "Oh, you know it excites you," she claimed to *Vanity Fair*. He'd sometimes pat her on the behind, and once asked her to hang a head shot of him taken by a celebrity photographer above her bed.

Madoff employees say those kinds of sophomoric sexual shenanigans were not untypical of Bernie.

Bill Nasi, for one, often had to deliver documents to Bernie and usually handed them to Squillari, who he felt was "hot, so to speak." On one occasion, as he stood in front of her desk, Bernie strolled out of his office and "made this really sleazy, sexual comment, and I was embarrassed and shocked. He looked at Eleanor and said, 'Bill Nasi has a massive hard-on for you today.' Eleanor starts laughing and says to me, 'Oh, just ignore him—don't listen to Bernie.' He was probably making those comments to her on and off for years."

A lot of the time it seemed Bernie's actions were dictated by what was below his Gucci belt.

After Bernie's arrest, FBI agents found some interesting and amusing data in his address book that he had left in his briefcase in his private office.

Under the letter *M*, for instance, were the names of women he would often see in the middle of the workday, according to Squillari. The *M* stood for masseuses who presumably offered Bernie a happy ending with his rubdown. His secretary, who had spotted him scouring salacious escort ads in a magazine, had warned him that someone might think he was a "pervert" if they ever saw the notations. She told him, "Keep it up and it's going to fall off." The full-body massages presumably were paid for with the money of investors who would get a very unhappy ending.

But Bernie's massages were the most innocent and least costly of his philandering, Madoff sources reveal.

"Bernie wasn't so faithful to Ruth," says a veteran female Madoff employee with close ties to the family. Some years back when he was in his 50s he had started having affairs in and out of the office, cheating on Ruth like he would cheat his investment clients. The veteran employee continues, "He had affairs in the office. There were two women I know of. They were gorgeous. They were blonde. They were young. They were like baby Ruths—the same type as Ruth with the same hair color and eye color. Ruth found out and told him to stop, and to get rid of them. He had to buy a few women off—things got a little too crazy. One of them told me she got bought off. "

Another longtime Madoff employee supports the claim. "Some of these young girls that worked there for a year left with big hush money checks in their purses. Bernie was screwing some of those secretaries. The guy who signed the checks told me one of them left with $250,000 in her purse."

Having had his office romances nailed by Ruth and others at Madoff, where everyone kept their eye on everyone else there, especially Bernie, and gossip and rumors flew faster than an electronic stock quotation on the trading desk, Bernie consequently was forced to seek female companionship on the outside. According to a Madoff insider, Bernie had begun still another serious flirtation with a young executive secretary at another brokerage firm that BLMIS did business with. Says the person:

> Ruth told him to stop [playing around], but he started having affairs all over the place. Unfortunately, I knew because a friend of mine was a friend of the woman involved. She told me Bernie was always trying to woo this secretary, her friend, to have an affair. He gave her his card with his own personal cell

phone number. I'm not a prude. I know it exists. I know people do it, but I didn't want to believe it about Bernie. But my
friend showed me the business card and I knew it was Bernie's
handwriting.

After Bernie's arrest, a woman who had claimed an office affair
with him approached the *National Enquirer* through a publicist offering
a tell-all in exchange for $100,000. An editor says he felt her fee was
too high and didn't further pursue her story.

In late March 2009, the *New York Daily News*, in a story headlined
"Was Ponzi Man Bernie Madoff a Philanderer, Too?," quoted two
sources as saying that he had "carried on at least one affair" during his
marriage. The straphanger tabloid reported that Bernie "once had a
thing" with a woman at a "major media corporation" who was "attractive and Jewish. He was quite generous with her. He used to fly her
around." The paper quoted another source stating, "When Ruth found
out about it, Bernie agreed to end the affair."

Madoff was a mini Peyton Place, and even the sexual persuasion of
certain female employees were often bantered about. Bernie is said to
have enjoyed the girl-girl intrigue, especially because two of the lovers
had high profiles within the company.

Despite all of these the salaciousness, Bernie and his secretary,
Squillari, had a good working relationship. She apparently didn't mind
his off-color innuendos and didn't feel she was being sexually harassed,
or at least didn't make an issue of it because she had a good situation
working at Madoff—that is, until her boss was arrested, and then she
spilled some of the beans, talking about her years with the fraudster, his
wife, and sons to *Vanity Fair*, for which she was said to have been paid.
She parlayed the interview into a *Today* show appearance and secured
her 15 minutes of fame by becoming part of Madoff history. Though
she had worked closely with Bernie since the late 1980s, she claimed
no knowledge of his crimes.

At one point in their working relationship, Bernie had been asked
to fire Squillari—by no less a power than someone from the New York
Catholic Archdiocese. "The archdiocese had called Bernie and wanted
a dozen tickets for a Yankees game, but they only had 11," recalls Nasi.

"Someone there talked to Eleanor and she told them there wasn't an extra ticket, and they were really angry and asked to personally talk to Bernie. A few minutes later he came out of his office and told Eleanor, 'They told me I should fire the person they were talking to.' So Bernie told Eleanor, 'You're officially fired. You're not here anymore. I just fired you. I told them I would fire you to keep them happy. What assholes!' "

Nasi believed the archdiocese had called Bernie for the prized Bronx Bomber tickets because "they had invested with him. I heard they had a pretty nice bundle of money with him, so they wanted some free tickets."

■ ■ ■

Apparently, Jewish charities and organizations weren't the only victims of Bernie's fraud, as it turned out. Catholics also got nailed to his cross.

While the New York archdiocese didn't show on the massive Madoff victims list, the Redemptorist Fathers of the Baltimore Province, a worldwide order officially called the Congregation of the Most Holy Redeemer, suffered "significant" losses, and feared having to "reduce, suspend, or cancel" some of their ministries. They'd been invested in Madoff since the early 1990s, and money from their investment was "used to fund Catholic-school scholarships for inner-city children, to train future priests and brothers, to care for elderly members, and to fund other pastoral ministries, such as financial support to those suffering from the ravages of Hurricane Katrina and the Tsunami of December 2004."

The Redemptorists were among at least three Catholic groups listed as victims. Others included the St. Thomas diocese in the Virgin Islands, which lost a reported $2 million, and St. Thomas Aquinas High School in Fort Lauderdale, Florida. The St. Thomas Aquinas High School campus housed a new and ultramodern arts center named after Michael Bienes, the Jew turned Catholic who along with Frank Avellino ran one of Bernie's earliest feeder funds. Bienes had pledged $2.5 million to the school, but after Bernie admitted the scam Bienes claimed he was taken, too, and couldn't meet all of his pledge to the school. Listed as the representative for the St. Thomas account was Monsignor Vincent Kelly, who was the supervising principal and reportedly a Bernie victim. (Monsignor Kelly later denied that the school was an active investor in Madoff, but said it had been back in the 1990s.)

Known for his glibness, Bill Nasi observes that Bernie was an equal-opportunity crook.

"On Mondays and Tuesdays he wore a turban, on Tuesdays and Thursdays he wore a yarmulke, and on Sunday he wore a bishop's miter."

■ ■ ■

Shana Madoff, Bernie's niece, was the source of much office gossip and backbiting, mainly because she was considered bossy and demanding—a "royal bitch and pain in the ass," as one less than diplomatic Madoff veteran describes her.

Shana was a graduate of the University of Michigan, where her cousin Mark Madoff also had matriculated, and had graduated from her father's law school alma mater, Fordham. Soon thereafter, around 1995, she came to work for her uncle and father as the rules compliance officer in the market-making area of Bernard L. Madoff Investment Securities.

A tall, slim, sexy, dark-haired fashionista with a little-girl way of talking, the Madoff princess, then 26, fell in love with a handsome, charismatic knight in Armani by the name of Scott Ira Skoller, then 30, whose divorced mother, Trina, was a pediatric nurse in New Orleans. Skoller was a clothing salesman at Tyrone—the elegant men's clothier specializing in Italian designer sportswear and suits in Roslyn, on Long Island, where Bernie and his brood lived for years. Although Tyrone was on a par with upscale Trillion, Bernie's favorite Palm Beach haberdasher, Bernie never once set foot in Tyrone.

The lovebirds were married on December 7, 1997, the 56th anniversary of the Japanese attack on Pearl Harbor. Even though her elegant nuptials were held at the fancy Pierre Hotel on Fifth Avenue, her parents, Peter and Marion, were said to have rued the day—viewing their daughter's marriage as their own personal "date that would live in infamy," mainly because they felt she could have done better for herself, husband-wise.

"Peter said, 'My daughter's not marrying a clothing salesman,'" says a longtime Madoff family intimate. "Deep down, her parents were embarrassed by Scott's job, so Peter said he told Scott, 'You have to become a partner, not just a salesman,' and Peter started saying, 'Shana's not just married to a salesperson in a clothing store. I bought him into the business. I bought him a partial ownership in the place.'"

But that wasn't what had transpired.

According to Richard Bucksbaum, owner of Tyrone, Skoller never had an equity stake in the business; he was simply the clothing manager, but "the best" Bucksbaum ever had.

Bucksbaum says that from his perspective he never got any indication that Skoller's in-laws were unhappy with him.

He observes:

Scott was a charming man and a great salesman, and I think that whatever Peter and Marion's darling daughter wanted was good enough for them.

If Shana wanted to marry this guy, Daddy was fine with it because the Madoffs had all the money in the world.

Marion's jewelry alone was *phenomenal*. They were probably the richest family out here, so who Shana married didn't really matter to them. And Scott was *so* presentable, and *so* charming to people that it didn't matter what he did for a living. It wasn't like he was a ditchdigger.

He was always very well dressed, very good-looking, tall, athletic, a very good golfer and tennis player. He fit right in with anybody and everybody. He befriended people very easily. He liked the wealthy, and he definitely was a social climber.

Skoller had known Shana from high school on the north shore of Long Island, and the two reconnected later through a mutual friend, as Bucksbaum recalls Skoller telling him. "Scott was a bit of an opportunistic kind of person and saw a good thing when he found it—and that was Shana."

Bucksbaum was one of the guests at Shana and Scott's "lovely, beautiful, not over the top, in very good taste" wedding, and he and his wife sometimes socialized with the younger couple, who were living in a fancy condo on East 54th Street in Manhattan. After Shana had her daughter, Rebecca, mother and child would sometimes stop in the store to say hello. Peter Madoff also became a customer. "He wasn't snobbish, but he wasn't warmhearted, either," and he didn't become a feeder fund of customers for Tyrone. "I wish he had [referred his friends]," says Bucksbaum, "but he wasn't [a source of new customers]."

With all of Skoller's qualities, Bucksbaum was surprised that he wasn't brought into the royal court of the Madoff family business where Shana was said to be making at least $500,000 a year.

"I don't think Scott was asked to join the business," reckons Bucksbaum. "He wasn't a college graduate, and he had no financial acumen. I think eventually he wanted to own his own men's clothing store. That was his passion—clothing was his passion. That was what he knew, and Shana was making the money, so I don't think money was an object or problem for them."

Bucksbaum always had in the back of his mind that if he decided to retire, Skoller, backed by Madoff money, would have bought his store.

"But it never came to that because it was a short-lived marriage, about three or four years," he says. "Scott just came in one day and threw up his hands and said, 'I've had enough! I'm separating from Shana. Maybe I'll go back and maybe I won't.'"

He didn't, and they were divorced.

Years later, Tyrone was hit hard by the Madoff mess.

"I had a very upscale clientele until the Madoffs did in a good portion of them," maintains Bucksbaum. "The area that we are in is very close to Glen Oaks Country Club and Fresh Meadow Country Club, where the brothers recruited people as investors, and a lot of the people in the neighborhood got creamed. A lot of my customers got hit—and hit bad. There have been times we've called customers and told them, 'It's the beginning of the season—come on in,' and they'll say, 'Look, I lost a lot of money with Madoff, so call me when you're having a sale.'"

■ ■ ■

There was at least one commonality that Shana Madoff and her ex-husband had—both were clotheshorses. Black was the new black to Shana—the color she wore most of the time. Like her Aunt Ruth, Shana dressed chicly, but conservatively, favoring designers such as Narciso Rodriguez, whose dresses and shoes she came to admire when she was a law student and saw a photo of his clothes on the chic wife of John F. Kennedy Jr. She developed a relationship with a boutique in Manhattan's trendy meatpacking district, and every season the salespeople who dealt with her automatically sent Narciso's creations, and she was charged for everything that wasn't sent back.

Whatever Shana wanted she got.

In a profile of her and two other trendy fashion-forward types for the fall 2004 fashion issue of *New York* magazine, she described how she was leafing through a magazine while tanning on the beach in the Hamptons with friends. She suddenly left the crowd, cell phone pasted to her face, telling her pals she had to make an important call. It wasn't about Madoff business, however. In the magazine she was reading she was knocked out by an expensive tweed Prada bag, and she just had to order it; thus the emergency call.

"If I see something I like, I call around," she stated in the *New York* magazine piece. "I just don't have time to shop . . . because I could be doing so many other things that are so much more productive."

Co-workers at Madoff recall they got a hoot out of that one.

They say that Shana, described as "a diva," was constantly gallivanting off to shop during the workday—or having other Madoff worker bees run personal errands for her.

Toniann Astuto, hired at BLMIS as Shana's $40,000-a-year assistant in 2001 after the previous assistant threw her hands up and quit, characterized her as "an absolute princess."

Her attitude, and what she did, wasn't really professional. She'd leave in the middle of the day to go to a doctor's appointment or to go to yoga. She was very involved all the time with fashion. She wore all Diane von Furstenberg, and she was *always*

ordering clothes and shoes and sending them back and ordering them again. She was very fickle. She'd go and she'd order
all these shoes, and then she'd decide she only wanted one pair
and send the rest back.

Though Astuto was hired to assist Shana with her important compliance duties—making certain the BLMIS traders had proper registrations and followed other rules—she seemed to be spending most of her
time as Shana's personal slave.

She really didn't do much for herself. I had to make all of her
travel arrangements and take care of her personal mail, and
I was always sending stuff back to stores for her. She had a
housekeeper and a nanny and she had somebody who shopped
for her groceries.

Astuto asserts that Shana spent only half her time on the job—and a
lot of that was doing "human resources" work rather than compliance—
and the other half dealing with personal stuff. "When she really needed
to, she would spend more time on [compliance] work-related things,
like if we were being audited. She was always on top of the traders,
always monitoring their continuing education."

Another veteran female Madoff employee viewed Shana as "a
spoiled brat. She'd make the firm's chauffeur take her dog's specimens
to the vet. She was despicable. She had no sense of money, no sense of
responsibility. In one year she spent $50,000 on cell phones. Her dog
would break her phone, or her daughter would break her phone, and
she'd want new ones, the best and latest, all the time. She'd say, 'My
name is on the door. Do what I want you to do. I'm a Madoff.' She
relied on secretaries whose asses she worked off. Their responsibilities
were ridiculous, and she had many secretaries quit on her. She used
and abused her employees."

Others, however, took a far different view, and maintained that
Shana was driven and dedicated at her uncle's firm, and was well-
respected in the financial community.

The Girl Scouts of America, for instance, honored her as a "woman
of distinction" at the organization's 16th annual Women of Distinction

Breakfast a little over a month before her uncle was branded a crook. Deborah Norville, the anchor of the tabloid TV show *Inside Edition*, was the mistress of ceremonies. One of the Girl Scouts' benefactors was Uncle Bernie himself, a former Boy Scout. The underwriter of the event at the New York Hilton was the Bank of New York Mellon, where Bernie had assets that were frozen after his arrest.

Early in her Madoff career, Shana had spent a lot of time in Washington, D.C., where she rubbed shoulders with regulators. She served on the compliance advisory committee of the Financial Industry Regulatory Authority (FINRA), and in the same capacity at the Securities Industry and Financial Markets Association, the lobbying arm for the industry. After Bernie was arrested, she resigned from those groups. While at sessions involving such organizations, she met her future second husband, Eric Swanson, formerly of the Securities and Exchange Commission.

The two were married in late September 2007 at the trendy Bowery Hotel attended by more than a hundred guests, many of them soon to be Ponzi victims. At the glam affair, Bernie jokingly stated that his niece was marrying "the enemy." Also in 2007, while sitting on a business panel discussing the workings of his firm, Bernie talked about SEC regulation and got a chuckle out of the audience when he bragged that he had a "very close" relationship with an SEC lawyer, and "in fact, my niece even married one."

Curiously, while there was a wedding announcement in the *New York Times* for Shana Madoff's first marriage, none could be found for her fancy nuptials with Swanson, which raised the question: Did the Madoffs feel it was better not to advertise the union because it might raise red flags—a big announcement that the compliance officer and family member of a firm already suspect was betrothed to a former lawyer for the government agency that polices such firms?

Those who contended that she was a devoted workaholic pointed out that while the newlyweds were on their honeymoon in the Caribbean, according to a source who talked to the *Wall Street Journal*, Shana spent so much time arranging for speakers for an industry event that her groom "threatened to throw her BlackBerry into the ocean, or lock it in the hotel safe."

People close to the Madoff-Swanson merger wondered whether it would last longer than the Madoff-Skoller marriage.

■ ■ ■

Meanwhile, back at the office before Bernie's niece remarried, Astuto says she spent more time dealing with Shana's social schedule and making arrangements for her personal travel than handling official business.

"She would change her mind on a whim," the former assistant states. "She'd say she wanted to go to St. Bart's and stay at a certain hotel and leave and arrive at a certain time. I'd make the arrangements, and then she'd say, 'I changed my mind. I don't want to leave that day. I want to leave the next day.' And then of course she'd get there and hate the hotel. She'd call me at all hours and say, 'This hotel isn't nice enough. Find me a nicer one.'"

After her divorce from Skoller and before she met Swanson, she got a reputation among her office associates as a partier. Her lifestyle was alluded to by her own brother, Roger, in his memoir. Astuto says that Shana was always asking her and other younger women in the office who were "wild" to go out clubbing with her. (Astuto therefore was relieved when she transferred from running errands for Shana to working for Madoff Energy, headed by Andy Madoff.)

That wild period of Shana's life was the source of much chatter around the watercooler at Madoff.

"She brought some of the guys she dated into the office," asserts a colleague with close ties to the Madoff family. "They were really the low of the low. She must have met these people in clubs at three in the morning. They were all losers. And then I finally met Eric [Swanson] and I thought, 'Oh, God, he's a nice guy.'" This person felt speculation was absurd that Shana had become involved with Swanson because of his SEC connections. "I think she's cold. I think she's shallow. I have zero respect for her. But who the hell would really marry someone just to protect her uncle's business? That's going too far. I would *think* that the girl had to have a little more self-respect."

Bernie didn't particularly like his niece, whether or not she got into bed with "the enemy."

At Ruth's suggestion, Bernie always had expensive orchids ordered for the office—"off the charts in terms of cost"—and also delivered to the homes of family members. Since Bernie liked black and gray, Shana took it upon herself to have all the orchids delivered in black porcelain pots to match the office décor.

A colleague recalls:

Bernie freaked.

He says, "What the fuck's going on? Who did this? The orchids are supposed to be in clay pots like always." When the person who followed Shana's instructions explained the situation to Bernie, Bernie called Shana on the carpet. "The only fucking people that decorate this office are me, Ruth, and Susan Blumenfeld. Don't nobody listen to Shana." She said, "But Uncle Bernie, everything is black." It blew up in her face.

When they got orchids for the office, every Madoff got extras, which the firm's drivers had to deliver to their respective houses. Shana's mother, Marion, who was nice, but prissy nice—that's the way Bernie felt about her, and he put her down a lot behind her back—had a temper tantrum because the stem of one orchid leaned over a little. She called the office and said, "Get these out of my house—and if someone's not here in an hour . . ."

■ ■ ■

While the relationship between Shana and her husband was under a prosecutorial microscope for any possible conflict of interest, her cousins, Mark and Andy Madoff, also being looked at by investigators, were hit with bombshell lawsuits in mid-June 2009 that alleged they knew about their father's Ponzi scheme, assertions that had long been denied by them.

The suits were filed in Manhattan Supreme Court just two weeks before their father was to be sentenced.

For all of the Madoff principals in BLMIS, it seemed as if the walls were closing in.

The suits, seeking $1.77 million—miniscule in comparison to other lawsuits in the overall Madoff scandal—were brought by Reed Abend and Richard Stahl, both of whom worked in BLMIS's proprietary trading business. The brokerage, the legitimate arm of the Madoff empire, was sold for as much as $25.5 million—to be distributed to Madoff victims—to a Boston firm formerly known as Castor Pollux Securities. The principals, Frank Petrilli, former chief of TD Waterhouse, and Robert Mazzarella, former president of Fidelity Brokerage Services in Boston, renamed the new acquisition Surge Trading Company. Pending approval by the Financial Industry Regulatory Authority, Surge Trading was scheduled to be operating by late summer 2009 in the same space in the Lipstick Building that Bernie's firm utilized before he was arrested.

In the court papers, the former Madoff traders, Abend and Stahl, alleged that the Madoff brothers "perpetuated a fraud of their own on their employees," and charged that Mark and Andy "had long known that their father's advisory business was an illegal enterprise" but failed to disclose it "to induce plaintiff (and others) to continue to earn legitimate profits."

The Madoffs had claimed no knowledge of their father's crimes, and were the ones who had turned him in to authorities after he was said to have admitted to them that he was a fraud.

Stahl, who demanded $1.3 million, and Abend, who sought $474,000 in his suit, charged that they were promised $75,000 salaries plus 25 percent of the profits from their trades. Stahl said he made $5 million in profits and Abend $2 million before the firm was liquidated "and did so during the worst market sell-off in recent memory." They asserted they were not paid the money Madoff owed them for 2008.

They both stated in the court papers:

It is universally recognized that while most of Madoff Securities was a giant Ponzi scheme, the trading business managed by the Madoff sons was a legitimate enterprise that earned legitimate profits. . . . It is now clear that the Madoff sons had long known that their father's advisory business was an illegal enterprise, and that criminal conduct threatened the trading business and each of its employees. Nevertheless, in order to perpetuate their father's lawless conduct, the Madoff sons made false statements to plaintiff (and other employees) and failed to disclose Madoff Securities' criminal actions in order to induce plaintiff (and others) to continue to earn legitimate profits.

The 10-page complaints brought up the *Barron's* red-flag-raising article in 2001, and revealed how the Madoff brothers allegedly brushed it off.

... the Madoff sons told the employees of the trading business ... that suspicions raised by the article were not true. The Madoff sons went on to state falsely that Madoff's investment advisory business was completely legitimate. The Madoff sons knew that these statements were false when they made them, as evidenced by, among other things, that the Madoff sons were Madoff's children and assisted in the management of the business.

About a month and a half after Bernie was arrested and his firm became a crime scene, the out-of-work Abend saw the 42-year-old Andy Madoff buying take-out chicken on Manhattan's Upper East Side and confronted him, demanding to know, "Where's my money?" Andy is said to have responded, "What about *me?*" The two sparred back and forth as Abend followed Andy to his car, where the divorced Madoff son's fiancée, Catherine Hooper, waited. According to a report in *Vanity Fair*, Abend shouted, "Is that your new whore girlfriend?" With that, Andy slugged him, got in his car, and sped off.

■ ■ ■

In many ways Andy and Mark were mirror images of the first-generation brothers of the Madoff dynasty, Bernie and Peter. Like his uncle Peter, Andy was thought by friends and associates to be the smarter of the two brothers. He was Ivy League, and had studied in an undergraduate Wharton School program at the University of Pennsylvania. He was the brother who knew the technical side of the business, the computer-savvy guy, while Mark was a chip off the old man's block—he even pledged Sammy, Sigma Alpha Mu, when he was at Michigan, the same party-boy Jewish fraternity that Bernie had joined during his one year at the University of Alabama.

Mark was the outside guy, so to speak—the gregarious one whom everyone at BLMIS seemed to like. He was hailed for running the firm's trading arm with an even hand, whereas Andy was considered tough, standoffish, and outright rude at times.

For one thing, Andy didn't particularly like Charles Wiener, the director of administration for BLMIS, who was the son of Bernie's sister, Sondra. Charlie, as he was known, had started on the trading desk in the 1970s. The general feeling was that he was there only because he was Bernie's nephew, and a relative to whom Bernie didn't particularly take a liking.

"He always wanted to fire him, but Bernie kept him around because of his sister," says a BLMIS and Madoff family insider. "Charlie was a sweetheart, adorable but not the brightest light in the chandelier."

Andy Madoff kept Charlie at a distance, but he found himself together with him one summer day as they were headed to the Hamptons in an SUV for the Madoffs' annual summer party. When they reached Bernie's Amagansett manor, Andy let loose on his cousin, according to the Madoff insider.

> Charlie says to the driver, "Can you wait a minute? I just want to go in and say hello to my uncle." And Andy turns around, glares at him, and yells, "What the fuck are you doing? It's bad enough my father has to see your face all week long. The last thing he wants is to see you tonight when he's got to see you for the rest of the weekend!"

■ ■ ■

Besides the Ponzi scandal, Andy had a tough period, having had cancer but surviving it, unlike his cousin Roger.

His marriage also fell apart after 14 years.

In January 1993, in a beautiful ceremony presided over by a rabbi at the very WASPy Union League Club in New York, 25-year-old Andy had married 24-year-old Deborah Anne West, daughter of Douglas West, a New York investment broker, and Susan L. West, then the managing editor at the Bantam Doubleday Dell Publishing Group. At the time, the bride, a graduate of Duke University, was a book promotions consultant.

Their wedding announcement in the *New York Times* described Andy's mother as the "director of administration" at Bernard L. Madoff Investment Securities.

At the time of their wedding, Debby was working in publishing for a children's book club, and by coincidence was the assistant to the young woman who would marry Mark Madoff. She was described as "cute and sexy" by a friend of the couple. "Her family didn't have anywhere near the money the Madoffs had. As my mother would say, Debby 'stepped in shit' when she married into the Madoff family—meaning she hit it big in a family with lots of money and a majestic lifestyle."

The Madoffs had two girls, who were sent to one of the best private schools in New York.

After they separated in 2007, Andy began dating Catherine Hooper—a cute, fresh-faced, outdoorsy, formerly married young woman who stands a foot and half shorter than Andy. One thing the two had in common was fishing, of all things. Hooper had been a cover girl for a magazine called *Fish & Fly*, which did a profile on her and her love of fishing. A 1994 graduate of Bryn Mawr College, she once wrote an article for the alumni magazine about a trip to Venezuela "to learn to fly-fish for bonefish." The article was accompanied by a sexy shot of her, all wet in the water holding a big, slimy bluefin trevally. "In the space of two years," she wrote, "fishing has taken me to places I would never have dreamt of, has introduced me to people whom I am blessed to know, and helped me overcome the barriers of fear that held me back from fully enjoying my life."

The world of Madoff was one of those places.

Like his father, Andy was an avid fisherman—back in high school Bernie had made up that story about a fictitious book he had read called *Hunting and Fishing*, and among his prized possessions were his luxurious sportfishing boats. Andy headed an investment group that bought a fishing-related company called Abel Reels, and had also invested in a Manhattan fishing supply store called Urban Angler Fly Shop. Hooper, whom Andy planned to marry just around the time his father was arrested, was reportedly a former co-owner of Urban Angler.

■ ■ ■

Like Andy and cousin Shana, Mark Madoff also had a first marriage that failed even though he and his wife were considered a "golden couple—a Jewish Barbie and Ken."

A woman who was in the Madoff boys' circle growing up in Roslyn on Long Island, where both Madoff boys went to the public high school, recalls how girls swooned over Mark.

> He's always been incredibly handsome—Robert Redford handsome—and was about as straight an arrow as you're ever going to meet. Andy was the smart one. But they were both very popular in high school, and Mark was certainly *very* popular at Michigan.
>
> He was sort of a golden boy—a good athlete, a great skier, you know, the sort of privileges that come with being a rich kid. He did everything well, was sophisticated, traveled all over with his family. Every vacation was like a ski trip or summers in the south of France, and this was as he was growing up and it continued into college. Mark was a very likable Jewish prince—but conservative. In college he drove a Honda Accord. He was definitely a *mensch*.

The woman became a member of the Madoff family circle and bonded with Ruth, who she says was "always perky, warm, lovely. Anytime I did anything with the family they were wonderful to me. Bernie would take us out to dinner when we'd go to Montauk. They just could not have been warmer and more inclusive."

Noting the stories about Bernie's obsessive-compulsive problem, and how he wanted everything in his offices to be black and gray, and how he wouldn't let Ruth sit on their penthouse antique furniture, she says he was the same way at home at the Montauk beach house.

"It's fairly austere and impeccable, and it's all grays," says the woman, who worked in publishing. "Bernie was *so* strict about how things should look. He gave us strict orders on how to fold the comforters a certain way. If someone tracked sand into the house he went bananas. He demanded that everything be in the proper place. But the only person who stood up to him was Mark's wife, Susan. She was not afraid of Bernie. She did not take any of his shit. She would just tell him to fuck off."

It was Bernie and Ruth's longtime friends the Kavanaus—Joe and Jane—who played Cupid, sort of setting Mark up with the daughter of close friends, pretty Susan Freeman from Rye Brook, New York, who also went to the University of Michigan, as did the Kavanaus' daughter. Jane Kavanau recalls:

I said to Susan, "Oh, you're going to Michigan, too. I know a very cute guy going there. He's handsome," and I said in jest, "He has *lots* of money." I told Ruth about Susan, too, and eventually Mark and Susan met, so in a way we were sort of responsible. Mark was so handsome and Susan so adorable.

"They *were* the golden couple," says a close friend of the former Mrs. Mark Madoff who was also at Michigan at the same time. "They met freshman year, fell in love, and saw each other through all four years of college. Susan and Mark actually look like brother and sister—both are blond and beautiful—the Jewish Barbie and Ken. Susan was very bright, popular, sharp, a lot of fun, from just a kind of average middle-class family."

After graduating from college, the two lived together in a spectacular midtown Manhattan doorman-attended apartment building owned by Bernie's pal Fred Wilpon, who also owned the New York Mets and was one of the victims of Mark's father's fraud. In their mid-20s, Susan Freeman became Mrs. Mark Madoff in "a classy and lovely, understated and tasteful" wedding held at the Fresh Meadows Country Club in Great Neck—known as the "Madoff country club" where later a number of wealthy members became Bernie victims.

Mark and Susan had two "adorable" children, and eventually moved, the close friend says, "to a house that was like to die for"—a $6 million mansion in ritzy Greenwich, Connecticut.

Then the marriage went south.

"Susan's a very feisty girl. As one of our mutual friends said, 'She's always full of piss and vinegar.' She likes to fight, have lots of drama, and I think she just kind of got bored with Mark. It was sort of like a midlife thing. They were in a rut."

The two got divorced, and both remarried—the former Mrs. Madoff married a man with whom she had gone to high school, the friend says—and both Susan and Mark had children with their new spouses.

Like everyone else, the close friend was dumbfounded when the Madoff scandal broke. She says, "I do not believe Mark had any involvement, because he's such a straight arrow. He told some friends, mutual friends, that he had no idea what Bernie was doing, and he hasn't spoken to his parents since it happened. As shocked as I am about Bernie, I would be more shocked if Mark and Andy knew."

■ ■ ■

In late October 2007, 14 months before Bernie admitted to committing the largest known fraud in history, he was invited to be the honored guest alongside other Wall Street icons such as Muriel Siebert at a panel session to discuss the future of the stock market.

The session was sponsored by the Philoctetes Center for the Multidisciplinary Study of Imagination, and held at the organization's Manhattan headquarters. The center encouraged discussions on all sorts of subjects, including business.

After Bernie's arrest it was revealed that the foundation that funded the center's work was heavily invested in Madoff and was a victim of Bernie's massive fraud.

The foundation was the brainchild of wealthy New York commercial real estate mogul Norman Levy, who died in 2005 at 93. In a paid death notice in the *New York Times* he was hailed by a friend who wrote: "Your spirit and love of life have changed all who knew you. You taught me so much. I'll cherish our friendship forever."

The friend was Bernie Madoff.

Though Bernie was a quarter century younger than Levy, the two had developed a close bond and immense trust. Levy was like a father figure to Bernie. He had invested heavily in Madoff, though suspicions were later raised that Levy—who once owned the Seagram Building skyscraper in New York—might have had knowledge about some of what Bernie was up to.

In any case, Norman's son, the novelist Francis Levy, had financed the Philoctetes Center with $950,000 of Levy Foundation money. It was the younger Levy who invited longtime family friend Bernie to appear on the panel at the center and discuss the world of Wall Street and investing.

After Bernie was arrested, Levy quoted his late father as declaring, "If there's one honorable person, it's Bernie."

One would never have guessed in a million years watching Bernie pontificate and boast at that panel session moderated by Justin Fox, *Time* magazine's "The Curious Capitalist" columnist, that this hero of Wall Street was nearing the nadir of his secret criminal scheme. Bernie appeared relaxed, confident, articulate, and funny at times. Wearing a black suit, his long hair expensively cut, a crisp white shirt open at the collar, his legs crossed, he seemed to all concerned like the Master of Universe he was—at that moment in time.

In introducing Bernie, the low-key, boyish-looking Fox noted:

> That name may not say a lot to you, but go over to Madoff and you talk to Bernie and he mentions, "Oh, by the way, 10 percent of stocks traded in the United States are going through this firm right now." It's one of those really important parts of our financial system that doesn't show up in the headlines.

Later, after Bernie was behind bars awaiting sentencing and with dozens of tentacles of his crime stretching around the world, Fox, a veteran business reporter, acknowledged that he wished he had done some hard research on Bernie beyond a routine googling before moderating the panel discussion and tossing softball questions.

He told the author he was unaware of the earlier *Barron's* story and didn't know anything about the allegations Markopolos had made. "I googled Bernie to see who he was. I had never heard of him before I was asked to moderate." He acknowledged that "at some level" the session was like a virtual infomercial for Bernie, "but that's what most of these panel discussions end up being. They're not the same as journalism. I had no idea he basically had a giant hedge fund on the side."

Several weeks before the event, Fox says, he was invited by Bernie up to his office in the Lipstick Building to "brainstorm" what would be discussed. "When he called I thought he was offering lunch, but there was no lunch on offer. We talked about the panel, and how to make it work." He says Bernie asserted no ground rules.

> Then he walked me around the office, but sadly not to the 17th floor. His offices were just very weirdly quiet and uninhabited. I actually asked him about that, and he said that since 9/11 he had a backup facility "so I basically have to have desks for everybody in both places." That was questionable. My take on him was that he didn't project this I'm-a-big-deal-CEO thing. He was much more a little bit aw-shucks, but then occasionally hitting you with things about how important he was. He's good at that, actually—kind of throwing in "I helped set up Nasdaq, but I'm just Bernie Madoff, the boy from Queens."

However, a careful analysis of some of the things Bernie had to say that day, according to a transcript and video, was quite revelatory in view of what came to be known about him.

Bernie told the gathering, "Wall Street is one big turf war . . . by benefiting one person you're disadvantaging another person, and the basic concept of Wall Street, which sometimes regulators lose sight of, as do the academics, is it's a for-profit enterprise," which got a big laugh from the audience. He noted that Wall Street "is one of the few industries where the cost of doing business had dramatically increased" for firms like Madoff, and "the cost of regulation has dramatically increased. Now, no one is going to run a benefit for Wall Street"—more laughter—"so whenever I go down to Washington and meet with the SEC and complain to them that the industry is either overregulated or the burdens are too great, they all start rolling their eyes."

He revealed that "the big money on Wall Street is made by taking risks."

Firms like BLMIS, he noted, were forced into taking risks because they "couldn't make money charging commissions . . . because of the regulatory infrastructure you had to have dealing with clients," and he stated that the "great majority" of income came from "risk taking. . . . That's where the money is made."

He even gave Mrs. Madoff a big plug, and made her sound much more like a decision maker at the family firm than had been previously known.

When the discussion turned to the types of people who work for a firm like BLMIS, he recalled how he'd hired MBAs as traders, and how that wasn't the perfect situation. "Then we went through another stage. Actually it was my wife [the math whiz in high school and college] who said, 'Why don't you hire math people? Why don't you go to MIT and hire math people, because everything you're doing is related to algorithmic trading and they're probably the best people.'"

Bernie said Ruth's suggestion didn't work out because, "They just spend too much time thinking. . . . You could actually watch them; they would deliver an order. My brother and I and my sons would look at them saying, 'Well?' And they would say, 'I'm getting there.' By that time the price would usually have moved against us."

He said that BLMIS, like all brokerage firms, was "very carefully enforced and surveilled. It doesn't mean there are not abuses, for sure, but by and large in today's regulatory environment, it's virtually impossible to violate rules. . . . If you read things in the newspaper and you see somebody violate a rule, you say well, they're always doing this. But it's impossible for a violation to go undetected, certainly not for a considerable period of time."

As one participant who was present at the session observed after Bernie's arrest, "If there had been a bullshit detector present in the room, it would have exploded."

■ ■ ■

Another who asked some questions at the session and didn't feel he got straight answers was Daryl Montgomery, a 49-year-old independent equities trader, who headed a group of people interested in the stock market called New York Investing Meetup.

Montgomery says he was aware of who Bernie was, that he had headed Nasdaq and was helping to run markets, "but not that he was the biggest crook on earth." After seeing and hearing Bernie for the first time, he states, "He was not a great intellect, and was fairly insubstantial, but that is very common for people that have these big positions—pleasant but don't seem incredibly bright."

Montgomery is further convinced that people who invested in Bernie and got big returns didn't want to hear anything bad about him, whether it came from *Barron's* or Markopolos. That's why they continued to invest. He says:

> The people investing with Madoff were for the most part multimillionaires, and those people would never have believed, no matter what anyone would tell them or what could have been explained to them, that Madoff was a crook.
>
> We actually predicted the credit crisis in July 2007. We said the Fed was not going to be able to fix the problem. We said the stock market was going to peak. We said in September 2007 there's a recession. We pointed out that Bear Stearns was going to go under. We predicted Lehman would go under many months before it did. And every time we did this, people left the group.
>
> They'd tell me the economy is more resilient, America is more resilient, these things can't happen. People do not like to hear negative news. In fact, there is some psychological research that indicates that even if you explain to people that something is an investment scam, it might make them more likely to invest in it.

Many of Bernie's victims, as it turned out, felt that way.

Chapter 14

Another Arrest, and Blood Relatives Get Taken to the Cleaners

Despite all the suspicions and investigations and proliferating civil lawsuits, the only other person arrested in the Madoff scandal in the days after Bernie's guilty plea was his accountant, handsome 49-year-old David G. Friehling, who more resembled the character Carlo Rizzi in *The Godfather* than a nerdy numbers cruncher. But according to prosecutors, Friehling was quite creative.

Amazingly, virtually none of Bernie's thousands of hoodwinked investors, or other financial advisers, ever questioned the fact that the financial messiah in whom they had so much trust, the Wall Street guru whom many begged to take their money, had an accountant who worked out of a dumpy 13-by-18-foot storefront office in a drab strip

of offices in the hamlet of New City, across the Hudson River and
about 45 minutes from Madoff headquarters.

He was a red flag, if there ever was one.

It was like the equities trader Daryl Montgomery observes—no
one questioned or wanted to believe that Bernie was a rotten egg, as
long as those beautiful earnings statements arrived in the mail, and
extraordinary returns kept coming despite all the warning signs.

For more than a decade, Friehling, of the firm Friehling &
Horowitz—Horowitz being Friehling's father-in-law, Jeremy, who had
retired to Florida in 1997 and later died of cancer at the age of 80,
curiously on the morning Bernie pleaded guilty—handled all of the
auditing for Bernie's crooked investment advisory business.

Charged with securities and investment adviser fraud linked to
the Ponzi operation, Friehling surrendered to federal authorities in
mid-March 2009, about a week after Bernie was sent to jail, and was
released on $2.5 million bond.

The six-count criminal complaint charged that Friehling, who was
licensed with New York State as a certified public accountant (CPA)
in 1987, "deceived investors by creating false and fraudulent certified
financial statements for Bernard L. Madoff Investment Securities LLC
and its predecessor Bernard L. Madoff Investment Securities and caus-
ing those certified financial statements to be filed with the United
States Securities and Exchange Commission and sent BLMIS clients."
The government also charged that Friehling "caused false and mislead-
ing certified Bernard L. Madoff Investment Securities audit reports to
be filed with the SEC" beginning in December 2004 and continuing
through December 2007.

In exchange for his services that had escaped detection for years,
Friehling received handsome returns from Bernie—he was paid
$12,000 to $14,500 per month between 2004 and 2007, the government alleged.

"Mr. Friehling is charged with crimes that represent a serious
breach of the investing public's trust," declared acting U.S. Attorney
Lev Dassin, who was in charge of the Madoff investigation. "Although
Mr. Friehling is not charged with knowledge of the Madoff Ponzi
scheme, he is charged with deceiving investors by falsely certify-
ing that he audited the financial statements of Mr. Madoff's business.

Mr. Friehling's deception helped foster the illusion that Mr. Madoff legitimately invested his clients' money."

Beyond Friehling's alleged rubber Madoff stamp, the accountant and his wife had a more than $500,000 account with BLMIS.

Friehling was initially scheduled to appear in court on June 17, 2009, and the expectation was that he would either be indicted by a federal grand jury or cop a plea. There was speculation among knowledgeable observers that he was cooperating with prosecutors in exchange for a lighter sentence, or in the best-case scenario for immunity if he had hard evidence that went beyond Bernie's admissions—evidence of conspirators, evidence of where the billions went. He faced a maximum of 105 years in prison if found guilty, and also faced civil charges by the Securities and Exchange Commission (SEC).

But the June date came and went after prosecutors received a 30-day extension—until July 17, 2009—stating they were seeking a possible "disposition"—boilerplate legal jargon that left it up in the air as to whether a plea deal was in the works. What it did mean was that talks were ongoing between the prosecutors and Friehling's lawyer. In mid-July 2009, he pleaded not guilty, waiving an indictment, which meant no grand jury review. Another hearing was scheduled.

Before his fall, Friehling had been on the board of the Rockland County, New York, chapter of the New York Society of Certified Public Accountants, and had once served as its president.

The day Jeremy Horowitz died in Florida, his son, Irwin, posted the following tale of woe on a web site:

> The irony that Bernard Madoff pled guilty to 11 counts of fraud, perjury and money laundering on this day is beyond measure. My father's passing has become part of this great American tragedy. He served as Mr. Madoff's auditor for over three decades, before handing it off to my brother-in-law. He never suspected the crime that was happening.
>
> These last three months, since the Madoff scheme became public, have been a living nightmare for my entire family. This has been especially true for my father, who had spent his entire life building up both a reputation for honesty and integrity as well as an investment nest egg that would provide for my parents'

retirement. His reputation has suffered mightily simply from the association with Mr. Madoff.

■ ■ ■

No investor with Bernie appeared to have been left unscathed—not even Ruth's own older sister, Joan Alpern Roman, and her husband, Bob Roman. He also swindled his own sister, Sondra (Sonnie) Wiener, and her son, Charlie, the head of administration at BLMIS.

In mid-June 2009, with Bernie's sentencing looming, the Romans filed claims in the Madoff bankruptcy case—Joan for $2.7 million, and her husband, Madoff's one-time insurance agent, for $8.7 million. Three of the Romans' daughters also had Madoff accounts, according to the BLMIS victims list, but they hadn't filed any claims. It was possible, since the list covered all past and present investors in Madoff, that they had taken their money out. Whether Joan and Bob Roman had taken money out through the years was not revealed. Also of interest was whether it was Ruth rather than Bernie who had enlisted her sister into Bernie's investment advisory-cum-Ponzi scheme.

"Joan's very nice and *totally* unlike Ruth," observes a Madoff family intimate.

> While they're sisters, their personalities and mannerisms are like night and day. Ruth is prettier, dressed better, but Joan is down-to-earth, a lovely person. Unlike Bernie, Ruth generally did like her sister. They shared times together. They made time for each other with or without their husbands.
>
> Bob was the firm's insurance agent, and Bernie didn't like him. But he felt he was stuck with him because of Joan. So in the end he screwed them all, and in the end Ruth had to know her sister was getting screwed. Bernie felt he was stuck with all these people because he had to appease Ruth.

The Romans were among the blood relatives, like Mark and Andy Madoff, who had received those bizarre packages of gifts that Bernie had sent out on Christmas Eve 2008 after his arrest—care packages supposedly set aside by Ruth during their marriage that included what his attorney described as "sentimental personal items." The goody bags included about $1 million in jewelry—Cartier and Tiffany watches, a ring, a diamond necklace, and other bling. When the prosecutors learned what Bernie had done, they charged that it was a way for him to "dissipate" assets, while Bernie's lawyer contended it was all done in innocence as a way for Bernie to "reach out" to beloved family members.

The Romans, in their early 70s, young-looking, sprightly, in very good health, and living the snowbird Florida lifestyle, were in desperate straits after Bernie was arrested, according to a close Madoff family friend who grew up in Laurelton and also knew the Romans in Florida. Until the time of Bernie's arrest the Romans didn't have a worry in the world, living quite comfortably in a beautiful Boca Raton condominium.

Says the friend:

> The reality is that they were basically retired and definitely happy and contented—and now they're working very hard to make ends meet.
>
> Joan lost a lot of money. She's certainly not in the financial position she was in before the scandal. They had been living very nicely. She told me she was "stunned like everybody else, just absolutely *stunned*!" She couldn't believe what happened, and she didn't believe that Ruth was involved. Joan is not a devious person at all. She's very quiet, straightforward, and honorable. In the early years she had a career, an interesting job— she worked for Time-Life in an administrative capacity—and had nothing to do with Bernie's business.
>
> After they lost all the money, Joan was very eager to have an income. She's quite discreet, good at office-type work, so she got together with a woman in Florida who was starting a business and who needed part-time help, and Joan got the job that is basically like a clerk. It's very sad and very depressing and shocking that Bernie would do that to his wife's sister.

If he financially wiped out his sister-in-law, he seemed to have had no qualms about taking his own 74-year-old sister for at least the $3 million she had invested with him. Sondra Madoff Wiener and her husband, Marvin, now a retired dentist, had even been introduced to each other back in Laurelton by Bernie and his high school friend, Elliott Olin. Because of her brother's scam, the Wieners were forced to put their gated 3,409-square-foot, three-bedroom home in the very upscale Ballen Isles Country Club area of Palm Beach—the same exclusive water-view enclave where Serena and Venus Williams lived—on the market.

Like the Romans, the Wieners also reportedly received Bernie's Hanukkah gift package and were forced to return it. Afterward, they put their home up for sale at $950,000 in a dreadful south Florida real estate market. Their real estate listing said the house had a pool and spa, included a golf cart, and offered the "best water view" with sunsets every evening. Country club membership in the Wieners' complex ranged from $35,000 to $115,000—and was a requirement when they bought the property in 2003 for $650,000.

The *New York Post*, under the headline "Madoff Blistered His Sister," quoted her son, David, as saying, "My family's a victim. More so than anybody else. It's very painful."

His brother, Charlie Wiener, the 30-year veteran BLMIS executive, was also victimized by his boss. Having lost an investment in the millions, he and his wife, Carolyn, were forced to put their four-bedroom, ranch-style Centerport, Long Island, home with a dock on the market for $1.3 million. "I can't afford it anymore," he told a reporter. "We have to move." He called what Bernie did to him "emotionally devastating to our entire family. . . . [We suffered] a devastating financial loss. It's been a painful experience."

Around the time Peter Madoff's son, Roger, was struck down by leukemia, the Wieners' daughter was stricken with a form of blood cancer, but fortunately recovered.

As with regard to his sister-in-law, Joan, his brother-in-law, Bob, and his nephew, Charlie; Bernie didn't appear to care much for his own sister, Sondra.

"Charlie told me that he felt Bernie didn't like his mother," says a former BLMIS veteran. "When Sondra would call Charlie at the office and after they chatted for a while, she'd ask his secretary to be transferred to Bernie. She'd be switched and Bernie could see on caller ID that his sister was on the line, and he would tell Eleanor [Squillari] to tell her he wasn't available, that he was in a meeting or out of the office. He'd just ignore her. He didn't want to deal with her. He had no time for her."

■ ■ ■

A number of Madoff employees, an estimated 20 percent of the 180 or so who worked for the firm, were wiped out by Bernie's swindle. Some lost more than $1 million, their life savings. Moreover, most couldn't find jobs because of the dark cloud of the Madoff name that was now part of their resumes. The only bit of luck they caught was that their 401(k)s had been transferred to a third party outside of BLMIS to be administered, so they at least had those—although much of their savings in the 401(k)s had been devastated in the stock market crash.

While Bill Nasi wasn't invested in Madoff, he says his 401(k) had lost $30,000. "But thank God someone in that company had the foresight to say that the pension plan would not be handled in-house. Thank God they farmed them out to Fidelity. But I told the guys at work, 'Why couldn't Bernie get arrested back in June or July before the great Wall Street meltdown? We wouldn't have lost as much.'"

Nasi offers that he wouldn't know what to say to Bernie if he was given the opportunity to sit down with him face-to-face in prison. "That would be very difficult to do," he observes, "because I think I would just start crying. Here's a guy who just destroyed all of us, all my friends, all my co-workers. Forget about the nameless, faceless charities and the people that have really big money. He screwed up the lives of everyone who worked for him, all my friends there, even the ones that didn't have any money invested. I considered these people almost like family members, and he screwed all their fucking lives up."

Some fell into deep depression because of their losses, and others went into hiding. Still others had to find jobs—and that was not easy. Besides the recession with few companies doing any hiring, they carried the toxic stain of the infamous Bernie Madoff.

Toniann Astuto, who had a newborn and a five-year-old, went job hunting and was greeted with outright contempt and disdain.

> I went to one employment agency and one of the women there was really unpleasant to me. She first says, "That's a horrible suit you're wearing." And I said, "All right, I'll wear a different suit." And then she says, "I don't like the typing on your resume. I don't like the font." And the list was going on and on and on. I finally said, "Well, I did have a job. I do have excellent experience."
>
> And then she finally glared at me and said, "Just look at who you worked for. You worked for *Madoff*! Why don't you go from one criminal organization to another? Go apply to the Mafia!" I was in shock. I said, "Are you kidding me? If I had skimmed off some of the $50 billion, do you think I'd be here looking for a job?"

■ ■ ■

Stanley Shapiro wasn't a full-time Madoff employee, but he showed up on the firm's list of employees as being one, had the use of a desk and a phone, and enjoyed being around the action. A multimillionaire who had made a fortune in the women's apparel business, he was in his 80s, owned a Park Avenue co-op, had a place in the Hamptons, and wintered in Palm Beach. He was a high roller, and one of Bernie's loyal cronies going back many years.

"Bernie used to come into the office and say, 'Where's that *alta kocker*? Send him to me so we can kibbitz,' " recalls a Madoff insider. "He and Bernie hobnobbed all the time—dinners in Palm Beach, lunches together in New York. Stanley wasn't on salary. I think Bernie may have had him listed as an employee for insurance purposes—so Stanley could get insurance. He used to come in every day and pay his bills and schmooze about the stock market. Bernie just wanted one of his old friends to feel young."

Some years back Shapiro had been part of the triumvirate that included Bernie and Bernie's longtime associate, Martin Joel. And like the late Joel and his survivors who lost a bundle in Bernie's fraud, Shapiro was also a victim of his longtime friend with whom he puffed $10 Davidoffs in the fancy cabanas at the Breakers in Palm Beach.

Shapiro "took a real beating" in Bernie's fraud, says a friend. "Stanley was flipping out. Besides his own investments with Madoff, Bernie did the trust of Stanley's four grandchildren. His health has suffered."

Shapiro—short, thin, extremely sharp and erudite—was at his desk at BLMIS the day Bernie was arrested. Bill Nasi says Shapiro, in a state of shock, walked over to him and said, "I just lost $100 million. I'm like I'm 19 years old again. I have to go back to work. I have to find a job."

Shapiro says a business associate introduced him to Bernie in the 1960s when he was just starting out hawking over-the-counter and penny stocks, and he started "directly" investing with him. "It was a one-on-one because my associate, who I considered to be very well informed, told me he was doing well with Bernie. I had every reason to believe that Bernie was just buying and selling stocks on my behalf."

Shapiro invested with BLMIS for at least four decades, and got Bernie's monthly statements. "I don't recall taking money out," notes Shapiro, "but I do recall giving."

By the 1970s, Shapiro had gone from being simply an investor to becoming a part of Bernie's social circle, a "friendship which grew more in the 1980s and 1990s and this century."

Until he became a victim, Shapiro had had great affection for his investment messiah and friend.

> He had a great sense of humor, he was very considerate, and it's now going to sound peculiar, but I actually trusted in him. Our relationship was always very congenial, and very easygoing. Bernie was very giving of his time, and of his money, and of his possessions. He was not the kind of guy who would ever quibble—"It's my plane, it's my boat." He never was possessive of those things. He was always very sharing with them, and on top of that, so was Ruth. Ruth was socially more than acceptable. She was always vibrant, always happy, and always charitable in complimenting people and sensitive to their needs. It's very

funny in retrospect that they were a very congenial couple, and always pleasant to spend time with.

And then came Bernie's arrest, and the revelation of his mind-boggling fraud.

"My wife and I are still in shock over the whole thing," says Shapiro. "She and Ruth became at least as close as Bernie and I."

■ ■ ■

In the weeks leading up to Bernie's sentencing, U.S. District Judge Denny Chin, who was applauded for ordering Bernie incarcerated and out of penthouse detention after he pleaded guilty, received letters from more than a hundred victims—ranging from their 30s to their 90s—telling their hellish stories, and asking the jurist who would pass sentence to give no hope or forgiveness. The victims called Bernie a "monster" and a "serial criminal." The letters were made public.

A 61-year-old widow who lost everything wrote, "Mr. Madoff has wreaked havoc on our family."

Another woman wrote, "I can't tell you how scattered we feel. It goes beyond financially. It reaches to the core and affects your general faith in humanity."

A man wrote, "According to Madoff's last statement for November 2008, I had $2 million. Two weeks later I was bankrupt."

A New Jersey man explained that his parents had lost their life savings—money that was put away to help "my brother, who is mentally retarded."

A 76-year-old Korean War veteran said Bernie's swindle had left him destitute. The man said he was forced sell his car and his home, could no longer afford health insurance, and was now living with his daughter.

A woman investor noted in her letter about Bernie, "You are a murderer. You committed generational theft."

An 81-year-old woman from Pennsylvania declared, "He has condemned his investors to a life of hell, while his hell will be the prison you sentence him to."

Another stated, "At the age of 89, I find myself and my wife (86) devoid of future hope. I find it hard to believe what he did to us and . . . all the charities affected by this Bastard."

A mother of three who had lost her life savings wrote, "I often feel as if life is futile. Why bother to do 'the right thing' when it doesn't mean anything?"

A 52-year-old Florida victim wrote, "Due to his egregious deeds, Mr. Madoff deserves no better than to live under a bridge in a cardboard box, scavenging for his food and clothing, living the existence which he has undoubtedly relegated some unfortunate victims to. Instead, he will be allowed to serve his sentence in the relative comfort of prison, being guaranteed food, shelter, clothing, medical care, and treatment."

And a former Madoff employee, an 18-year veteran, wrote, "In December 2008, we lost our jobs, our health coverage, and most importantly, our trust in a company that we worked tire-lessly to build."

A woman who noted that her elderly father had lost his life savings wrote, "I thought no day would be as bad as 9/11. . . . Bernie deserves a longevity pill—not death—so he can watch each generation suffer and watch what he did."

It's one thing to lose one's life savings; it's another thing to lose one's life.

Bernie, the swindler, could also be thought of as Bernie, the mur-derer. As he spends the rest of his life behind bars, he does so with blood on his hands because two of his Ponzi victims, depressed about being fleeced, committed suicide.

The first was the French aristocrat and co-founder of the money management firm of Access International Advisors, 65-year-old Rene-Thierry Magon de la Villehuchet, whose body was discovered at his desk in his 22nd-floor office in a Manhattan building. He had slashed both of his wrists and a bottle of pills was found nearby, but he had left no suicide note. What was known, however, was that he had placed $1.4 billion of his investors' money into Madoff, and all of it was lost. And his entire life savings were wiped out.

After his suicide three days before Christmas 2008, while Bernie relaxed in his plush penthouse under house arrest, de la Villehuchet's Parisian brother, Bertrand, told reporters, "For him, it was a positive act of honor. He brought his friends and clients, and a lot of them were his friends, to a catastrophic situation."

More to the point, though, were the comments of de la Villehuchet's widow, Claudine, who a week before Bernie's sentencing broke her silence and declared in a TV interview, "He killed my husband. I think he's a murderer."

The other suicide victim who had been fatally attracted to Bernie's promises of financial wealth and security was 65-year-old William Foxton, a retired British army major, who shot himself to death on a Southampton, England, park bench in February 2009 after losing everything he had invested with Bernie. Foxton's 28-year-old son, Willard, pledged to himself to find out who this guy Madoff was and how and why he did what he did to his father and others. "I wanted to take all the medals my father had won for gallantry and throw them into Bernie Madoff's face, to make Madoff know the sort of man he killed," Foxton told the BBC. On his U.S. journey to probe Madoff he encountered other victims, such as a woman named Norma Hill, who after her husband had passed away decided to discuss his investments with Bernie.

She met with him personally. She told the BBC:

> He appeared to be a really nice, kind man, sort of like anybody's grandfather. He put his arm over my shoulder and he looked at me and he said, "Don't worry, everything's going to be fine."

She believed him and left her husband's investment with him for two decades. She lost it all, and expected she'd have to sell her home.

The former New York City police officer who served as Bernie's bodyguard during his penthouse confinement and who accompanied him to court says that Bernie never for a moment showed any remorse for what he had done, or any compassion for any of his victims during the time he spent with him. His only concern, the ex-cop said, was that the SUV that transported him didn't have blackout windows, allowing news photographers to take pictures of him. Bernie left that complaint on the bodyguard's answering machine, the tape of which was played on *20/20*.

■ ■ ■

The emotional words and the immense losses of regular middle-class, everyday Americans who were hoping through Bernie, or through a Madoff feeder fund, to have a better life and a secure future made it difficult for many to have much sympathy for another breed of victim of his crimes—the big-name celebrities from the world of entertainment who claimed losses.

As one close observer of the Hollywood and entertainment scene notes:

> There was great schadenfreude beside the pool at the Beverly Hills Hotel when it became known that the likes of Steven Spielberg, who has more money one can ever imagine, and Larry King and Kevin Bacon and others like them, who generate huge incomes and are treated like royalty, had lost money to Madoff. Hollywood and the entertainment world are all about greed and making more and more money. Bernie Madoff underscored the Hollywood vibe. They'll all continue to do well. No need for tears for them.

Most, if not all, of the celebrities taken to the cleaners by Bernie had invested through feeder funds and did not even know of Madoff until he was arrested.

For some, like 51-year-old Bacon, best known for his role in the film *Footloose* a quarter century ago, the publicity his victimization generated in the media was possibly worth more than his loss, which was never disclosed. His story was carried around the world and constantly referred to in the media. A few weeks after Bernie's arrest, the actor offered a few a boo-hoo words to a celebrity weekly: "We'll march on. We have to. There's nothing you can do about it," he was quoted as saying. And he announced, "I don't have anything lined up right now, but I need to work, for obvious reasons." (He later claimed to the web site The Daily Beast that he was misquoted and taken "so out of context.... I'm hoping that story becomes old news as soon as possible. . . . I'm working on stuff, you know, developing stuff." But the first interview in *Life & Style* got all the attention and garnered all the sympathy.)

His interview appeared in mid-January. A month later, however, he had a presumably well-paid starring role in a well-received HBO film appropriately called *Taking Chance*. Moreover, his actress wife, Kyra Sedgwick, star of the popular TV series *The Closer*, earned a reported $300,000 an episode. In mid-June the high-earning Sedgwick, who had just been honored with a star on the Hollywood Walk of Fame, went public, acknowledging, "We did not lose everything. We lost hard-earned money that we worked very hard for that was [in] what we thought . . . [was] a safe place. It's painful, but a lot of people lost a lot more."

Actress Jane Fonda, ex-wife of billionaire Ted Turner, was starring in a hit Broadway show in the weeks right after the Madoff scandal struck. Between acts during rehearsals, she jumped on her laptop to blog to her fans about everything from doing "pilates" with someone named Kimberly, to rehearsing for the second act and being "blown away by the set and the lighting," to getting fleeced by Bernie.

She wrote:

I was thinking today on my way to the theater how grateful I am to be working, never mind doing something really exciting. So many aren't. I ache when I read about the layoffs. I've lost a lot but it's nothing compared to friends of mine who have lost everything they had because every penny they saved over their entire lifetimes was invested in one of Maddoff's [sic] schemes. I read a few days ago that Maddoff [sic] was complaining that he felt like a prisoner in his own penthouse! I want to shake him till his teeth fall out. No matter what happens once this play opens, I won't be complaining. I feel blessed. I also feel tired. Enough.

A commenter on the Fonda blog, which had a huge fan base, responded, "The nerve of that Maddoff [*sic*]. Not that I'm rich or any-thing, but I just opened a pension plan and I freak out every time I hear about that guy in the news."

Lawrence Harvey Zeiger, better known as popular $7-million-a-year CNN interviewer Larry King, reportedly lost more than $1 million in the Ponzi scheme. King and Bernie had a few things in common. Both had been born in Brooklyn, and, like Bernie, Larry had faced criminal charges once upon a time himself. On December 20, 1971, he was charged with grand larceny involving $5,000, and had his mug shot taken at a police station, resulting in his suspension from a job he had at a local Miami radio station. "My lawyer thought we could beat the charges," King wrote in his 2009 autobiography. In the end, though, the case was dismissed because the statute of limitations had run out.

After Bernie was in the slammer, the eight-times-married King interviewed Donald Trump and asked, "How did he [Bernie] get away with it?" Answered The Donald, "Because people were stupid enough or foolish enough to just keep pouring money into his accounts. . . . They'll probably change the name of Ponzi to Madoff. It was really the ultimate scheme."

After he was fleeced by Bernie, King privately consulted over corned beef sandwiches at his favorite Beverly Hills deli hangout, Nate'n Al, with another poster child of Wall Street greed, "Junk Bond King" Michael Milken, who went to prison for almost two years in the late 1980s for securities violations stemming from an insider trad-ing investigation. The tabloid celebrity web site TMZ ran an exclusive photo of Larry sitting opposite Milken in the deli. The caption said, "Larry did a lot of listening during the meet as Michael spoke almost nonstop."

Spielberg's and Jeffrey Katzenberg's Wunderkind Foundation suffered some losses. Former baseball great Sandy Koufax, the Hall of Fame pitcher, was listed among the Madoff victims, as were the actor John Malkovich and the estate of John Denver. The Hollywood screenwriter and Madoff investor Eric Roth, who had won a Golden Globe for *The Curious Case of Benjamin Button*, told the *Los Angeles Times*, "I'm the biggest sucker who ever walked the face of the earth."

■ ■ ■

In her 90s and confined to a wheelchair after having suffered strokes, the famous-for-being-famous Hungarian-born Gabor sister, Zsa Zsa, and her ninth husband, 65-year-old Prince Frederic von Anhalt, lost practically all they had salted away for their old age through a feeder fund that placed celebrity money with Madoff.

Von Anhalt says that he had been personally advised to meet with a representative of the fund by Zsa Zsa's close friend Merv Griffin, the billionaire creator of *Wheel of Fortune* and *Jeopardy*. Griffin, a one-time popular TV talk show host who made a fortune in everything from hotels to casinos to real estate development, died at 82 in August 2007.

"We lost about $10 million," says von Anhalt, speaking from a cell phone in his Rolls-Royce outside the Beverly Hills mansion Zsa Zsa bought with the proceeds from her divorce years earlier from the hotel baron Conrad Hilton, the late great-grandfather of party girl Paris Hilton. "We invested in a California company and they in turn invested in Madoff. We didn't know anything about Madoff—never met him, never heard of him. Nothing."

Von Anhalt says he was having lunch with Griffin at the trendy Café Roma in Beverly Hills and mentioned that he and Zsa Zsa wanted to invest some money and get a decent return.

> Merv was a very good friend of my wife, Zsa Zsa, and her sister, Eva. Everybody knew and trusted Merv. He was a great guy, very rich. He always invested very well, and he recommended me. I told him, "We want to invest some money. I want a good return. What can I do? You're the master. You're very rich. Give

me some advice." And he said, "I know a good company. I have somebody very good if you want a big return. I have somebody you can trust in." I trusted Merv, and I invested in good faith.

There was no problem for about five years, the length of time the money was locked in. Von Anhalt continues,

We got great returns, about 8½ percent quarterly, better than a bank. We could live on the interest. We could pay our bills. It was wonderful. It was like life insurance. And we still had our $10 million. When the contract ended, I planned to renew for another five years, but I wanted to take $2 million out, and wanted to lock in the remaining $8 million.

He made the request for the money but it was not forthcoming. When he questioned why, he says he was told, "We're having a problem. It's going to take a little longer." All of a sudden everything was blocked. "I called my lawyer, and then I heard about Madoff and I was told that's why I wasn't getting the money. So I said, 'I don't give a shit about Madoff. I invested in you.' "

Six weeks later Bernie was arrested, and the money was lost.

Von Anhalt said he and Zsa Zsa might be forced to sell their house "if we don't get money flow. I don't know what's going to happen. We're in a big hole. We have big overhead. We may have to take things to a pawnbroker, but I don't want to think about that."

He said the investment was a mix of Zsa Zsa's money and his.

I took all my money from German banks and put it into this fund. It was only earning 3½ percent in Germany, but I should have left it. But people get greedy and you think you can make more. And everything *was* wonderful. It worked out perfectly—until I wanted to take out some money. Now I've got nothing. When I told Zsa Zsa what happened to our money she nearly had a heart attack. I had to defend myself in front of my wife, which wasn't easy because when this first happened the finger was pointed at me and I was accused of putting the money in another corner. But she trusted me.

He said that if he had an opportunity to meet with Madoff he wouldn't say anything to him.

"I would take a baseball bat and hit him over the head."

■ ■ ■

John Robbins and Bernie Madoff were as different as chopped liver and tofu.

While Bernie was considered a Wall Street guru before his Ponzi scheme caught up with him, Robbins became a guru of the vegetarian movement. He had everything growing up that Bernie didn't have— enormous wealth and luxury, all of which he later turned his back on.

His father was Irvine Robbins, the son of Polish and Russian immigrants, who took a $6,000 bar mitzvah gift and parlayed it into what became the Baskin-Robbins ice cream chain, with more than 1,600 stores throughout the United States, Canada, Japan, and Belgium. Along with his brother-in-law, Burton Baskin, the two entrepreneurs conceived such offbeat flavors as Pink Bubblegum and Daiquiri Ice. Their logo, a cherry and chocolate sign along with the "31 Flavors" concept—one flavor for each day of the month—became a pop culture icon and a symbol for a great American dessert treat. The two men became extremely wealthy.

In John Robbins' home growing up in Encino, California, the swimming pool was shaped like an ice cream cone, and inside the spectacular Robbins manse was, naturally, a soda fountain that offered guests all 31 flavors. Everything was ice cream–related, even the family yacht that was christened *The 32nd Flavor.* Each and every day, John's father ate three or four scoops of ice cream. He lived to be 90, but had developed diabetes. He died in May 2008.

But John Robbins long before had turned his back on the family fortune and how it was made. In his early 20s, when his father hoped he'd take over the Baskin-Robbins empire, he expressed his negative feelings about the effects on health of eating dairy products, and about the materialistic world he saw growing up. He detested ice cream and felt it caused illnesses such as diabetes. In 1967, an uncle died of a heart attack. He believed the uncle's death and his father's diabetic condition were caused by consuming too much of the family's 31 flavors.

He believed in natural foods and the vegetarian lifestyle. "I didn't want to sell a product that hurts people's health. I made a choice for integrity."

In 1987 he wrote a best seller called *Diet for a New America*, an expose that targeted the fast-food, junk-food industry. One of his later books, *The Food Revolution*, dealt with environmentalism and food consciousness.

To some, he lived a Spartan, almost hippie-like existence in Soquel, California, in the Santa Cruz Mountains, with his wife, Deo; son, Ocean; daughter-in-law, Michelle; and twin grandsons, River and Bodhi, who had disabilities. He sought a simple but honest lifestyle. Unlike his boyhood home, his own house, including three offices, operated on self-generated solar energy and encompassed eight rugged acres.

Still, Robbins was entrepreneurial like his father. He was the leader of a movement and his books sold almost as well as ice cream cones, and he didn't despise money. A guest appearance on *Oprah* gave him national recognition and enormous book sales.

Robbins started investing in Madoff through a friend and attorney he trusted in Marin County, California, Richard Glantz. Like so many others, he received steady and favorable returns. While capitalism wasn't part of his lifestyle, he didn't feel he was violating any of his principles, and eventually put all of his book royalty earnings and speaking fees, which were substantial, into Madoff through the lawyer's feeder fund. Robbins knew others who had similarly invested—many of them were enormously wealthy—so he felt his money was in good hands.

When the 61-year-old vegetarian author's name showed up on the list of Madoff victims—he lost his entire life savings of more than $1 million, 98 percent of his family's net worth—the vegetarian movement took action and began a fund-raising drive for Robbins and his family. They were so financially devastated by Bernie's Ponzi scheme that Robbins and his wife were forced to take in tenants, and she had to work part-time jobs.

"I don't see us as a charity case," he told a local newspaper. "There are people who are in worse straits. I appreciate the love that is coming to us."

As for Bernie, Robbins declared, "This wasn't a bad investment. This was a theft, a criminal action."

■ ■ ■

Richard Glantz, the 64-year-old trusted lawyer to whom Robbins had given his money for investment, told the author he created a Madoff feeder fund because:

> I wanted my family and some close friends to have access because I thought Bernie Madoff was an opportunity who could help people. I was not doing it for profit. I charged nothing. I've been with Bernie a very long time and made a lot of money with him. Bernie wasn't opening accounts for people [with] less than a million dollars, so I thought I was doing people a favor—and I actually was doing them a favor for many years. They had an opportunity to get 10 percent a year, or whatever the return was, and I know that outstripped what you [typically] see in the stock market.

Glantz is one of the few Bernie feeder funders who has spoken out about his dealings through the years with Madoff.

Asked whether he ever questioned the steady and continual returns in good and bad economic times, and whether he saw such returns as a red flag of a possible scam, Glantz says that when he asked Madoff about what was going on he got all kinds of complex answers, gobbledygook about split strike conversions that Bernie claimed was his strategy, one that few understood.

Glantz had personally invested with Bernie, too, he says.

> I would never put anyone in anything that I wasn't in—and I lost everything. I lost millions of dollars. *Everything.* I have to sell my homes.

Glantz had learned about Bernie from his now-deceased accountant father, Edward Glantz, who had a long, complex history with Madoff. The senior Glantz along with his then accounting partner, Steve

Mendelow, were feeders for another Madoff feeder fund, the one run by Frank Avellino and Michael Bienes. Glantz and Mendelow had offices on the same floor as Avellino & Bienes in a New York office building and, according to an SEC complaint, collected $89 million in investor money for Avellino & Bienes that was then funneled to Bernie Madoff. All of that ended when the SEC shut down the Avellino & Bienes firm in 1992.

"My father told me what he was doing," says Glantz, "and I was skeptical. But after I watched him invest with Bernie with our family money, I decided I'd do it also—you know, the guy was head of Nasdaq, he had a high rating as a wholesale dealer, and a wholesale dealer is an insider."

In 1988, John Robbins had started an international nonprofit organization called EarthSave to promote healthy, environmentally sound food choices and to raise awareness of "the ecological destruction and cruelty linked to the production of food animals." The organization's headquarters were in New York, and each year it held a vegetarian food festival called "Taste of Health."

Robbins had named his friend Glantz to the board of directors of EarthSave after Robbins' book, *Diet for a New America*, "had made an impact on me, and many people of my generation," says Glantz. "John and I became friends. I loved John and cared for him, and somewhere down the line I said, 'If you want, you can try out what I'm doing,'" which was putting money in Madoff. "I told him what I thought the return would be—10 to 13 percent. I considered I was very fortunate [to be investing in Madoff], so I brought John in. I brought friends in."

Asked how many investors he had enlisted, Glantz declined to answer.

"All I can say is I brought in friends and family, and one of them was John Robbins."

In all the years Glantz was investing and feeding friends to Bernie, he claims he never once met the big man himself:

> I always talked to Frank—Frank DiPascali. He answered my questions. I thought his answers were legitimate. I got the Madoff statements. They looked like [legitimate] broker statements. The trades were always accurately shown, and when you wanted money it was always there.

He says through the years he took money out. "I lived off it. I never touched the principle."

When reminded that Bernie had admitted that he hadn't made a trade in some 13 years and just kept investors' money in a bank account, Glantz responded, "Apparently. It's mind-blowing, isn't it? Half the world went upside down. I have a 91-year-old mother, and all her money was in with Madoff. All *my* money was with Madoff. But Bernie had credentials. He had a three-floor brokerage in New York and an office in London. I had a client who called up Bernie himself and told him he wanted to put in $100 million and Bernie told him no, he wasn't taking it. I think he was afraid of big money because the people would want to send in people to do due diligence."

Glantz says he has not been questioned by the FBI or the SEC since Bernie's arrest.

Asked what he would say to Bernie if he had a chance to visit him in jail, Glantz says:

I wouldn't give him the time of day to visit him. I don't give a damn about him.

But Glantz says he's convinced that Bernie didn't act alone as he claimed to federal prosecutors.

I have no idea how he set up his Ponzi scheme. Do I think Frank DiPascali knew? Yes. Do I think Bernie overpaid people either in London, the Bahamas, or his back office in New York to help him? Yes. What I don't understand is, if he's done his fraud for 16 years, why no one left and turned on him. Why didn't Bernie cop a plea? His only cooperation now is to turn in his family, and he's not going to do that.

Asked what John Robbins' reaction was when he told him all of his money was lost, Glantz says:

I don't have clarity on that. I don't remember. It was such a sad time to call him, to call my relatives and friends. For two or three weeks I was just grieving—grieving for the suffering I've created, not just my suffering.

Even now as I talk I feel such sadness. I just felt so bad speaking to John. John was very sweet. He called me a couple of days later and said, "Richard, I love you and I'm concerned for you." So here's this guy who I completely devastated and his reaction was love. John's a very remarkable man that way.

Remarkable, for sure.

In April 2009, with most if not all of his money gone and with the man who stole it behind bars, John Robbins made a lucrative deal with the publisher Ballantine to write a book appropriately entitled *The New Good Life*, described as "a manifesto for finding meaning beyond money, and a practical blueprint for living happily on less."

■ ■ ■

An odd event occurred a week before Bernie was scheduled to be sentenced to spend the rest of his life behind bars. At the Metropolitan Correctional Center where he had been held since pleading guilty to masterminding history's biggest Ponzi scheme, Bernie had a visitor. For three hours, he sat and talked with David Kotz, the inspector-general of the SEC. For months Kotz had been probing who at the regulatory agency might have known what Bernie was up to but did nothing with the information. Was Bernie suddenly cooperating? Was Bernie going to be a consultant for the agency he saw as his enemy—a consultant expert in spotting Ponzi schemes?

No one would comment on the meeting.

There was lots of other action, too, as the countdown to Bernie's historic sentencing began, overshadowed only by the sudden death of Michael Jackson and the passing of cancer victim Farrah Fawcett. One of those actions prompted the *New York Post* to declare: "Ponzi King Takes *Chutzpah* Crown."

The angry headline was sparked by Bernie's plea seeking leniency. In a letter filed in Manhattan federal court, Ira Sorkin, Bernie's lawyer, asked for a prison term for his client of no more than 12 years when he was facing a maximum of 150 years for his crimes.

"We seek neither mercy nor sympathy," he said in the letter. "Respectfully, we seek the justice and objectivity that have been—and we hope always will be—the bedrock of our criminal justice system." According to Sorkin's logic based on Social Security Administration statistics, Bernie had a life expectancy of 13 more years beyond his 71, and the lawyer felt that a sentence of a dozen years would be appropriate. He said that "mob vengeance" surrounded the Madoff case. The *New York Daily News* blared, "Has Bernie Madoff's lawyer gone mad?"

Immediately after Sorkin made his plea, federal prosecutors argued that because of the "unique scope and duration" of Bernie's crime he be given the maximum sentence. "Madoff's crimes were of extraordinary dimensions," the prosecutors said in a memorandum to U.S. District Court Judge Denny Chin, the sentencing judge. The prosecutors also made note of a letter from the trustee in the case, who stated, "Mr. Madoff has not provided meaningful cooperation or assistance to the Trustee since his arrest."

On the evening of June 26, three nights and a wake-up before Bernie was to be formally sentenced to prison for the rest of his natural days, he and Ruth were stripped of his stolen goods—declared to be $170 billion worth. The enormous amount was considered symbolic, and meant only that any future assets discovered by investigators would be seized and sold to help pay back the victimized investors.

But it also meant that Ruth would be penthouseless.

U.S. marshals were ordered by Judge Chin to sell the Madoffs' spectacular apartment, along with the Montauk beach house where in the summer of 2008 Bernie had held forth at his disgraced firm's annual beach party. Also to be put on the block was the Madoffs' Palm Beach house that was seized earlier. In all, the properties were valued at almost $22 million. Along with the homes, all the fancy cars and boats were to be sold off along with all personal property—from the antiques in the apartment that Ruth wasn't permitted to sit on, to the Steinway in the living room, the paintings on the walls, and whatever other expensive *tchotkes* were found anywhere in the Madoffs' possession.

Moreover, the forfeiture included millions of dollars in loans made over the years to family members such as Bernie's sons and brother, to friends, and to employees. In essence, the Madoffs were stripped bare of everything, except for $2.5 million that Ruth was permitted to keep "in settlement of the claims she would have otherwise brought against property," according to the prosecutors.

The infamous Madoff dynasty was clearly at an end. The family had virtually been reduced to nothing. The Ponzi King and his royal family had lost the riches accumulated over the years, much of it stolen from trusting investors.

The disgraced, reviled financier now awaited being told where his final resting place would be.

Epilogue

While the three months he spent behind bars awaiting formal sentencing didn't make him any more cooperative with investigators, or sympathetic toward his thousands of victims, Bernie Madoff did get one benefit from life inside: the chubby fraudster lost weight.

As he stood before U.S. District Judge Dennis Chin in the packed and emotionally volatile courtroom in downtown Manhattan, where the 71-year-old ultimate symbol of greed was sentenced to the maximum 150 years in prison on the sunny morning of Monday, June 29, 2009, he was visibly thinner. Bernie's custom-tailored Savile Row suit, one of the ones he'd had cut to match his ultrathin cell phone, hung on him and was no longer form-fitting as he stood to hear his victims' anger and the judge's declaration.

The historic day began with nine of Bernie's victims in his massive Ponzi scheme eloquently and emotionally asking the judge to impose the maximum sentence, not the dozen years the admitted swindler's attorney had requested, claiming "mob vengeance." Ira Sorkin told the court, "Vengeance is not the goal of punishment."

But that's not the way his victims saw it. They spent almost an hour of the 90-minute courtroom drama voicing their anguish.

"He stole from the rich. He stole from the poor. He stole from the in-between. He had no values," declared Tom Fitzmaurice. "He cheated his victims out of their money so he and his wife Ruth could live a life of luxury beyond belief."

Through the nine heart-wrenching soliloquy-like denouncements, Bernie kept his back to his victimized investors, his head bowed, his hands clasped before him or resting on a courtroom table, showing no emotion while some of the speakers wept openly.

Outside the courthouse at 500 Pearl Street, within walking distance of the financial district where Bernie went into business a half-century earlier, dozens of victims had gathered in a sea of reporters, photographers, and TV crews from around the world.

The public and his victims had not heard Bernie's voice since he pleaded guilty in March, but when the jurist asked whether he had anything to say, Bernie stood and spoke in a monotone, his Queens-based, Noo Yawk-ese accent seemingly stronger than ever. Alone for most of the time in his cell, he hadn't used his voice much at all.

But then he stood and spoke.

"I'm responsible for a great deal of suffering and pain; I understand that," he acknowledged, presumably using words prepared for him by his attorney. "I live in a tormented state now, knowing all the pain and suffering that I've created. I've left a legacy of shame, as some of my victims have pointed out, to my family and my grandchildren." He said he could not "offer any excuse for my behavior. . . . I thought I could get out of it. . . . For once in my life I have failed."

Speaking about his wife, Ruth—next to Bernie the most suspect and reviled in the enormous scandal, though she hadn't been charged with any crimes—he claimed, "She cries herself to sleep every night, knowing all the pain and suffering I have caused. That's something I live with as well. . . . How do you excuse lying to my wife and sons?"

He still asserted that none of his family members who were active in the firm knew anything about his crimes—not his wife, or his sons, Mark and Andrew, or his brother, Peter. None of them were in the courtroom, and none of them had sent letters asking the judge to give him mercy.

And then for the first time Bernie turned stiffly to face victims of his fraud who were sitting in the front row of spectators.

"I will turn and face you," he said, his voice emotionless. "I'm sorry. I know that doesn't help you."

The prosecutor, Lisa Baroni, one of a team of federal prosecutors who would continue to probe the crime—looking for the missing billions, and for conspirators—declared that Bernie deserved the maximum sentence, stating that he "stole ruthlessly and without remorse."

In the end, 55-year-old Judge Chin sent Bernie to prison for the rest of his life. The 150-year sentence was mainly symbolic since, at 71, Bernie had a life expectancy of about a dozen years.

"Objectively speaking, the fraud here was staggering," Chin told Bernie. "It spanned more than 20 years. . . . Here the message must be sent that Mr. Madoff's crimes were extraordinarily evil and that this kind of manipulation of the system is not just a bloodless crime that takes place on paper, but one instead that takes a staggering toll."

Bernie showed no emotion when Chin announced the sentence. When the hearing ended, he was led off. The Federal Bureau of Prisons would have the final say as to where he would live out the rest of his life. It was believed he'd be put away in a minimum-security prison in the Northeast.

It seemed almost anticlimactic.

Uptown, outside the fancy co-op building where Bernie and Ruth had lived in splendor—$18,000 in linen and bedding alone, and $8,500 in silverware—another contingent of reporters, passersby, and hangers-on waited in hopes of catching a glimpse of the fraudster's wife, who would soon lose all of her homes, though she was granted $2.5 million and there were lingering suspicions that more might be stashed away. With her husband's sentencing out of the way, prosecutors planned to focus more on other Madoff family members, and more arrests were possible.

The *New York Post* quoted sources on sentencing day who claimed that Ruth was having doors "slammed in her face" by landlords who were refusing to rent to her. "She has nowhere to go," an unnamed broker said. It also was reported that the Ponzi King's wife had begun using her maiden name, Alpern, because "No one wants someone with her name in their building. People like their privacy."

With Bernie headed up the river to the Big House for good, Ruth, probably on the advice of her legal team, decided finally to say something publicly. She also was placing distance between her and her husband of half a century.

In a written statement, but not facing anyone directly, she declared:

I am breaking my silence now because my reluctance to speak has been interpreted as indifference or lack of sympathy for the victims of my husband Bernie's crime, which is exactly the opposite of the truth.

From the moment I learned from my husband that he had committed an enormous fraud, I have had two thoughts—first, that so many people who trusted him would be ruined financially and emotionally, and second, that my life with the man I have known for over 50 years was over.

Many of my husband's investors were my close friends and family. And in the days since December, I have read, with immense pain, the wrenching stories of people whose life savings have evaporated because of his crime.

My husband was the one we (and I include myself) respected and trusted with our lives and our livelihoods, often for many, many years, and who was respected in the securities industry as well. Then there is the other man who stunned us all with his confession and is responsible for the terrible situation in which so many find themselves.

Lives have been upended and futures have been taken away. All those touched by this fraud feel betrayed, disbelieving the nightmare they woke to. I am embarrassed and ashamed. Like everyone else, I feel betrayed and confused. The man who committed this horrible fraud is not the man whom I have known for all these years.

In the end, to say that I feel devastated for the many whom my husband has destroyed is truly inadequate. Nothing I can say seems sufficient regarding the daily suffering that all those innocent people are enduring because of my husband. But if it matters to them at all, please know that not a day goes by when I don't ache over the stories that I have heard and read.

While there would be no annual Madoff company party on the beach in Montauk in the summer of 2009, the intensely scrutinized and pilloried Madoff mate received some welcome news to help her celebrate Independence Day. Reports surfaced in the *New York Post* and *Wall Street Journal* that for the present time there was no prosecutable evidence linking her to her husband's crimes, according to two unnamed sources. A few days later her passport was returned, allowing her to travel. The bad news was that Ruth was roofless after U.S. marshals evicted her and seized the Madoffs' prized penthouse, forcing her to find new and presumably less luxe lodgings. "Ruth left voluntarily," her lawyer, Peter Chavkin, stated. But there was a tad of regret as she surrendered the lap of luxury for the last time: The marshals wouldn't let her take one prized possession—a fur coat; all she was able to walk away with was a straw bag.

With all of the drama surrounding the swindler's petite and much maligned wife, it wouldn't take too much to imagine Barbara Walters, Diane Sawyer, and Oprah Winfrey burning up the lines trying to book Ruth for a teary-eyed, tell-all sit-down. With Bernie put away for good on July 13th in the medium security Butner Federal Correctional Complex in North Carolina, Ruth Madoff was the big media "get," next to the ghost of Michael Jackson. If she escaped the long arm of the law, one could also see a big book deal in her future: *The Ponzi King and the Woman Who Loved Him.*

■ ■ ■

Meanwhile, sources close to the investigation see the probe lasting through 2010 with as many as a dozen others being formally implicated and with close attention being focused on certain family members, top associates within Madoff, close colleagues of Bernie, and European links to the Madoff organization.

"Now that he's been sentenced, we have a long way to go, but we know who we're after and we're hoping they can lead us to the billions still missing," says a person with knowledge of the probe. "From intelligence it's apparent Bernie didn't mastermind this scheme himself. It's far from a one-man operation. It's just too vast. There are feelers out regarding organized crime here in the United States and abroad— the Russian mafia, the Israeli mafia, people in high places—*very* high places.

"When you have billions of dollars floating around across continents and oceans, there are some very bad people, and some very big people, who have a hand out, or a hand in. Was Bernie a puppet, a middleman who became the fall guy, who decided to fall on his sword? The radar is starting to show such blips. The other shoe is certain to drop, but it takes time. This is an enormous scheme that goes way beyond anything we've ever seen. It makes Watergate look like a smash and grab."

At Butner, a state-of-the-art prison where Bernie will spend the rest of his years, he has all the comforts of home. Well, not quite all. Living in a dormitory or two-man cell, the Big House is no penthouse or beach house in the Hamptons. But Bernie certainly has a lot more amenities than many of his destitute victims had after he robbed them.

Within the locked doors and barbed wire of Butner, located in a poor, rural community almost 500 miles south of his swank Upper East Side apartment, Bernie gets free cable TV, three free square meals a day, air conditioning in the summer, and the best medical care in the federal prison system—all at taxpayers' (and Madoff victims') expense. He has the freedom to order books and magazines, and he can receive visitors—although it is doubtful there is anyone, including members of his own family, possibly even prison widow Ruth, who would care enough to come.

His days aren't too bad. He's up and about at 6 A.M. for an all-day work assignment. Forget about the Hollywood prison movies of old where inmates broke rocks. At Butner Bernie can be assigned to plumbing or groundskeeping—after all, he was an expert at installing sprinkler systems, and his late father once fixed toilets for a living. And he even gets paid, as much as $104 per year. For relaxation after work there is always the well-equipped gym (no outlandish fees to pay), or he can walk the outside track or participate in sports. In his free time he can even teach a course—finance is one possibility—to some of his 4,800 fellow inmates.

Besides the robbers and rapists, Bernie has some once respectable prison mates as peers to schmooze with, such as the father-and-son team of 84-year-old John and 53-year-old Timothy Rigas, the Adelphi Communications founder and his scion, who were found guilty of securities fraud. Another is Franklin C. Brown, with whom Bernie will have even more in common—Brown is serving time for a $66 million Ponzi scheme.

If Bernie takes the advice offered him by his hired prison consultant, Herb Hoelter, he'll probably do okay in his golden years. That advice was, keep your space, respect fellow inmates, and "bring some meaning to your life." Hoelter, who waived his fee for the financially and morally bankrupt Prisoner #61727-054, release date November 14, 2139, believed his client would "do some good things" behind bars.

"He's sensitive enough and smart enough."

Author's Note on Sources

Since Bernie Madoff was a relative unknown until his arrest, his bibliography was limited to a couple of magazine profiles noted in the text of this book, a mention in at least one book about Wall Street, the subject of a couple of "red flag" articles such as the *Barron's* piece, and quotes and references here and there over the years in financial stories. In essence, not a whole lot.

Therefore, it wasn't until his arrest that Bernie became an ongoing, headline-making story wherever around the world people had been scammed by him. As of July 6, 2009, for example, there were 212 million Google references for his name, while President Barack Obama garnered 61.4 million.

Much of this book was based on interviews conducted by the author (see Acknowledgments), with much help from the daily newspaper chronicles and the few monthly magazines (and all their related web sites) that covered the ongoing investigation. Dozens of excellent reporters worked the story.

That said, I would like to point out that all persons directly interviewed by the author are quoted in the present tense. The past tense is used only for quotes or other material coming from newspapers, magazines, or court documents, and I've attempted to cite those sources in the text of the book.

In some cases I've interviewed persons in greater depth who were first mentioned in news accounts or online. I've attempted to differentiate the author interviews of those people by using the present tense where applicable.

Among the newspapers, magazines, and related and separate web sites used as reference and source material are:

The *Wall Street Journal*, the *New York Times*, the *Washington Post*, the *Financial Times*, the *New York Post*, the *New York Daily News*, the *Palm Beach Post*, the *Los Angeles Times*, the *Guardian* (London), the *Telegraph* (London), the *Daily Mail* (London), Reuters, Associated Press, Bloomberg News, ABC News, CNBC, CBS News, CNN, Fox News, *Vanity Fair*, *New York* magazine, *Traders Magazine*, *Portfolio*, *Forbes*, *BusinessWeek*, *Barron's*, *Newsweek*, *Time*, *Fortune*, and *Wall Street & Technology*, among others.

Other research sources were the web sites of the town of Laurelton, Far Rockaway High School, the University of Alabama, Hofstra University, Brooklyn Law School, Fordham Law School, *The Huffington Post*, *The Daily Beast*, TPMCafe, and various government web sites.

Acknowledgments

Bernie who?

He was someone few had ever heard of, who had committed a monstrous crime no one had been aware of.

But after his story began unfolding following his arrest in December 2008, Bernie Madoff became a household name overnight, the ultimate poster boy for extreme Wall Street greed, and the most reviled and cunning crook America and the world had ever come face-to-face with. He was compared to one of those psychopathic serial killers who murder anonymously, live among us, and are loved and respected by their friends and associates until someone comes across the bodies buried in the backyard.

In Bernie's case, the financial victims numbered in the thousands and his take was in the billions of dollars. Besides losing life savings, two of his investors had taken their lives. There was blood on his hands.

When the Madoff story broke—and headlines about his massive Ponzi scheme blared around the globe, for his victims were everywhere—I had just completed writing an expose of a company called *Toy Monster: The Big, Bad World of Mattel*, my ninth book.

While I was quite aware of the exploding scandal, my focus still was on *Toy Monster*, which had taken more than a year of intensive reporting and writing. But in late January to early February 2009 I was convinced that the story of Bernie's amazing rise and calamitous fall was a business crime story of historic proportions, and I dove into research and reporting.

As I stated in the Prologue, my goal was to tell the story of the man behind the scam. I was in for some tough competition. Some of the best business and investigative reporters in daily and magazine journalism had been on the Madoff case since day one.

But I wasn't trying to play catch-up. My goal was to find and talk to the people who knew Bernie intimately, who saw him in action, who knew him for what he was, from the days when he was playing stickball in the streets of Laurelton, in the New York borough of Queens, to playing hardball on the Street and beginning his giant Ponzi swindle.

With a lot of old-fashioned reportorial shoe leather and telephone work, I was able to track down dozens of people who had seen Bernie operate, who had gone to school with him, who had worked with him and under him, and who had been robbed by him.

This book could not have been completed without their gracious help, their candid memories, their on-the-mark perceptions, and their colorful anecdotes, which together morphed into a telling, frightening portrait of the man, ending with the drama of his being put behind bars for the rest of his life—his family and legacy forever demolished.

That said, I wish to offer my heartfelt thanks to those who opened their doors and took time out of their lives—many of those lives being tragically sad because of Bernie's victimization—to help me tell the story. I could not have done so without you. In no particular order of importance, hale and hearty thanks to:

Jennifer Madoff, Bill Nasi, Richard Glantz, Jay Portnoy, Ed Heiberger, Sheldon Fogel, Fletcher Eberle, Mike Gandin, Eli Greenbaum, Gordon Ondis, Carol Ann Lieberbaum, John Maccabee, Peter Zaphiris, Charles Lubitz, Sheila Olin, Martin Schrager, Andy Monness, Justin Fox, Robin Warner, Gale Hayman, Joe Kavanau, Cynthia Arenson, Amy Joel, Toniann

Astuto, Albert Reitman, Hoong-Yee Lee Krakauer, Miles Goslett, Ocean Robbins, Stanley Shapiro, Doug Abrams, J. M. Brown, Levi Touger, Jonny Lieberbaum, Gary Hartnick, Erin Robbins, Neil Fenwick, Jeff Nelson, Paul Finfer, Anthony Guerra, Howard Samuels, Richard Bucksbaum, Arnold Schotsky, Elka Weiner, Deb Kass, Sherry Fabrikant, Robert Gettinger, John Shoup, Frederic von Anhalt, Marsha Veit, Jane Kavanau, Patricia Samuels, David Neff, George Somlo, Nina Mehta, Justice Litle, Daryl Montgomery, Barbara Curreri, Leonore Feldman, David Arenson, and a number of others. If for some reason I missed offering an appreciation for your help, please accept my apology.

I'd also like to thank one of the best editors I've worked with in a long time, Kelly O'Connor, who put her fine touch on the manuscript.

I'd like to offer a very special thanks to my wonderful wife, the journalist, illustrator, and photographer Caroline Walton Howe, for helping me chase down sources, locate relevant materials, and conduct some interviews, particularly when the workload and hours seemed to be burying me. She deserves major kudos. This book is also being written in memory of our beloved Westie, Cuco, who at age 12 sadly had to be put to sleep on the day I began my reporting. May he rest in peace.

Index